W9-BDL-276

LEGENDS
of COUNTRY

Dalmatian
P·R·E·S·S
an imprint of dalmatian publishing group

LEGENDS OF COUNTRY

Published by Dalmatian Press, an imprint of Dalmatian Publishing Group.

Produced by Hylas Publishing, 129 Main Street, Irvington, NY 10533.

Publisher: Sean Moore
Publishing Director: Karen Prince
Art Directors: Gus Yoo, Brian MacMullen
Editorial Director: Aaron Murray
Senior Editor: Ward Calhoun
Editors: Suzanne Lander, Rachael Lanicci, Lisa Purcell
Designer: Gus Yoo
Proofreader: Glenn Novak

ISBN: 1-40373-721-5
16562-0607

07 08 09 10 SFO 10 9 8 7 6 5 4 3 2 1

LEGENDS of COUNTRY

LIZ MECHEM and CHRIS CARROLL

CONTENTS

INTRODUCTION

"The Sunday smell of someone's fryin' chicken." Kris Kristofferson sure nailed it when he wrote that line for Johnny Cash to sing in their classic "Sunday Morning Coming Down." Six little words that imply an entire hidden world of nuance and drama. The sinner who awoke to find his "cleanest dirty shirt" and then had beer for breakfast was taken aback by that evocative aroma. We listeners are affected too, along with the guy in the song: ". . . it took me back to somethin', that I'd lost somehow, somewhere along the way."

Kristofferson managed to evoke several of the essential themes of country music in that one short phrase. Yearning, nostalgia, loss, and pathos all contribute fundamentally to country music's palette of emotions. Country's all about using small stories to represent big themes, and using big themes to illuminate small moments. Those moments are both specific and universal enough that listeners can relate. Admit it, you can remember clearly where you were the last time you smelled chicken frying. You might not have been consumed with the sense of alienation and loss of Kristofferson's antihero, but you may well have your own fond memories of childhood kitchens.

Frying chicken is an apt metaphor on another level as well. There's perhaps no more fundamental act than the preparation of food. Everybody does it and is particularly partial to whatever variations they happened to enjoy in their youth. My grandmother's fried chicken was better than yours. But they all had roots in the same deep mysterious past. In the same way the Spanish brought their chickens to the New World, African, Irish, and Gypsy influences found their way into country music.

Country music itself is a uniquely American art form, composed of completely borrowed common elements that blend to make the modern jambalaya gumbo of music that we all enjoy today. And if the irreducible element in country is the song, the irreplaceable element of the song is the singer. Country doesn't have operas, or symphonies; country has songs. And singers sing songs, about people. Which is why this book is organized as a series of biographies. Whether you're a fan or are yet to become one, the people of country are the most interesting bunch of folks you'd ever want to meet. We intend to introduce you.

In the early '20s, a fellow named Ralph Peer was having great success making recordings of "colored" musicians in his New York studio. Working with Victor, the manufacturer of the studio recording equipment, he was able to miniaturize enough of the components to make a traveling studio possible. So it was that he found himself in a borrowed barn in Bristol, Tennessee, one sweltering morning in August 1926. He didn't know it, but the country music industry was about to come into being. By going to the heart of mountain country Peer found talent that never would have made its way to cosmopolitan New York. Beginning right then, country music's roots in the hills and hollows would interact and mix with big-city technology and industry. Victor's device, combined with the other new high-tech wonder, radio, allowed such simple hill folk as the Carter Family to eventually reach millions of listeners the world over.

Peer set up his equipment in a neighborhood barn and invited locals to come in and sing and play the music they'd been entertaining each other with for generations, and then brought the tapes back to his New York record label. That city/country dichotomy would persist in country music to this day. It was music of the people, from the hills, but nobody would ever have heard it without the intervention and indeed invention of the modern recording industry. Records and radio reinforced each other in a way unprecedented in modern marketing. Women grew used to ordering "a pound of butter, pound of flour, and the latest Jimmie Rodgers record." And through each succeeding decade, the oil and water of country and city is never burbling far beneath the surface of country music.

Peer recorded two local artists that crucial day in Bristol, the Carter Family and Jimmie Rodgers. Both would go on to be among the first stars of the burgeoning art form. They also each would epitomize a distinct branch of country: the establishment and the outlaw, respectively. Those branches would swing in the wind over the years like a pendulum; with the smooth Nashville Sound being countered by Bakersfield's rough and rowdy honky-tonk, New Traditionalists giving way to Garth and Shania, and everybody loving Willie.

The uniquely American stew Peer caught on wax that stifling day in a barn in Tennessee grew to encompass all of America's hopes and dreams. America is still a young country, full of the promise and terror of the frontier. Country music mirrors its muse, with all her wonder—but more than wonder, her flaws and imperfections. Just as America couldn't be America without having been birthed in blood, so country music revels in detailing the most basic human emotions and behavior. Yet through our common roots in the world of sin we can arise to new heights of redemption. You might not have cheated on your man or killed for honor today, or even had beer for breakfast. But drop a needle on a country record, close your eyes, and listen. Now do you smell the chicken fryin'?

He was the "father of country music"; they were the "First Family." Jimmie Rodgers (left), poses with the legendary Carter Family in the early 1930s. From left: Maybelle Carter, Alvin Pleasant Carter, and Sara Dougherty Carter.

ROY ACUFF

SEPTEMBER 15, 1903–NOVEMBER 23, 1992

The King of Country Music, Roy Acuff hit the Opry in 1938, and there he stayed, until the "great speckled bird" came to take him away. Serving as the courtly host and Grand Master of the Grand Ole Opry for much of his career, Acuff wore many other hats as well. Partnering with songwriter Fred Rose, Acuff was a music publisher, booking agent, and record label founder. Mostly, though, he was a hugely popular singer and fiddler, whose clear, true voice and earnest singing style made him the biggest male country star of the '40s. Nearly always seen with a fiddle in his hand, Acuff touched a nerve and won many hearts with his plaintive voice during the war years.

Country music's shift from old-time hillbilly string bands to newer star players with backing bands coincided with Acuff's own rise to fame. The son of a Baptist minister, Acuff was born in Maynardville, Tennessee, and later moved to Knoxville. The young Roy was a wild boy with baseball dreams; as a youth he even qualified for a tryout to the major leagues. But severe heatstroke, followed by a nervous breakdown, cut short his career in sports; Roy turned to music instead and at age 29 joined a traveling medicine show as a fiddler, singer, and all-round entertainer.

Soon Acuff had formed his own band; together they cut some sides in Chicago and were dubbed the Crazy Tennesseans by a DJ. The combo landed a spot at the Opry in 1938. Roy's delivery of the classic "Great Speckled Bird" got them invited back fast, though Opry management renamed the group the Smoky Mountain Boys. Hit records, movie appearances, and national tours followed throughout the '40s and '50s, with Bashful Brother Oswald on Dobro resonator guitar through it all. In 1962, Acuff was the first living member to be inducted into the Country Music Hall of Fame.

The Grand Ole Opry

Perhaps the most important institution in country music, the Grand Ole Opry is a weekly live music show broadcast every Saturday on Nashville's WSM radio and on Country Music Television. But it's much, much more than that: For over three-quarters of a century, the iconic Opry has been the premiere showcase for country acts, launching many a career, fending off controversy, and remaining true to its vision of traditional country music.

The Opry first hit the airwaves on November 28, 1925, as the WSM Barn Dance. The name change came about in 1927, when 30-year-old announcer George D. Hay (radio name "the Solemn Old Judge") joked that audiences had been listening to Grand Opera for the last hour (the Barn Dance followed a classical music show), and now it was time for some "Grand Ole Opry." The name stuck, and the show is now the longest-running radio program in the world.

In its many years as the center of country music performance, nearly every country luminary has crossed its stage—or hasn't, for some well-publicized reason or other. The Opry now includes four different venues: the Grand Ole Opry House, the Acuff Theatre, the Opry Museum, and the Opry Plaza, with occasional performances at the original Ryman Auditorium. Not bad for a barn dance.

"Any game you play, you got to lose sometime."—Roy Acuff

THOUGH A CHOIRBOY DURING HIS RAMBUNCTIOUS YOUTH, ROY ACUFF ASPIRED TO BECOME A BASEBALL PLAYER UNTIL A BOUT OF SUNSTROKE RUINED HIS CHANCES FOR A MAJOR LEAGUE TRYOUT.

GREATEST HITS

YEAR	SONG
1936	"Great Speckled Bird"
	"Wabash Cannonball"
1940	"The Precious Jewel"
1942	"Fireball Mail"
	"Wreck on the Highway"
1943	"Night Train to Memphis"
	"Pins and Needles"
1947	"Tennessee Waltz"

ALABAMA

1969–

Alabama (from left to right: Mark Herndon, Teddy Gentry, Randy Owen, and Jeff Cook) started out with first cousins Teddy and Randy and their distant cousin Jeff teaming up to form a group when they were all still in high school.

Without Alabama, you might not even be a country fan. The chart-topping, crowd-pleasing quartet brought the country sound to a newly wide and diverse audience. Crossing over into the rock and pop charts while staying true to their roots, Alabama was the first such group to sell millions of records and win fans on a scale unprecedented in country music, with 21 gold or platinum albums, dozens of #1 singles, and two Grammys to their name. The Academy of Country Music named them "Artist of the Decade" in 1989, followed by the Recording Industry Association of America, which in 1999 honored Alabama as the "Country Group of the Century." The group was inducted into the Country Music Hall of Fame on November 15, 2005. All this from a couple of cousins from Fort Payne, Alabama.

First cousins Randy Owen and Teddy Gentry played guitar and bass respectively. When they joined up in the late '60s with another family member, guitarist Jeff Cook, the group Wildcountry was born. Sticking to day jobs and local gigs for a few years, the three young men finally went on the road in 1973, taking their act to Myrtle

Big Heart Alabama

Alabama believes in giving back. So from 1982 to 1997, the group sponsored the June Jam, an all-day music festival in their hometown of Fort Payne, Alabama. Taking over a 40-acre field behind the high school, the likes of Garth Brooks, Vince Gill, and others joined Fort Payne's homegrown band, Alabama. The June Jam raised millions of dollars, benefiting a slew of local and national charities, most notably the Big Oak Ranch, a center for orphaned, abused, and troubled children.

But that's not all. In 1989, Randy Owen helped establish the "Country Cares" fund, which has raised over $225 million for the benefit of St. Jude's Children's Research Hospital in Memphis, Tennessee. Add to these good works the outreach Alabama has shown to service men and women, plus their fund-raising for victims of Hurricane Katrina, and you can see why they were awarded both the Bob Hope and the Minnie Pearl Humanitarian Awards.

ALABAMA

1969–

Beach, South Carolina, among other stops. There they made their mark at a popular club called the Bowery, putting in long, dedicated shifts, keeping their energy high, and winning over audiences along the way. Their appealing, popular sound incorporated elements of the Allman Brothers Band's Southern rock, along with influences ranging from pop to honky-tonk. In 1977 the group was renamed Alabama, and in 1979 they drafted rock drummer Mark Herndon as their final fourth man. Then things went big.

After a few singles on small labels GRT and MDJ, Alabama was invited to appear in the "New Faces" segment at Nashville's Country Radio Seminar. There they attracted the attention of RCA records, leading to a 1980 contract. "Tennessee River," the group's first single on RCA, hit #1, as did 20 more singles in the ensuing seven years.

During the '80s and '90s, Alabama kept up a rigorous touring schedule. Their live act was one of the first in country music to borrow a performance style from popular rock acts of the day, complete with lights, sets, and backup musicians. Young people embraced this stylistic fusion, and pretty soon the band's distinctive logo—equal parts 1880s Western and 1950s hot rod—became a T-shirt favorite.

Alabama has been showered with awards, and its members are the only entertainers to receive the Country Music Association's Entertainer of the Year Award three times in a row (1982, 1983, 1984).

"We're a great example of what can happen to people who just won't quit."—Randy Owen

GREATEST HITS

Year	Song
1980	"My Home's in Alabama"
	"Tennessee River"
1981	"Feels So Right"
	"Love in the First Degree"
1982	"Mountain Music"
1983	"Lady Down on Love"
	"Dixieland Delight"
1985	"Forty Hour Week (For a Livin')"
1985	"Can't Keep a Good Man Down"
1986	"She and I"
1989	"Song of the South"
1992	"I'm in a Hurry (and Don't Know Why)"
1993	"Reckless"

In 2002, Alabama announced its farewell tour, and the group spent much of the following two years saying goodbye to its loyal audiences. But Alabama rose again. While the band no longer tours, a year after their induction into the Country Music Hall of Fame, they released the album *Songs of Inspiration*, which hit #1 in 2006. This was followed by 2007's *Songs of Inspiration, Vol. 2*. It's pretty clear—you can't keep a good band down.

NUGGET: At the 2001 funeral for NASCAR great Dale Earnhardt, who was killed in a crash during that year's Daytona 500, Randy Owen sang an emotional version of the band's 1995 single "Angels Among Us," written by Becky Hobbs and Don Goodman. While the song never had great success on the charts, topping out at #28, this exposure made it an instant favorite, and it has since been included on a number of Alabama's greatest hits and compilation albums.

EDDY ARNOLD

May 15, 1918–

Eddy Arnold was a crooner. He sang from his diaphragm, naturally, in the nonchalant way that could only come from thousands of hours of work. He was perhaps the first crossover artist, bringing country sounds to the masses. Arnold preferred love songs over the nitty gritty honky-tonk numbers. From the '40s to the '60s and even as late as 1980, Arnold racked up 145 hit songs, 28 of them #1s.

"I'm trying to sell every audience something; that something is me."—Eddy Arnold

From humble beginnings as a Tennessee farm boy, Richard Edward Arnold worked his way up to being the Tennessee Plowboy, with stops on the way at the Grand Ole Opry and innumerable radio shows. He started making records and saw his first big hit with "That's How Much I Love You" in 1946. As the public began to hear Eddy's smooth straightforward singing, the hits piled up. But a funny thing happened to country music in the late '50s, a little something called rock and roll. Country artists like Arnold noticed they were losing sales to this nascent musical form. RCA producer Chet Atkins worked with Eddy on smoothing the "country" edges of his records, exchanging vocals and strings for steel guitars and gritty arrangements. Arnold and others began forging what would come to be known as the Nashville Sound.

Eddy Arnold succeeded in his goal of broadening the reach of his smooth vocals. In 1965 he had an international smash hit with "Make the World Go Away." Arranger Bill Walker surrounded Arnold's natural, clean voice with lush, evocative arrangements. The process worked, too, as Eddy Arnold transformed the Tennessee Plowboy into a suave, sophisticated entertainer, rolling out a string of sixteen straight hits throughout the '60s. Arnold took the act on the road, donning a tux and booking complete string orchestras to accompany him. And his slick, cosmopolitan presentation worked: In 1966 Arnold became the first country musician to play Carnegie Hall; both performances were sold-out shows. So much for keeping country on the fringes of mainstream.

GREATEST HITS

Year	Song
1955	"Cattle Call"
	"Just Call Me Lonesome"
1959	"Tennessee Stud"
1962	"After Loving You"
1965	"Make the World Go Away"
	"Tip of My Fingers"
1966	"Somebody Like Me"
1967	"Lonely Again"
	"Turn the World Around"
1968	"Then You Can Tell Me Goodbye"
1980	"Let's Get It While the Gettin's Good"

Arnold during a performance in the 1960s. By this time the handsome crooner had had forty-five #1 hits; his 100th record, *After All These Years*, came out in 2005.

Country Crooners

When you hear the word "crooner," perhaps the first singers to pop into mind would be Bing Crosby or Rudy Vallee. But country had its crooners too, epitomized by Eddy Arnold. Crooning became literally possible in the '40s and '50s as microphone technology advanced. No longer did singers have to virtually yell to reach the back of the house; now they could be as direct and soft-spoken as they liked. The all-hearing ear of the modern microphone caught every breathy utterance. Arnold's label mate Jim Reeves found success with a similar singing and production style. George Morgan is often mentioned in the same breath as Arnold and Reeves and was the last performer at the Grand Ole Opry when it moved from the historic Ryman Auditorium in 1974.

CHET ATKINS

June 20, 1924–June 30, 2001

Chet Atkins was never a huge country star, but he was a legend—one of those people whose influence touched an entire industry. He was a lifelong performer, but it was his work behind the scenes that made Chester Burton Atkins legendary. Production is such an ineffable art, it's no surprise that the public at large doesn't appreciate it. But ask any musician and they'll tell you about the importance of production. And listen to any one of dozens of records born in Nashville in the '50s, and you'll get it.

> *"Do it again on the next verse and people think you meant it."*—Chet Atkins

Among a cohort of industry leaders, Chet Atkins produced, tweaked, refined, and built what became known as the Nashville Sound. "Country" sounding pedal steel guitars and fiddles were replaced with smooth vocal arrangements and string sections. Chet Atkins produced a number of records for RCA before being promoted to vice president of RCA's Nashville studio. His slick, sophisticated arrangements brought new audiences to country. While some traditionalists never quite got over it, Atkins' deft touch on the dials expanded the palette available to artists like Eddie Arnold, Skeeter Davis, and Floyd Cramer.

For all his production expertise, Chet was a legend of the guitar as well. After he chanced across a Merle Travis performance on the radio, Chet perfected the thumb-and-finger picking technique for which he became renowned, earning the nickname "Mister Guitar" long before the eponymous album. He was so good, the Gretsch guitar company produced a "Chet Atkins" model for 25 years. As well as on his own records, Chet's smooth picking could be detected on hits by greats like Hank Snow, Jerry Reed, and Les Paul.

Chet continued to experiment and improvise over his entire career. He was the Country Music Association's Instrumentalist of the Year nine times between 1967 and 1988. In his later years, Chet's music was introduced to a new generation through a collaboration with Mark Knopfler, of Dire Straits fame.

The Nashville Sound

Steve Sholes was a producer at RCA Records during the '50s. He had a big hand in the huge success of a little rock act named Elvis Presley. Sholes mentored Chet Atkins, and began turning over more and more production to him, finally putting him in charge of all production at RCA's Nashville studios.

Atkins and Sholes, along with Owen Bradley at Decca, Don Law at Columbia, and Ken Nelson at Capitol, saw the success being enjoyed by their brothers at the rock and roll divisions of their record companies. They saw that success as coming at the expense of their country divisions. In response, they traded the honky-tonk roughness for slicker, more pop production values to broaden the appeal of traditional country. It worked. The nascent Nashville Sound caught on like wildfire. Singers like Patsy Cline, Jim Reeves, and Roger Miller benefited from their producers' newfound influence to create hits that quickly became legends.

Chet Atkins would have gotten rid of his first guitar, a Sears, Roebuck Silvertone, if his mother had not insisted that he hold on to it; the instrument now resides in the Country Music Hall of Fame.

GREATEST HITS

Year	Song
1955	"Mr. Sandman" "Silver Bell" (with Hank Snow)
1965	"Yakety Axe"
1968	"Country Gentleman"
	"Prissy"
1990	"There'll Be Some Changes Made" (with Mark Knopfler)

GENE AUTRY

SEPTEMBER 29, 1907–OCTOBER 2, 1998

Gene Autry taught himself to play on an $8 Sears, Roebuck guitar. He began developing his singing cowboy persona on local Oklahoma radio, and when he hit New York City he began recording for five different companies. In 1931, Autry received the first Gold Record ever, for a duet with Jimmy Long, "That Silver Haired Daddy of Mine."

In the summer of 1934, a guest appearance in a Western, *In Old Santa Fe*, led to Autry starring in his own series of Westerns. The role of singing cowboy suited him, and before long he had become known as "the Singing Cowboy." By 1940 Autry was voted fourth most popular movie star—not bad for an Oklahoma kid with an $8 guitar.

Autry blazed a trail later ridden by the likes of Roy Rogers and Tex Ritter. He always seemed to play himself in the movies, or a character suspiciously like Gene Autry. Astride his horse, Champion, and alongside frequent foil, Smiley Burnette, Gene triumphed over the odds with gentle humor and straightforward midWestern goodness. He wore a six-shooter but rarely used it, preferring to wield his guitar for such classics as "Tumbling Tumbleweeds" and "Back in the Saddle Again."

FROM COWBOY CROONER TO COMPOSER OF CHRISTMAS CLASSICS, GENE AUTRY IS THE ONLY ENTERTAINER TO HAVE FIVE STARS (FOR LIVE PERFORMANCE, MOTION PICTURES, RADIO, RECORDING, AND TELEVISION) ON THE HOLLYWOOD WALK OF FAME.

As successful as his career in film, recording, and radio was, Autry hewed to his own code and left the saddle to serve in the Army Air Corps, flying transports in the Pacific Theater in World War II. Returning stateside after the war, Autry continued to record. "Here Comes Santa Claus," "Rudolph the Red-Nosed Reindeer," and "Frosty the Snow Man" supplanted his Western persona with a friendly Christmas delivery, beloved by generations of listeners. Never just an empty hat, Autry produced his own movies and in 1950 saw the promise of a burgeoning medium and starred in *The Gene Autry Show* on CBS Television. He later purchased the California Angels baseball team; the club's management was so impressed by Gene's marketing ideas, they offered him the entire team. Autry will always be most fondly remembered as the Singing Cowboy—straightforward, honest, and armed with a ready smile and an easy song.

GREATEST HITS

YEAR	SONG
1931	"That Silver Haired Daddy of Mine"
1935	"Tumbling Tumbleweeds"
1938	"South of the Border (Down Mexico Way)"
1939	"Mexicali Rose"
	"Back in the Saddle Again"
1947	"Here Comes Santa Claus"
1949	"Rudolph the Red-Nosed Reindeer"
1950	"Frosty the Snowman"

The Cowboy Code

The Singing Cowboy went so far as to publish a "Cowboy Code" prescribing proper and ethical behavior for his legions of young fans. An updating of the ancient chivalric code, Gene's rules for living right included admonitions to help those in need, stay clean, and act respectfully and truthfully.

DEFORD BAILEY

DECEMBER 14, 1899–JULY 2, 1982

DeFord Bailey, the Grand Ole Opry's first solo star, was known to audiences as the "Harmonica Wizard." In fact, Bailey was there in 1927 when the Opry became the Opry. Right after DeFord's performance of "The Pan-American Blues," announcer George D. Hay spontaneously changed the show's name from the WSM "Barn Dance" to the "Grand Ole Opry."

Born in rural Smith County, Tennessee, Bailey lost his mother when he was just a year old and was raised by his aunt and uncle. Young DeFord contracted polio at age 3, which stunted his growth; as an adult, Bailey stood only 4 feet, 10 inches. Music was at the center of DeFord's family life, and he soaked in the secular style he called "black hillbilly" music. DeFord's father, grandfather, and uncle taught him banjo, fiddle, guitar, mandolin, and, of course, harmonica.

"Music is like a disease. You either got it or you don't."—DeFord Bailey

Bailey's big break came by accident, the way they often do. The first thing he did right was to move to Nashville in 1918; the second was to wander into Dad's Auto Parts in 1925. The owner happened to be Fred "Pop" Exum, who was soon to launch a radio show on WDAD station; before too long, another performer, Dr. Humphrey Bate, brought Bailey along to WSM's Barn Dance, and the rest was history.

History, though, can't forget the few sour notes that hover around DeFord Bailey's virtuosic career. Touring the South during the '30s with the likes of Roy Acuff, Bill Monroe, and fellow Opry star Uncle Dave Macon, DeFord experienced the indignity of the Jim Crow laws, which forced this first-class musician into second-class status. A sharp dresser with impeccable manners, DeFord nevertheless remained positive and professional. Then, in 1941, Bailey was dismissed from the Opry on the grounds that he wouldn't learn any new songs. The reason turned out to be a convoluted problem with publishing rights, but many of DeFord's fans suspected racial prejudice. The Harmonica Wizard quit professional music, opened a shoeshine parlor, and died in near poverty in 1982. But country hasn't forgotten; in 2005, DeFord Bailey was finally inducted into the Country Music Hall of Fame, taking his rightful place among country music's greatest.

THOUGH DEFORD BAILEY WAS A GRAND OLE OPRY FAVORITE FOR A TIME, THE AFRICAN-AMERICAN PERFORMER WASN'T IMMUNE TO DISCRIMINATORY PRACTICES IN THE WORLD AT LARGE.

Blowin' the Train

"I'm just like a microphone," DeFord Bailey once said. "I pick up everything I hear around me." The locomotive was one sound DeFord picked up, practiced, and perfected. Some of his most famous songs, "Pan-American Blues," and "Dixie Flyer Blues," were imitations of train sounds. They start off slow, pick up speed, and continue down the track, the steam engine whistling a long steady whine, just like the real thing. He even gets the Doppler effect: The approaching sound is higher pitched than the receding one. Said DeFord: "I worked on that train for years, getting that train down right . . . I got the engine part. Then I had to make the whistle. It was about, I expect, seventeen years to get that whistle." So go ahead and try it at home—got 17 spare years?

GREATEST HITS

YEAR	SONG
1927	"Pan American Blues"
	"Hesitation Blues"
1928	"Dixie Flyer Blues"
	"Lost John Blues"
	"Cow Cow Blues"
	"Alcoholic Blues"
	"Fox Chase"
	"John Henry"

CLINT BLACK

February 4, 1962–

Honky-tonk lives, and it was personified in the '90s by Clint Black. Tall, dark, and handsome, Black could belt out a hard-rocking barn burner, then slide into a crooning ballad for the ladies. He was the point of the spear for the "new country" movement, which would shake up the staid world of traditional country music.

"The only easy day was yesterday."—Clint Black

His loyal legion of fans helped this multiplatinum-selling artist land a star on the Hollywood Walk of Fame in 1996.

Clint Black's 1989 debut album, *Killin' Time*, featured an old-time honky-tonk style, updated with modern studio production values. And it killed, sitting atop the Billboard country charts for more than half a year, earning Clint six different categories of Country Music Association awards, and yielding five #1 hits. Black toured heavily, borrowing rock staging conventions to create a new amalgam of traditional country brought into the MTV age. He co-wrote, recorded, and released yet another huge album, which would produce two #1 hits. Oh, and managed to meet, woo, and marry *Knots Landing* beauty Lisa Hartman. Not a bad couple of years.

Of course, what storybook life would be complete without a little turmoil? Shortly after being married, Black sued his manager in an acrimonious split. The bitter legal battle didn't seem to hurt his creativity or drive though, as 1992's *The Hard Way* received great critical acclaim and claimed five hits in the top five. In 1993 Clint Black's version of the Eagles' "Desperado" became one of the top radio hits from *Common Thread: Songs of the Eagles*.

In 1994 Clint took up acting. He went on to appear on television in shows like *King of the Hill*, *Hope and Faith*, and *Hot Properties*, and scored roles in movies, including *Maverick*, *Anger Management*, and *Going Home*.

Mrs. Clint Black

Lisa Hartman was hot. She played the "whoa, Nellie, look how she's grown up" witch Tabitha Stevens on TV. Then really hit her stride as *Knots Landing*'s Ciji Dunn. The character was murdered, a common fate in soap operas. But uncommonly, fan outcry was so huge, producers brought Lisa back, in the guise of the suspiciously monogrammed Cathy Geary. So when Lisa Hartman went backstage after Clint Black's New Year's Eve blowout in 1991, it was a good thing the sparks didn't ignite the big top. "Flash in the pan," they all said. Country star, TV leading lady—right, that sounds like a sure recipe for domestic harmony. But despite all odds, Clint and Lisa (now credited as Lisa Hartman Black) made their marriage work and are well along in its second decade. Along with occasional projects together, Clint Black and Lisa Hartman Black released *The Love Songs* in 2007.

GREATEST HITS

Year	Song
1989	"Better Man"
1990	"Put Yourself in My Shoes"
1991	"Burn One Down"
1992	"Desperado"
1993	"No Time to Kill"
1996	"Like the Rain"
1998	"Nothing But the Taillights"

GARTH BROOKS

February 7, 1962–

Garth Brooks? Who is this guy? From seemingly nowhere, in 1989, boom, there he was. You'd never heard of him, then suddenly it was as if you'd always known him. His self-titled first album initially sold well. After it had been out a year or so, the fourth single pushed Garth Brooks beyond the boundaries of country music. What had been a successful album became a monster smash. "The Dance," a bittersweet song of nostalgia for roads not taken, was accompanied by a compelling music video.

"If you do it for the money you won't last very long, because money is the opposite of music." —Garth Brooks

Garth Brooks was on the way to becoming a certified legend. Gradually, it wasn't just country fans who were digging the hardworking scrappy persona; even rock fans were beginning to catch on. Brooks' live shows shared stagecraft with the glitzy rock spectacles of the time, then upped the ante. Garth wasn't movie-star tall, dark or handsome. But his athletic and explosive antics on stage went even Bruce Springsteen one better. An early adopter of the wireless microphone and guitar, Brooks was free to gambol and cavort around his enormous stage unencumbered by cables or microphone stands. And he did it all in that hat. Who was this guy?

No Fences, released in 1990, sat in the #1 spot on the country music charts for nearly half a year. But a curious thing happened; it also went to #3 on the pop music charts. The country music scene had seen huge stars before, but never had a country artist found such success with rock audiences. Brooks went where no country star had gone before. "Friends in Low Places," which would become his signature anthem, was an unrepentant paean to proletarian values. Right, a drinking song. People who had never bought a country record in their lives were either trying to join Garth in that low A-note or tailing behind as he effortlessly slid a few octaves up to the "beer chasers." Everybody loved the guy who "showed up in boots and ruined your black tie affair."

Garth Rocks!

Never one to pigeonhole himself, Garth Brooks shocked many in 1994 by contributing to the hard rock *Kiss My Ass* tribute to Kiss. Not only did he not do a country version of "Hard Luck Woman," he did a straight rocking version with Kiss themselves. And while fans may have been a little disappointed to see Kiss during their "no makeup" phase, the shock was undoubtedly heightened by Garth, in his trademark hat and bright blue, yoked cowboy shirt, front and center, belting out the words on *The Tonight Show*.

With his incredible crossover success, Garth Brooks has been instrumental in bringing country music to a wider audience.

No Fences also contained the track "The Thunder Rolls." This song's unflinching portrayal of spousal abuse and murder was originally shunned by radio and video outlets but was eventually embraced as one of Brooks' most powerful statements.

Retirement?

Though he remained mostly retired, Garth did pop back into the public eye several times in the new century, usually supporting a charitable cause. In 2005 Brooks and Tricia Yearwood performed the John Fogerty classic "Who'll Stop the Rain" for the national Hurricane Katrina telethon. Garth also released a new single that year, "Good Ride Cowboy," a tribute to his late friend, rodeo star, and country singer Chris LeDoux. It was good old Garth, all slinky guitars and honky-tonk fiddle, with a barroom chorus of ". . . crossed that River Jordan, with Saint Peter on the other side, singing good ride, cowboy, good ride!"

Country artists had crossed over into rock and pop markets before, but not like this. Garth Brooks' third album sold 4 million copies. Before it was even released. *Ropin' the Wind* entered the pop charts at #1, an unprecedented feat for a country artist. Brooks' entry into pop culture was certified. While it could still fairly be considered a country album, *Ropin' the Wind* rocked, no doubt about it. "Rodeo," despite the title, was all about the guitars. The record's barn burner was a Billy Joel cover called "Shameless." And "Papa Loved Mama" gently tweaked country stereotypes with affectionate humor.

Garth Brooks owned the '90s. If somehow one had managed to remain oblivious to the feisty little guy in the big hat, August 7, 1997, was the wake-up call. Some 700,000 went to see a concert in the park. In a little town not previously known for tolerating country music. A little town called New York City. Literally millions more watched on live television. Billy Joel and Don MacLean stopped by to share some tunes. And he killed. He was on top of the world.

And then, he took an unexpected artistic chance. *Garth Brooks, in . . . The Life of Chris Gaines* was an album by an imaginary rock star, played by Garth. Though the album sold respectably for an album by a new rock musician, it didn't reach anywhere near the sales heights Brooks' records usually attained. Both critics and fans seemed mystified by the concept of Garth being somebody other than Garth, and plans for a film and additional albums were shelved.

NUGGET: It doesn't get any lower than a foxhole in the desert. So it should come as no surprise that some of the most ardent fans of "Friends in Low Places" were soldiers fighting in the first Gulf War.

In October 2000 Garth hung it up, retired, to spend more time with his family. He said he wouldn't record again until his youngest daughter turned 18. And other than an occasional benefit recording he has stayed retired. Brooks married country superstar Trisha Yearwood in December 2005, and they live in Oklahoma.

Prior to becoming a country music superstar, Garth attended Oklahoma State University on a track scholarship (for javelin throwing) and majored in advertising.

GREATEST HITS

Year	Song
1989	"If Tomorrow Never Comes"
	"The Dance"
1990	"Friends in Low Places"
	"The Thunder Rolls"
	"Unanswered Prayers"
1991	"Rodeo"
	"Papa Loved Mama"
	"Shameless"
1992	"We Shall Be Free"

BROOKS & DUNN

1991–

BETWEEN PERFORMANCES, (FROM LEFT) BROOKS & DUNN MAKE MUSIC ON THE ROAD, COMPOSING NEW MATERIAL AS THEY RIDE THE TOUR BUS. HERE, THEY PERFORM AT FARM AID.

With Brooks & Dunn around, those other guys just don't stand a chance. What other guys? Just about any country duo that wants to stay alive in the charts, that's who. This hard-hitting twosome has racked up more awards than you can count. Kix Brooks and Ronnie Dunn took home the Country Music Association's Vocal Duo Award every year but one between 1992 and 2006. Add in all those Album of the Year and Entertainer of the Year awards, the multi-platinum albums and singles, and you get the idea. These guys hit a nerve with modern country fans, and as long they keep the kickin' tunes and the high-voltage shows coming, Brooks & Dunn are the big-time honky-tonk favorites of our time.

"In Oklahoma and Texas, if they don't dance, you're dead." —Ronnie Dunn

Country music has a long history of singer-songwriter duos, but most of them were brothers who came up strumming or singing together: the Delmore Brothers, the Louvins, the Everlys, and so on. Brooks & Dunn didn't exactly grow up together—in fact, they didn't even meet until they'd each had some commercial success on their own. But something clicked; the brand-new partners' first album, 1991's *Brand New Man,* stayed on the Billboard country charts for a solid five years, yielding a string of #1 hit singles and selling more than 6 million copies.

Born in Shreveport, Louisiana, in 1955, Leon Eric "Kix" Brooks moved around some as a young man—first to Alaska, where he worked with his dad on an oil pipeline, then to Maine, and then to Nashville, where he landed in 1979, ready for anything. He began writing songs, with some success; the Nitty Gritty Dirt Band's #1 hit "Modern Day Romance" was penned by Kix. His own record releases weren't the chart toppers he'd hoped for. Still, there was that something.

Ronnie Gene Dunn was born in 1953 in Coleman, Texas, and

GREATEST HITS

YEAR	SONG
1991	"Brand New Man"
1992	"Neon Moon"
	"Boot Scootin' Boogie"
1993	"She Used to Be Mine"
1994	"She's Not the Cheatin' Kind"
1995	"You're Gonna Miss Me (When I'm Gone)"
1996	"My Maria"
2001	"Only in America"
2003	"Red Dirt Road"
2005	"Play Something Country"
	"Believe"
2006	"Building Bridges" (with Sheryl Crow and Vince Gill)

raised mostly in Tulsa, Oklahoma. He felt the pull between his hard-living truck driver father, who did time in Leavenworth Prison, and his devoutly religious mother. The eternal conflict between those two paths still enriches Dunn's songwriting. For a while, Ronnie studied theology at Abilene Christian College, but the honky-tonk won out over the pulpit. Back in Tulsa, Ronnie started singing as well as playing bass, and wound up winning the Marlboro Country Music Talent Search. Then, in 1990, Tim DuBois at Arista Records introduced Ronnie and Kix, and the cocktail proved to be potent indeed. A new era of muscular, hard-rocking country was born.

NUGGET: The Olympics and Corn Flakes: you can't get more champion than that. Brooks & Dunn have appeared on both, gracing the "Breakfast of Champions" box, and performing at the 2002 Winter Olympics.

Kix and Ronnie's chemistry has rewarded them well—and not just as performers. In addition to penning nearly all their own songs, they also know how to put on a hell of a show. The duo can kick up some dust on stage, Ronnie mostly taking lead vocals, while Kix cuts it up with the crowd. Brooks & Dunn's three-time traveling "Neon Circus and Wild West Show" let them share the stage with name artists and up-and-coming acts to boot. And the duo has hosted the CMA awards since 2004.

Some of Kix and Ronnie's best moments have come when they return to their elemental country roots. Brooks & Dunn are nothing if not versatile, turning out aching ballads and heartfelt anthems along with their beer-joint, rabble-rousing, up-tempo numbers. But their middle period left a few fans wondering, with 1999's *Tight Rope* producing not a single #1 hit. The boys returned with a vengeance. First *Steers and Stripes*, then *Red Dirt Road*, and now *Hillbilly Deluxe* show that Brooks & Dunn are the masters of their game. They get it—the sense of love and longing, the stumbles and falls and mistakes and triumphs that none of us can shake. And then they shake it all up into a pure, distilled shot of country.

I Dance the Line

You remember line dancing. Don't pretend you didn't indulge in a little Electric Slide back in the early '90s. No? Well, you missed a good time. And Brooks & Dunn's "Boot Scootin' Boogie" helped start it up. It's pretty near impossible to sit still when you hear that song, with its infectious rhythm, slinky fiddle, and boogie-woogie piano.

The line-dance craze got so hot that in 1993, Denim and Diamonds, L.A.'s city-slicker version of a country honky-tonk, opened up a 16,000-square-foot outpost in New York City. And the place was jammed, leading some old-timer skeptics to dub the new country converts "yuppie cowboys."

At least the supply of sawdust held out until the craze ran its course.

When they're not on the road, the two spend time in the studio perfecting their craft. Both men write, sing, and play the guitar.

"Only in America"

"Only in America," one of Brooks & Dunn's most straight-up patriotic anthems, has had some pretty good traction. Sure, it hit #1 on the country charts in 2001, but it stayed there only a week. It definitely got a lift from B&D's performance at President George W. Bush's first inauguration ceremony that same year.

Then something else happened, on September 11, 2001. The tragic events of that day gave new life to "Only in America." Suddenly it felt urgently, fervently right. Maybe people remembered the video, which showed a patchwork of racial diversity, unity, and the old-fashioned American dream of opportunity for all. The lines meant something: "Only in America, where we dream as big as we want to. We all get a chance, everybody gets to dance." The song hit on the ideals we hold most dear, and touched a chord in those days and weeks following the attacks of 9/11—before anyone started pointing fingers at their fellow Americans. No blue states, no red states, just "dreaming in red, white, and blue."

President Bush adopted the anthem as the official song of his 2004 campaign.

GLEN CAMPBELL

April 22, 1936–

Glen Campbell was always a natural on the guitar—self-taught and early out the gate with his signature style. When Glen hit the West Coast, he immediately found work, playing lead guitar for bands like the Champs, right after they'd had a hit with "Tequila." He put out a few records, but mostly gained renown as a session musician. Frank Sinatra, Bobby Darin, Dean Martin, Merle Haggard—all benefited from the dulcet tones of Campbell's guitar. He even toured with the Beach Boys when Brian Wilson couldn't join them on the road.

"I like to start the day early; it keeps me out of trouble."

—Glen Campbell

Glen's dad, an Arkansas sharecropper and father of 12, recognized the boy's talent early and encouraged him with the purchase of a Sears, Roebuck guitar that the kid had mastered by the age of 10.

Glen had the first hit he could call his own in 1967, with "Gentle on My Mind." Though it never charted above #26, it had staying power; in 1990 it was voted the fourth most-played song of all time on radio. Over the next several years, the hits came fast and furious: "Wichita Lineman," "By the Time I Get to Phoenix," "Galveston," and "Where's the Playground, Susie?" All featured Campbell's smooth guitar picking, winsome voice, and vividly drawn characters penned by Jimmy Webb—and more often than not, a palpable sense of longing. The arrangements included strings and backup vocals, in what came to be known as the "Countrypolitan" style. As the name implies, Campbell's records were country but appealed to a wider, cosmopolitan audience as well.

GREATEST HITS

Year	Song
1967	"Gentle on My Mind"
	"By the Time I Get to Phoenix"
1968	"Wichita Lineman"
1968	"Dreams of the Everyday Housewife"
1969	"Galveston"
	"Where's the Playground Susie?"
1975	"Rhinestone Cowboy"
1977	"Southern Nights"

What A Playground, eh, Susie?

Although Glen Campbell's aural and screen personalities were easygoing, confident gentlemen, his off-screen escapades were frequently much more tempestuous. Three divorces and well-documented drug and alcohol problems throughout the '70s culminated in a tumultuous 1980 engagement to country firecracker Tanya Tucker. Glen cleaned up his act during the '80s and continues to perform and record to this day. In fact, he's working with songwriting partner Jimmy Webb again, and the two are due to release an album together in late 2007.

Campbell's telegenic looks just added to his appeal. From 1969 to 1972 he hosted *The Glen Campbell Goodtime Hour*, a variety show that featured guest stars such as Willie Nelson, Merle Haggard, Johnny Cash, and regulars like Anne Murray, Mel Tillis, and Jerry Reed. And the silver screen came calling too, with Glen taking a star turn opposite John Wayne in *True Grit*.

Campbell had an additional string of hits in the late '70s, beginning with "Rhinestone Cowboy." A bittersweet look at the artifices and tradeoffs of fame, it became Glen's signature tune and was later the title of his autobiography. "Southern Nights," despite its pure country title, was an out-and-out rocker.

BILL CARLISLE

DECEMBER 19, 1908–MARCH 17, 2003

In the 1920s *The Carlisle Family Saturday Night Barn Dance* radio show began broadcasting to great success on radio stations in Kentucky and Tennessee. The family included young Cliff and Bill Carlisle, who played Dobro (a resonator guitar) and guitar, respectively. Cliff split off from the family group first and by the mid '30s had gotten a nice little career going. He invited Bill to join him, and the brothers soon found success on radio and record. Cliff was the bigger star, but Bill was working on his own act, playing a character named Hotshot Elmer, yodeling and pratfalling all over the stage.

NUGGET: Bill put paper in the strings of his guitar to accentuate their rhythmic brightness, in order to contrast with Chet Atkins' jazzy riffs on "No Help Wanted."

While the brothers played together often, they also played solo gigs and recorded individually. Bill had a succession of hits with ribald songs of double entendre, like "Copper Head Mama" and "Jumpin' and Jerkin' Blues." Even for the times they were risqué propositions, but hugely popular nonetheless. After some 15 years of the brother act, Cliff retired, leaving Bill as a solo artist. Shortly, Bill did pretty much exactly what you wouldn't expect: started a group called the Carlisles, which contained no Carlisles other than, well, Bill himself. During this period Bill revived his old Hotshot Elmer character. He began cavorting about on stage, jumping over chairs, falling off the steps, and generally creating havoc. His routine was so affecting, he earned the nickname "Jumpin' Bill." And his legs weren't the only thing jumping—his fingers flew along the fretboard. Carlisle's rockabilly guitar work prefigured the nascent rock and roll genre.

JUMPIN' BILL CARLISLE (CENTER) WITH HIS EPONYMOUSLY NAMED GROUP. THE 2005 COMPILATION CD *GONNA SHAKE THIS SHACK TONIGHT* FEATURES THIS IMAGE ON ITS COVER.

By the '50s, tastes had taken a distinct turn for the conservative, and ribald wasn't what the market was screaming for. Bill Carlisle continued to write and perform novelty tunes, but he cooled it with the scatological references. "Too Old to Cut the Mustard," "Is Zat You Myrtle?" and "Knothole" all shared a loopy evocation of the scatological songs of yore, without upsetting the increasingly prudish audiences of the day.

And for all the rock and roll affectations of his Jumpin' Bill persona, Carlisle remained country; he and the Carlisles were invited to join the Grand Ole Opry in 1953. He played there for the next 50 years, until literally days before his death in 2003.

GREATEST HITS

YEAR	SONG
1934	"Copper Head Mama"
1935	"Jumpin' and Jerkin' Blues"
1952	"Too Old to Cut the Mustard"
1953	"No Help Wanted"
1953	"Tain't Nice to Talk Like That"
1954	"Honey Love"

Straight Man

Though ultimately remembered for his long career of novelty songs, Bill Carlisle wrote some enduring "straight" songs as well. "Rattlesnake Daddy," Bill's first single, went on to become a favorite bluegrass number beloved by audiences and artists alike. And "Gone Home" has become a gospel classic.

THE CARTER FAMILY

1927–1943

THE CARTER FAMILY (FROM LEFT: MAYBELLE CARTER, ALVIN PLEASANT CARTER, AND SARA DOUGHERTY CARTER) KEPT PERFORMING EVEN AFTER SARA DIVORCED A. P. AND MARRIED HIS COUSIN.

What if A.P. Carter hadn't come across young Sara Dougherty sitting under that shady tree back in 1914, strumming her autoharp and singing "Engine 143"? Who knows if we'd even have country music at all? Well, he did (or so legend has it), fell in love with both the girl and her lovely alto voice, the two married, and they began a journey that would change the face of American music for generations. When Sara's young guitar-playing cousin, Maybelle Addington, joined the pair in 1925, they became the Carter Family. (Maybelle became a Carter by marrying A. P.'s brother Ezra.) Their music brought to light the deep vein of our rich folk music tradition and became a ray of sunshine for a nation in the throes of the Great Depression. Without the Carter Family and their seminal early recordings, we might not be singing a fraction of the songs we are today. It's only fitting that they should be known as the First Family of Country Music.

Alvin Pleasant Delaney Carter was the son of a farmer in Maces Springs, Virginia, near the Tennessee border. A.P.'s father was an able banjo player, his mother sang folk songs, and his uncle had taught him music using the shape-note technique. When he met Sara, A.P. was on a mission to sell fruit trees; after marriage his ambition changed course, and he became an avid collector of traditional songs, which he, Sara, and Maybelle began to perform: A.P. fiddling and singing some, Sara playing autoharp and singing lead, and Maybelle playing guitar.

It was largely Maybelle's guitar style that gave the Carters their distinctive sound. Strumming the rhythm on the upper strings, she'd simultaneously pick out the melody on the bass strings—a style known alternately as "flatpicking," the "thumb-brush" technique, and the "Carter scratch." It produced a lot of sound—nearly two guitars' worth. Maybelle, who'd been playing since the age of 12, picked up the technique from local African-American musician Lesley Riddle, who was also instrumental in helping A.P. collect songs to add to his repertoire. At the time, it was still unusual to hear a guitar as a lead instrument—a banjo, fiddle, or harmonica were much more common in country or folk music. You can rightly say that Maybelle opened the way for nearly all popular, guitar-based music as we know it. Her influence is truly monumental.

In 1927, the Carter Family traveled 26 miles—an all-day trip—to Bristol, Tennessee, for a recording session that Johnny Cash later called "the single most important event in the history of country music." Producer Ralph Peer of Victor Records held a kind of open-mike, which he'd advertised in local circulars. A. P. jumped at the chance; when he arrived, he was told that a musical act with a female lead singer would never make it, but go ahead anyway. The Carters took home $300 for the six songs they recorded that weekend. Peer also recorded Jimmie Rodgers, the Johnson Brothers, and Ernest Stoneman during

NUGGET: Shortly before A. P. was born in 1891, his pregnant mother, Mollie, was nearly struck by lightning. She claimed it was this near miss that gave A. P. that tremor you hear in his voice.

In a photo from the early 1930s, the Carters pose with the Singing Brakeman, Jimmie Rodgers. Rodgers would succumb to tuberculosis in May of 1933.

NUGGET: Woody Guthrie's "This Land Is Your Land" is built on the bones of the Carters' "When This World's on Fire." Same tune, different words. Bob Dylan did the same thing with "The Wayworn Traveler," which became his "Paths of Victory." He then modified that song, changing the time signature, and it became his "The Times They Are A'Changin'."

those sessions. Bristol has since become known as the birthplace of country music.

A year later, convinced by the staggering sales figures, Peer brought the Carter Family to New Jersey to record a dozen or so more songs, and then moved them on to a number of different labels, finally landing at Decca. During all this time, A.P. had continued rambling the country looking for songs; Sara, left at home alone in poverty and with children to feed, eventually fell in love with one of A.P.'s cousins, Coy Bays. His family packed him up and moved to California, but Sara divorced A.P. in 1936.

Though broken as a family, the Carters continued to play together professionally and in 1938 landed a radio gig on XERA border radio, located in Mexico just across the river from Del Rio, Texas. The station broadcast at a powerful 500 kilowatts, carrying it far and wide across the southern United States. The signal was so powerful, in fact, that when Sara dedicated "I'm Thinking Tonight of My Blue Eyes" to her faraway friend Coy Bays, the young man heard it all the way in California. He immediately traveled to Texas, where he and Sara were married in 1939.

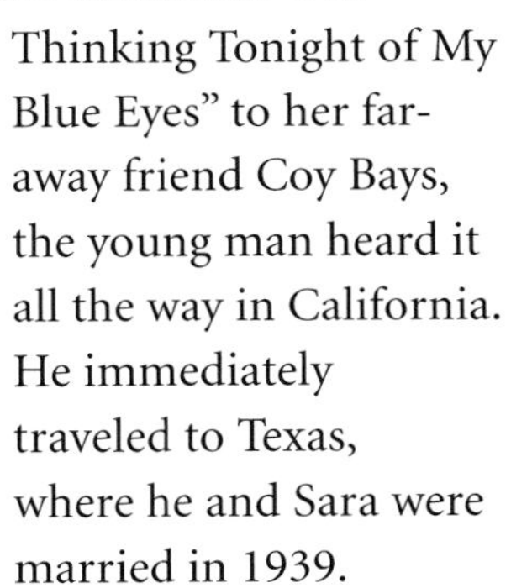

1941 saw the breakup of XERA radio, and the Carters moved to North Carolina, where they'd been offered a gig at a Charlotte station. Sara was hesitant to leave Coy for that long in California, and after two seasons, she moved west to stay. The year 1943 was the end of the Original Carter Family, as they are sometimes called, but their legacy can be heard nearly any time you drop a needle on a record.

Generations

The Carters proved there are second acts in showbiz. With her three daughters, Helen, June, and Anita, Maybelle went on performing as Mother Maybelle and the Carter Sisters. Helen was the ace guitarist, June was the actress and comedienne, and Anita was considered the best singer. June, of course, went on to marry Johnny Cash and wrote his big hit "Ring of Fire." Her daughter Carlene Carter had a respectable singing career of her own, as did Johnny's daughter Rosanne Cash (she's June's stepdaughter).

During the late '60s folk revival, interest in the Carter Family was running high. Artists like Bob Dylan and Joan Baez recorded a number of their songs. Sara and Maybelle saw their moment and joined up for a tour or two, playing to enthusiastic, adoring fans.

GREATEST HITS

Year	Song
1927	"Bury Me under the Weeping Willow Tree"
	"The Storms Are on the Ocean"
	"Single Girl, Married Girl"
	"Poor Orphan Child"
1928	"Keep on the Sunny Side"
	"Wildwood Flower"
	"John Hardy Was a Desperate Man"
1929	"I'm Thinking Tonight of My Blue Eyes"
	"My Clinch Mountain Home"
	"Will the Circle Be Unbroken"
1930	"Worried Man Blues"
1936	"The Wayworn Traveler"

JOHNNY CASH

February 26, 1932–September 12, 2003

Johnny Cash was serious as a heart attack, the baddest badass in country music. The Man in Black. When he sang it sounded like the truth. How could it not? That booming, deadpan, yes, biblical bass voice was a unique and unequalled instrument. Even singing near-novelty songs like "Boy Named Sue" or "One Piece at a Time," that voice resonates with the knowledge and finality of the other man in black, the grim reaper. Violence, mayhem, and death were never far offstage in Cash's songs. And Johnny's personal voyage from the bottoms of despair to the heights of redemption make his story a great American parable.

Johnny Cash's first musical experiences were singing in the fields, picking cotton with his family. When he auditioned for Sam Phillips in 1954, he sang gospel songs, like a good boy. Sam told him to "go home and sin, then come back with a song I can sell."

"Abraham Lincoln, with a wild side."—Kris Kristofferson

"Sunday Morning Coming Down"

In 1969 aspiring songwriter Kris Kristofferson was mopping floors at a music studio in Nashville, picking up occasional work as a commercial helicopter pilot. At the studio, he ran into Johnny Cash and managed to pass him some songs. Cash promptly filed them in the circular file and forgot all about it. But Kristofferson sure didn't. Next time he was in a chopper he headed directly to Cash's spread and landed smack dab in the front yard. Having gotten his attention, Kris was able to get Johnny to take a closer look at his songs. And indeed, "Sunday Morning Coming Down" was a huge hit for Johnny the following year. Good thing too, as Kris later said, "If I hadn't known him, he'd probably have shot me out of the sky."

So he did. Sun released "Hey Porter," "Cry, Cry, Cry," and "Folsom Prison Blues." They all did pretty well on the charts, but merely paved the way for "I Walk the Line" to become a #1 smash hit. A personal declaration very much in the first person, it became Johnny's signature song. Simple, clean orchestration, rough edges showing—you can even hear Johnny humming to hit that note right in the beginning. Then, a straight declaration of self, sitting squarely atop a railroad train of rhythm: pure Johnny Cash.

Clean and sober and happily married to June Carter Cash, Johnny performed on many a tour date in the '70s.

Johnny switched labels to Columbia in the late '50s. He had hits there too, notably "Ring of Fire." Surprisingly, for all its brimstone imagery, the song is about the perils of love. June Carter wrote it when she knew she was in love with Johnny but couldn't do anything about it because they were both married. "It burns, burns, burns, the ring of fire . . ." is not the way most people think about love. Nevertheless, the song struck a chord with the public and became an instant classic.

The mid-'60s were a difficult time for Cash. He had run-ins with the law, drug problems, and his first marriage ended. He married June Carter in 1968, and she helped him conquer his drug addictions and wrangle his personal demons. In January 1968, Cash recorded a performance at Folsom Prison. Of course he sang "Folsom Prison Blues," along with every other prison song he knew. The recording crackled with energy and perhaps a hint of a threat. The captive audience was nonetheless appreciative. The deadpan-macho Johnny Cash performance

"Hello. I'm Johnny Cash." Johnny playing at London's Hammersmith Odeon in 1966.

All of the featured acts in this winning 1967 bill for *The Johnny Cash Show* were acclaimed artists in their own right.

GREATEST HITS	
Year	Song
1955	"Hey Porter!"
	"Cry, Cry, Cry"
1956	"I Walk the Line"
1959	"Don't Take Your Guns to Town"
1963	"Ring of Fire"
1964	"The Ballad of Ira Hayes"
1968	"Folsom Prison Blues"
1969	"A Boy Named Sue"
1985	"Highwayman" (with the Highwaymen)
1994	"Delia's Gone"
2002	"Hurt"

style had found the perfect environment. The following year Cash released the companion San Quentin concert album, to equally great acclaim and sales. "A Boy Named Sue," penned by cartoonist Shel Silverstein, became Johnny's biggest hit, ever. It of course went to #1 on the country charts, but it also rose to #2 on the pop charts.

Johnny Cash continued to tour prolifically throughout the '70s. But the hits grew fewer and farther between. He tried acting, appearing in a number of movies and TV hits (including, notably, playing a singer who looked an awful lot like Johnny Cash on *Columbo*—except this one murders his wife and almost gets away with it). Daughter Rosanne became more successful than her father at this stage of the game.

Then, in 1990, when most thought the best days of Johnny Cash were over, an unexpected thing happened. A hippie-punk-rock-rap kid from Long Island rediscovered Johnny. That kid was named Rick Rubin, and he had a record label, American Recordings. He was smart enough to stick Johnny in front of a

Rosanne

Imagine being Johnny Cash's daughter, thinking you might want to be a singer-songwriter. Sure, it's the family business, but boy, talk about having big shoes to fill.

Known to her dad as "The Brain," Rosanne Cash could have done all sorts of things besides make records. She could have written stories, as her widely praised 1996 collection *Bodies of Water* showed. Or penned children's books, like the equally well-received *Penelope Jane: A Fairy's Tale*. But beginning in 1979, Rosanne did what was so clearly in her blood: made records. And did pretty well at it, too, scoring eleven #1 country singles over 20 years.

Though considered a country artist because of her Nashville roots, Rosanne draws on a wide variety of styles and collaborators. She's covered songs by Tom Petty, the Beatles, John Hiatt, and, of course, her father.

Within a two-year period beginning in 2003, Cash lost her father, stepmother, stepsister, and mother. She poured her pain and loss into the music and turned the devastating period into an artwork documenting a journey into redemption: *Black Cadillac*. The very first thing on the album is father Johnny's voice, recorded decades earlier. Horns blare, reminding one of Johnny's signature song, "Ring of Fire." Then Rosanne's rich alto pondering "One of us gets to go to heaven, one has to stay here in hell…" on the title track. "I Was Watching You" imagines Rosanne watching with mixed feelings from above as her father starts a new life with June. "The Lake House" and "Burn Down This Town" each provide a more nuanced and complex portrait of her family seen through the lens of real events. Though it didn't contain any hits, *Black Cadillac* was rightfully hailed as a remarkable achievement. As a document of the process of learning to negotiate relationships with the dead it is a mile-stone achievement. Incredibly, it is simultaneously an album chock-full of compelling melodies and haunting vocals.

microphone with nothing but his voice and a guitar between us and the truth. American Recordings hit the rock and country worlds like a sucker punch. From the first phrase of "Delia's Gone" people stopped what they were doing and listened with mouths agape. "If I hadn't of shot poor Delia, I'd of had her for my wife." The old tradition of murdering songs was a healthy shock to the system for the digital age. No doubt about it, Johnny could still bring the goods. Stripping away the big, lush orchestration that had become de rigueur was a stroke of genius on Rubin's part, and the songs (and Cash's career) gained new life with nothing but "The Voice" and a guitar to propel them.

Rubin and Cash produced three more American Recordings albums, the last two while Johnny was quite ill. Continuing Rubin's predilection for interesting song choices, Cash sang a Nine Inch Nails song on *American Recordings IV: The Man Comes Around*. The song and video for "Hurt" is considered by many to be his epitaph.

June Carter Cash passed away from complications due to heart surgery in May 2003; Johnny was gone less than four months later. The doctors officially called it "complications from diabetes" and "respiratory failure," but most of us all believe that the Man in Black died from a broken heart.

Married in 1968, June and Johnny had seven children—Rosanne, Kathy, Cindy, Tara, John Carter, Rosie, and Carlene.

Johnny playing in Copenhagen in the 1980s. For his first performance at the Grand Ole Opry, he wore his trademark black while those around him dressed in rhinestones. "I want them to notice my music," he stated, "not my clothes."

Man in Black

Plenty of musicians dress in black. It's slimming, goes with everything, doesn't show dirt, and yes sir, it looks cool. Roy Orbison, Jim Morrison, and even Jerry Garcia pretty much wore exclusively dark wardrobes, but only Johnny Cash earned the moniker The Man in Black."

Cash wore black for a reason. Several, in fact, which he chronicled in 1971's "Man In Black." Johnny wore black to remind himself and others of those who needed their help: "I wear black for the poor and beaten down . . ." Further, he pledges: "But 'til we start to make a move to make a few things right, you'll never see me wear a suit of white." Then, in the last verse, Cash explains that it would be wonderful to be able to wear as many colors as he'd like, "But I'll try to carry off a little darkness on my back, 'til things are brighter, I'm the Man in Black." He didn't just wear black to remind us of the ills of the world—no, Johnny Cash hoped to salve those ills by bearing the weight of its sins directly on his black-clad shoulders.

RAY CHARLES

SEPTEMBER 23, 1930–JUNE 11, 2004

CHARLES HAD A MULTIPLATINUM ALBUM WITH HIS POSTHUMOUSLY RELEASED *GENIUS LOVES COMPANY* (2004), A SERIES OF DUETS WITH MANY MUSIC NOTABLES, AND HIS 250TH RECORDING EFFORT.

You may not immediately think of Ray Charles as a country great. But you'd be wrong. Ray and country go way back—to 1962, in fact. That was the year he made *Modern Sounds in Country and Western Music.* All of Nashville's music scene was up in arms about this record during production: "A black blues and soul singer is going to do what?!" When they heard it, though, they all changed their tune. This seminal album combined Charles' big-band rhythm-and-blues style with country classics, to great effect. Songs made popular by country artists such as Hank Williams and Eddy Arnold were given new life; tunes like "You Win Again," "Half as Much," and "Hey Good Lookin'" swung like they never had before.

Willie Nelson said, "With his recording of 'I Can't Stop Loving You,' Ray Charles did more for country than any other artist." Charles' inventive application of conventions from different genres to country showed the possibilities alive within the country standards of the day. The Genius earned his nickname on that album; by bringing urban swing to country, he was simultaneously bringing country to the city. Fully five certified hits emerged from what had initially been an experiment. And his album of country tunes sat atop the pop charts for three months. The second single was Charles' reimagined version of the Eddy Arnold hit "You Don't Know Me."

NUGGET: "Georgia On My Mind," the old Hoagy Carmichael and Stuart Gorrell gem, became identified with Ray Charles. In 1979 it was made the state song of Georgia. And Willie Nelson sang it at Charles' funeral in 2004.

Over the years, Ray returned occasionally to the country fold. Most strikingly, in the bicentennial year, Charles released his recording of "America." Brother Ray's version quickly insinuated itself in the American psyche as the standard. It's country all right, but it's also big and huge and makes you want to cry, just like America herself.

Brother Ray on the Ten?

Shortly after his death in 2004, an Internet petition began circulating. Signers, and as of publication there were nearly 10,000 of them, stated that they believed Ray Charles should have his picture on the $10 bill. Never mind that only long-dead presidents or statesmen had previously appeared on U.S. currency. It is an amusing thought that perhaps someday, high-rolling hotshots will be trading in their rolls of "Hamiltons" for some "Rays."

"You better live every day like your last, because one day you'll be right."—Ray Charles

GREATEST HITS

YEAR	SONG
1962	"I Can't Stop Loving You"
	"Born to Lose"
	"You Win Again"
	"Hey Good Lookin'"
	"You Don't Know Me"
	"You Are My Sunshine"
1966	"Crying Time"
1971	"Love Country"
1976	"America the Beautiful"
1984	"Little Hotel Room" (with Merle Haggard)
	"We Didn't See a Thing" (with George Jones and Chet Atkins)
2004	"It Was a Very Good Year" (with Willie Nelson)

GUY CLARK

NOVEMBER 6, 1941–

Guy Clark came from Monahans, out in the oilfields of West Texas, a bit west of Midland. And though he moved around plenty before settling in Nashville, those dusty hills and plains are always present in his songs. Clark has made numerous albums and is now into his fourth decade of touring, but he's primarily renowned as a songwriter.

Shortly after Guy and wife, Susanna, moved to Music City in 1971, their dining room table became the fulcrum of a songwriting circle. Steve Earle, Rodney Crowell, Emmylou Harris, and whoever else happened to be in town would sit around that table, passing around the guitar. The writer of whatever song voted best that night would be humorously threatened with grievous bodily harm. The atmosphere was so conducive to songwriting that Susanna, previously a successful fine-art painter, put down her brushes and picked up a guitar herself. Guy's own tunes were ingenious little gems: concise, clever, and rhythmic.

Guitar Man

While still a young man looking for his big break in music, Clark was living in Southern California. He got a job building Dobros at the Dopyera Brothers' guitar factory in Long Beach. He continued to build guitars even after he began making his living songwriting. He is an accomplished luthier and generally plays his own guitars in concert and on record.

Clark has spoken about writing with "a sharp pencil and a big eraser." He hones his songs, trimming and massaging them until they're all meat: tight little packages that tell big stories. Whether it's his hobby of fishing, his former vocation of guitar building, or songwriting itself, Clark's patience and persistence pay off. He's talking about boatbuilding, but might as well be discussing his songs when he sings, "I'm gonna build me a boat, with these two hands, it'll be a fair curve, from noble plans . . ."

AFTER RECEIVING A FLAMENCO GUITAR WHEN HE WAS 16, GUY CLARK ASSUAGED HIS CURIOSITY ABOUT THE INSTRUMENT BY TAKING IT APART AND PUTTING IT BACK TOGETHER, HIS FIRST ENTRY INTO THE REALM OF GUITAR CONSTRUCTION.

"There's only two things that you can't buy, and that's true love and home-grown tomatoes." —Guy Clark

Clark had a particular connection with fellow singer-songwriter Townes Van Zandt, and the two were friends until Van Zandt's death in 1997. Clark has put one of Van Zandt's tunes on almost every one of his albums since. In 1995, Guy Clark, Townes Van Zandt, and Steve Earle played a concert together and recorded it. It was released in 2001 as a live album; Clark titled it *Together at the Bluebird Café.*

Johnny Cash had two hits in the '70s with Guy Clark songs. By the '80s others had discovered Clark's songwriting gifts. Ricky Scaggs had a #1 hit with "Heartbroke," Vince Gill had a hit with "Oklahoma Borderline," the Highwaymen hit big with "Desperados Waiting for a Train" (originally covered by Jerry Jeff Walker), and Rodney Crowell had yet another #1 hit with "She's Crazy for Leaving" (cowritten by Crowell and Clark).
Guy Clark continues to record and perform, most recently touring with Joe Ely, John Hiatt, and Lyle Lovett in 2007.

GREATEST HITS

YEAR	SONG
1975	"Desperados Waiting for a Train"
1992	"Boats to Build"
	"I Don't Love You Much, Do I?"
1997	"Homegrown Tomatoes"
	"Heartbroke"
	"The Last Gunfighter Ballad"

ROY CLARK

April 15, 1933–

An all-around entertainer, Roy Clark could, and did, do it all. Though originally renowned as a prodigy on stringed instruments, Clark later developed talents for singing, writing, and performing. He would even guest-host *The Tonight Show* several times. But he started his career as a guitar prodigy, appearing on the Grand Ole Opry at the ripe old age of 17.

Clark had his first recorded hit in 1963, with "The Tips of My Fingers." But even then, Clark knew he wanted to expand the possibilities of a country guitar picker. He parlayed the guitar hits into guest gigs on TV shows. A guest role on *The Beverly Hillbillies* led to invitations to return as a recurring character. Clark even hit the mean streets of New York City, playing "Malagueña" on *The Odd Couple*.

While Clark has a great affinity for country music, he has also played with such varied performers as the Boston Pops and the late Clarence "Gatemouth" Brown.

In 1969, producers were looking for hosts for their new project, a country answer to *Laugh-In*. Thus *Hee Haw* was born. Clark was hired, along with guitarist Buck Owens. Owens picked and Clark grinned. And then some. Roy appeared in multiple comedy skits on every episode, as well as hosting, performing songs, and singing an a cappella gospel number at the end of every show. He remained with the show for its entire 25-year run.

GREATEST HITS

Year	Song
1963	"The Tips of My Fingers"
1969	"Yesterday, When I Was Young"
1970	"I Never Picked Cotton"
1972	"The Lawrence Welk Hee Haw Counter-Revolution Polka"
1974	"Honeymoon Feeling"

Branson: Sin City, Minus the Sin

In 1983, Roy Clark opened the Roy Clark Celebrity Theater in Branson, Missouri. Branson was a nice little town, mostly known for being a crossroads of lumber shipping. Roy saw the potential and realized he could have the fans come to him rather than endlessly touring. By owning the venue, he didn't have to split ticket income with promoters or managers. This brilliant idea was noted, then quickly copied by various other country acts. Soon Wayne Newton, Glen Campbell, Jim Stafford, Andy Williams, Mickey Gilley, Boxcar Willy, and Ray Stevens joined Roy at their own theaters in Branson. Stars who had a following but either didn't wish to, or didn't have the market pull to do national tours, could get some space in Branson and play shows at their own pace, in their own comfortable environment.

With each country star to announce they were taking their show to Branson, the attraction grew. A critical mass developed, and suddenly the little town smack dab in the center of the country could picture itself as Sin City without the sin. And though the portion of Highway 76 that runs by all the theaters was renamed "The Strip," no strippers, gambling, or racy entertainment could be found here. Branson was wholesome enough for the whole family.

And the whole family came, and brought everyone else with them. Myriad attractions followed the country artists, and Branson remains a hugely popular vacation and entertainment destination.

Louis Marshall "Grandpa" Jones, a *Hee Haw* costar, got his nickname when he was in his early 20s because he was grumpy about working on an early-morning radio show.

Pickin' and Grinnin'

By a quirk of fate, America knows Roy Clark best as the "pickin' and grinnin'" good ole boy cohost of *Hee Haw*. Country's answer to *Laugh-In*, this televised variety show combined live musical performances, scantily clad "farmer's daughters," and cornpone humor. Combining a variety show format with a cast of colorful characters, the residents of the fictional Kornfield Kounty made fun of the country culture while perpetuating every small-town, hick stereotype the writers could jam into an hour.

Pretty much every country artist of the time guest-starred on *Hee Haw*. But nobody was exempt from competing for screen time with a beloved cast of regulars, often doing variations on the same sketch. Each week a different guest would receive the "Where Oh Where Are You Tonight?" treatment, which involved trading nonsense verses with Archie Campbell. The guest began the sketch with his back to the camera, and only revealed himself upon being elbowed by Campbell.

The humor was antimodern. It was the epitome of corny—not surprising, since several of the set pieces of *Hee Haw* involved an actual cornfield set. But the humor was never biting, risqué, or mean. Sexist, maybe. Though a few female performers guested, the female cast members generally were chosen for how they looked in tight little outfits. While the jokes made fun of hillbilly mores and practices, the show clearly shared a lot of the sensibility the jokes were aimed at.

The regulars all had their shticks. Junior Samples—large, laconic, be-overalled—would offer up the lamest piece of metal ever to be called a car. Grandpa Jones would answer the cast's call, "Hey Grandpa! What's for supper?" with a recitation of the delicious meal to come, accompanied by the studio audience's cheers or groans (depending on the menu). Minnie Pearl, trademark tag hanging off her hat, would try to control a classroom of unruly "students." "Stringbean" would read the latest "letter from home," after searching through all the pockets of his overalls looking for the letter. He'd find it "right over my heart," which would usually turn out to be in his back pocket. All these jokes and more were generally packed into every episode.

But for all the humor and shenanigans, most episodes ended with a totally straight song from the Hee Haw Gospel Quartet. Roy Clark, Buck Owens, Grandpa Jones, and Kenny Price would belt out a gospel song, a cappella. These performances were so beloved that several were released as recordings.

PATSY CLINE

SEPTEMBER 8, 1932–MARCH 5, 1963

ALTHOUGH SHE WAS VOTED THE #1 FEMALE ARTIST FOR THE TWO YEARS BEFORE HER TRAGIC DEATH (IN 1963), PATSY WAS NOT INSTALLED INTO THE COUNTRY MUSIC HALL OF FAME UNTIL 1973!

Listen. There! That tinkly piano, descending in a glissade, then some Jordanaires close harmonies. There, before she even begins singing, Patsy's hooked you. Boom. One line is all it takes. Hell, one word: "Crazy." The biggest jukebox hit in history. Ever. Willie Nelson wrote it, Patsy hated it, but she got talked into recording it. The rest is, well, go ahead, you can sing along, you know you want to. Cline's voice is wistful, smoky, lonely, tragic, and compelling. That little catch—was she actually crying?

"Carnegie Hall was real fabulous, but you know, it ain't as big as the Grand Ole Opry."—Patsy Cline

Patsy Cline lived a life that could well have been described in one of her tearjerkers. Broken homes, multiple marriages, bad business deals—Cline lived them all, then died tragically. Since being forced to support the family at 15 when her father abandoned them, she pursued her singing career with single-minded determination. Patsy began performing in clubs and on the radio. She began to have some success and in 1954 landed her first recording contract. That contract was a mixed bag; she began a long association with producer Owen Bradley, but she also had legal wrangles with the company over compensation and royalties.

Cline put out four singles, to no great acclaim. But all that changed one night in January 1957. Arthur Godfrey's *Talent Scouts* featured Patsy Cline singing "Walkin' After Midnight." The crowd went wild, and the song rose to #2 on the country charts. Patsy felt she had finally made it, and spent the next year touring all the radio shows playing her hit single. And then? Nothing. That was it. What looked like the beginning of a promising career started to look a lot more like the trajectory of a one-hit wonder. By the end of 1957, Cline retreated into retirement, at the ripe old age of 25.

At the end of this period, Patsy managed to get out of her original recording contract, signed with Decca, and continued working with Owen Bradley. Bradley was an early proponent and creator of what later would be called "the Nashville Sound," and Patsy was one of his main projects. Though initially dubious, Cline trusted Bradley's instincts. She allowed him to orchestrate her next single with strings and the smooth-singing Jordanaires on backup vocals. "I Fall to Pieces" may not have rocketed up the charts, but it sure cruised. Eight months later, it was #1. More huge hits followed shortly, produced under the sure hand of Bradley.

NUGGET: In Patsy Cline's hometown of Winchester, Virginia, is a bell tower. Erected in memory of Patsy, it chimes hymns every evening at 6 to memorialize the hour Patsy died.

GREATEST HITS

YEAR	SONG
1957	"Walkin' after Midnight"
1961	"I Fall to Pieces"
	"Crazy"
1962	"She's Got You"
1963	"Leavin' on Your Mind"
	"Sweet Dreams"

Songs like "She's Got You" and "Crazy" were not only hits on the country charts, they were crossing over into pop territory. For perhaps the first time, a country artist was being embraced by the masses.

Cline traded the cowgirl getups for sophisticated and glamorous cocktail dresses, worn with spike heels, no less. Perhaps the first crossover superstar, Patsy headlined at Carnegie Hall and the Hollywood Bowl. She had actual gold dust installed on the tiles in the bathroom of her dream house. Patsy Cline had arrived. And then, shockingly, it was over. After playing a benefit in Kansas City, Cline, Cowboy Copas, and Hawkshaw Hawkins took off in a small plane piloted by Cline's manager, Randy Hughes. After a stop in Dyersburg for fuel, the foursome took off into inclement weather and high wind. Only 13 minutes after takeoff the plane had crashed, killing all aboard.

Even after her untimely death, Patsy continued to chart hit records. "Leavin' on Your Mind," "Sweet Dreams," and "Faded Love" were all released posthumously and went on to become classics. The bittersweet irony is that Patsy Cline's tragic death made her an even bigger star than she'd been while alive.

PATSY ATTRIBUTED A BOOMING SINGING VOICE "LIKE KATE SMITH'S" TO A NEAR-FATAL THROAT INFECTION SHE HAD AT AGE 13.

AS A CHILD, PATSY HAD IDOLIZED SHIRLEY TEMPLE AND WANTED TO BE A DANCER. AFTER WINNING A KIDS' DANCING CONTEST, SHE LOST INTEREST AND TURNED TO PIANO, FOLLOWED BY SINGING.

Premonitions

Patsy Cline had been nearly killed in a car accident in 1961. She had been thrown through the windshield; this was before the wide adoption of seat belts. When Dottie West arrived, she found Patsy on the ground in a spray of shattered glass and blood. While picking the glass from her hair, Patsy reportedly insisted the other driver be treated first. She suffered cuts on her face, a broken wrist, and a dislocated hip. She was hospitalized for nearly a month and was later forced to wear wigs to cover the scars on her forehead. Upon emerging from the hospital, she went right back on tour, supported by crutches.

As early as September 1962, Patsy Cline confided in friends Loretta Lynn, Dottie West, and June Carter that she felt a premonition of her own impending death. Mere months later the predictions had come true. Nashville was in shock at the simultaneous death of three stars. And it would get worse. Singer Jack Anglin died in an auto accident on the way to Patsy Cline's memorial service. Then, several weeks later, Opry star Texas Ruby perished in a fire. That brought to five the number of Opry members killed that month, a tragic record happily not surpassed in the ensuing years.

FLOYD CRAMER

October 27, 1933–December 31, 1997

When Floyd Cramer hit Nashville in 1952 there weren't really any session piano players. There was Owen Bradley, who was moving into production but still tickling the ivories as well. That was about it. Mostly, it seemed, there wasn't really any call for studio piano players. Back then country was all guitars, banjos, and pedal steel. There may have been a little tinkly honky-tonk-style piano on a few songs, but there wasn't enough work to support any session players.

So Floyd made some contacts but then headed back to Shreveport. He commuted up to Nashville for a couple gigs over the next few years, until producer Chet Atkins convinced him there was enough work for it to be worth his while to stay. He moved to Nashville in January 1955. Within two years, he was playing sessions night and day.

"I don't practice. I call it play. That's because I enjoy it. Practice I don't enjoy."—Floyd Cramer

Floyd Cramer's piano was heard on songs by Elvis Presley, Brenda Lee, Patsy Cline, Jim Reeves, Roy Orbison, and so many more. You can run out of breath just an inch into the list. Floyd's arrival in Nashville had been perfectly timed. Producers like Bradley and Atkins were developing "the Nashville Sound." Rough and rural steel guitars and banjos were out; slick, sophisticated, strings, piano, and smooth backing vocals were in. Floyd's playing was an integral part of the Nashville Sound. And he played on literally scores of records, by almost every country star of the time.

Cramer's arrival in Nashville coincided with a need for keyboard session players. So in demand was the self-taught pianist that he declined to join Elvis Presley's touring band.

Floyd Cramer gained renown beyond Nashville insiders in 1960, when he had his own hit with "Last Date." He had been working on gestating the slip-note style of playing and wrote "Last Date" specifically to showcase it. And though it did all right on the country charts, it absolutely rocked the pop charts. It never made #1 because some guy named Elvis was hogging the spot with "Are You Lonesome Tonight?" Didn't bother Floyd much, as he'd played on that session too.

Cramer went on to regularly create and release albums of his music for RCA records throughout the '60s and '70s. For nearly 15 years he would record two albums a year, usually with Chet Atkins in the producer's chair.

Appoggiatura

Appoggiatura is a fancy Italian name for what is otherwise known as slip-note playing. Floyd Cramer first heard it up on a demo tape for Don Robertson's "Please Help Me, I'm Falling" and used the style at the gig. The player "slips" from one note down up into the real note. Floyd later reported he was trying to imitate Mother Maybelle's autoharp technique. But no matter its origins, when Cramer's "Last Date" hit the airwaves, nobody could ignore it. The song was a huge hit, and the sound went on to be a staple of the burgeoning Nashville Sound.

NUGGET: In the free-for-all atmosphere of a recording session, job descriptions sometimes get blurred. On Jimmy Dean's "Big Bad John," Cramer was pressed into service to "play" the pickax sound effects by banging on an iron doorstop with a hammer.

GREATEST HITS

Year	Song
1958	"Flip, Flop, and Bop"
1960	"Last Date"
1961	"On the Rebound"
	"San Antonio Rose"
1977	"Rhythm of the Rain"
1980	"Theme from Dallas"

VERNON DALHART

April 6, 1883–September 14, 1948

By the standards of his day, Vernon Dalhart was barely a country singer. Never mind that in 1924 he recorded the first million-selling country record. Never mind that he was born on a ranch in Texas and worked as a cowboy. Never mind that he knew heartache firsthand, his father having been killed in a fight with Vernon's own uncle. The fella sang opera, moved to New York City, and owned a tuxedo. So by the country standards of his day, Vernon Dalhart was a little bit suspect.

Today, we know better. Dalhart's early recordings of hillbilly songs and country ballads brought the Southern sound to a new audience through the relatively new media of both records and radio.

"There should be music in all our lives. It would take away much of the grimness and sorrow." —Vernon Dalhart

Born Marion Try Slaughter in Jefferson, Texas, Try and his mother moved to Dallas after his father's death. There, Try studied music at the Dallas Conservatory, and he made his way to New York City in 1910. Adopting the name Vernon Dalhart from two West Texas towns where he'd worked as a cowboy, he achieved some success on New York's opera stages.

When he first arrived in New York City, the classically trained Dalhart found employment at a sheet music store and subsidized his income by singing at funerals.

Light opera was Dalhart's natural genre, but the early recording industry was looking for novelties. Vernon had what it took, moving easily between minstrel, Irish ballad, and Hawaiian styles. But he hit the jackpot with "The Wreck of the Old 97," which he recorded twice in 1924, first for Edison and then for Victor, who backed it with "The Prisoner's Song," a lilting ballad. That disc made Dalhart a star, selling 7 million copies.

Dalhart stuck with hillbilly and cowboy songs after that success. He played harmonica and Jew's harp, and paired up with guitarist, singer, and whistler Carson Robison on many of his recordings. Often using pseudonyms, Dalhart cut thousands of sides for a slew of labels. His songs resonated with the public at large—workingman's themes like train wrecks and mining disasters, smoothed over with his classically trained tenor. Dalhart primed American ears for the likes of the Carter Family, opening the path for the greats to come.

Disaster!

What is it about a disaster that makes people sing? We're not exactly sure, but country songs are full of them. Vernon Dalhart wasn't the only one to latch on to those disaster songs, but he had a good run with them. Partly, it was the storytelling that appealed to populist sentiments: the hapless engineer pushed to go too fast by the greedy railroad company (that's your "Old '97"). Or the famously trapped Kentucky spelunker—Dalhart tells you all about it in "Death of Floyd Collins," which ends with the words "we too must meet our doom."

Fires, hurricanes, floods, train wrecks, shipwrecks, car crashes, mining accidents—you name it, there's a country song about it. Disaster songs carry on a longstanding folk tradition that goes back to our oldest oral history roots. They're how we tell, honor, and remember.

GREATEST HITS

Year	Song
1917	"Can't Yo' Heah Me Callin', Caroline?"
1924	"Wreck of the Old 97"
	"The Prisoner's Song"
1925	"Death of Floyd Collins"
1925	"The Santa Barbara Earthquake"
1927	"The Gypsy's Warning"
1929	"Low Bridge Everybody Down"
c. 1931	"The Runaway Train" (with Adelyne Hood)

CHARLIE DANIELS

OCTOBER 28, 1936–

DUE TO HIS DEDICATION AND LOTS OF PRACTICE, CHARLIE LEARNED TO MASTER THE BANJO, THE FIDDLE, THE GUITAR, AND THE MANDOLIN.

"The Devil went down to Georgia . . ." OK, that tears it—best opening line to a story since "Call me Ishmael." Charlie Daniels' hit song of the same name burst on the scene in 1979. The dramatic tale of an epic fiddle battle with Satan soared to #1 on the country charts and clocked in at #3 on the pop charts.

Charlie Daniels had been playing as a session musician in Nashville during the '60s and '70s, recording with the likes of Bob Dylan, Marty Robins, and Leonard Cohen. In 1971 he made his own record and shortly after that assembled the Charlie Daniels Band. They've played together ever since, and beginning in 1974 hosted Charlie Daniels' Volunteer Jam. These frequently recorded sessions have continued to this day, apart from a brief three-year respite during the '80s.

Charlie Daniels Band was hard-core country. They wore big hats, included fiddles and mandolins in their orchestration, and worked the redneck angle heavily. But on top of that foundation, CDB rocked; their live performances crackled with rock and roll's energetic sense of chaos. And they were loud. When that crescendo came, you weren't sure if you were listening to a freight train or a song, but then suddenly, back into the pocket, hitting a tight groove for Daniels' dangerous tales.

"I just thank God I can make a living doing something I love as much as I do playing music."—Charlie Daniels

Daniels' cinematic yarns combined dramatic and humorous tales with dramatic musical accompaniment. When the Evil One strikes his fiddle in "The Devil Went Down to Georgia," you can almost smell the brimstone. And when the unlikely hippie of "Uneasy Rider" is chasing the redneck villains around the parking lot you can just picture the hapless erstwhile threats running circles in herky-jerky Keystone Kops fashion. Many of Charlie Daniels' songs shared that quality of being just on the edge of novelty, but remaining catchy and compelling enough to transcend that label.

Politics started dominating more and more of Daniels' songs by the '80s. "In America" was a comment on the Iran hostage crisis of 1979. Charlie may have been a proud right-winger, but he was an American first: "We'll all stick together, you can take that to the bank. That's the cowboys and the hippies and the rebels and the yanks."

What So Proudly Yet Waves

Charlie Daniels published *Ain't No Rag: Freedom, Family and the Flag* in 2003. It includes letters such as "An Open Letter to the Hollywood Bunch" in defense of George W. Bush's Iraq policies. Daniels runs his own Web site, where he shares his political views and invites readers to join right in and post their own views on "The Soapbox."

GREATEST HITS

YEAR	SONG
1972	"Uneasy Rider"
1975	"The South's Gonna Do It"
	"Orange Blossom Special"
	"Long Haired Country Boy"
1979	"The Devil Went Down to Georgia"
1988	"Uneasy Rider '88"
1985	"American Farmer"
1993	"America, I Believe in You"

JIMMIE DAVIS

September 11, 1899–November 5, 2000

"The Singing Governor," Jimmie Davis is best known for his hit single and reputed authorship of the classic "You Are My Sunshine." Serving two terms as Democratic governor of Louisiana, once in the '40s and again in the '60s, Jimmie Davis enjoyed his biggest musical success while serving his first term in office. Davis traveled a musical path from risqué early country-blues tunes such as "Red Nightgown Blues" and "Tom Cat and Pussy Blues," a stint doing Western swing, and then onward to traditional gospel during the '50s.

NUGGET: Jimmie Davis married Anna Carter Gordon of the gospel group the Chuck Wagon Gang in 1969, a few years after he lost his first wife, Alvern.

Though he was born into a poor sharecropper's family of 11 children in Beech Springs, Louisiana, James Houston Davis went on to earn a master's degree in 1927 from Louisiana State University in Baton Rouge. There he sang in the glee club and in a vocal quartet. Moving to Shreveport soon after graduation, Davis broke in to radio, ably imitating Jimmie Rodgers, complete with the bawdy double entendres and deft cowboy yodeling. After a string of unsuccessful singles for Victor, Jimmie signed to Decca records in 1934; his first Decca recording, "Nobody's Darlin' But Mine" finally yielded a hit.

Jimmie Davis didn't have to choose between politics and music; he just combined the two, and the formula worked. During the late '30s and early '40s, Davis campaigned with a speech and a song, or even a whole set of songs, hillbilly style. The technique—and doubtless his civic dedication—got him elected first to municipal and state offices, and then finally as governor in 1944. He even made time for movies, appearing in five different Hollywood productions during the '40s; these included one title with Ozzie and Harriet Nelson, and his own 1947 biopic, *Louisiana.* When his first term as governor was up in 1948, Davis began singing full time, turning to the smoother country style that was coming into vogue. The '60s saw Davis serving as governor again and dedicating himself to gospel music, which he did for the rest of his long career.

In his first run for governor, Davis used his hit "You Are My Sunshine" as his campaign song, helping him to beat out incumbent Huey Long.

GREATEST HITS	
Year	Song
1934	"Nobody's Darlin' But Mine"
1936	"It Makes No Difference Now"
1940	"You Are My Sunshine
1944	"It Is Too Late Now"
	"There's a Chill on the Hill Tonight"
1945	"There's a New Moon over My Shoulder"
1952	"Suppertime"
1962	"Where the Old Red River Flows"

"A song is the most intangible thing in the world."—Jimmie Davis

Whose "Sunshine" is it, Anyway?

Every schoolkid knows it by heart: "You are my sunshine, my only sunshine." Trouble is, there's no "only" author of the song. Jimmie Davis made it a hit in 1940, and Gene Autry and Bing Crosby gave the tune fine workouts themselves. Davis claimed he penned "Sunshine" while in graduate school, but the story isn't airtight. Hard up Depression-era songwriters would sometimes sell off their creations for a few bucks; this may have been the case with Paul Rice, of the Rice Brothers, who claimed authorship of the song himself. Of course, Rice borrowed the words from another guy, and so on. It was named official state song of Louisiana in 1977, and Jimmie Davis went to his grave insisting that "You Are My Sunshine" was his.

THE DELMORE BROTHERS

1931–1952

"Gas was low, tires were bad, and I didn't hardly know the way to Nashville." When Alton and Rabon Delmore drove down from the hills of Alabama in 1931, bound for the Opry, their cousin Jake Williams was at the wheel; that was his take on the trip. Well, they found the Grand Ole Opry, and the folks there liked the Delmore Brothers' soft voices, close harmonies, and bluesy, gospel-tinged songs enough to sign them on.

"The Delmore Brothers, God, I really loved them! I think they've influenced every harmony I've ever tried to sing." —Bob Dylan

The Delmore Brothers enjoyed a relatively short but very productive run at the Opry; by the time they left the show in 1939, they'd penned hundreds of songs; many of these, like "Blues Stay Away From Me" and "Alabama Bound," have since become standards. During the '40s the brothers cycled from gospel to boogie-woogie to full-tilt rockabilly. The Delmores were among the first to mix black players and musical influences with white country traditions, a cross-pollination that gave birth to rock and roll.

GREATEST HITS	
YEAR	SONG
1931	"Got the Kansas City Blues"
1933–41	"Alabama Lullaby"
	"Beautiful Brown Eyes"
	"Brown's Ferry Blues"
	"Gonna Lay Down My Old Guitar"
	"Lonesome Yodel Blues"
1943–52	"I'm Alabama Bound"
	"Southern Moon"
	"Hillbilly Boogie"
	"Blues Stay Away from Me"
	"Freight Train Boogie"

Other Brothers: The Louvins

Like the Delmore Brothers, the Louvin Brothers came up singing gospel together, and they took the act big, joining the Opry in 1955. Their 1960 album, *Satan is Real*, featured Charlie and Ira in Delmores-style close harmony, praising the righteous path—and of course, warning of the dire alternative. The Louvins gave a nod out to their inspiration, with their album *Tribute to the Delmore Brothers*. Brother Ira lost his life in a car crash in 1965, but Charlie is still going strong; on a 2007 album, Charlie sings Louvins classics, joined by the likes of George Jones and Elvis Costello.

Music was like the gospel in the Delmore family; mother Mollie was a composer of shape-note songs, and Alton, the elder brother, began composing along with her, becoming a deft guitar-picker in the process. Singing together came naturally, and by the time Rabon was 10, the brothers were playing and singing at local gatherings. Alton remained the primary songwriter, and the brothers stayed together as an act until Rabon died in 1952.

The Delmores' post-Opry years saw a musical change of pace. They amped up the whole operation and got themselves signed to King records. The brothers brought in Merle Travis on guitar, and Wayne Raney, who played a mean "choke" harmonica. Alton also joined up with Merle Travis, Grandpa Jones, and Red Foley to form the gospel quartet the Brown's Ferry Four. But in spite of all the moving around (Cincinnati, Memphis, Chattanooga, Houston—you name it) and all the slam-dunk tunes (about a thousand of them), the Delmore Brothers never really hit the big time.

MOST OF THE DELMORE BROTHERS' HONORS WERE DELIVERED POSTHUMOUSLY; THEY WERE INDUCTED INTO THE COUNTRY MUSIC HALL OF FAME IN MAY 2002.

LITTLE JIMMY DICKENS

DECEMBER 19, 1920–

They make pretty big boots these days. But no matter how big they make them, none can do anything to make Jimmy Dickens break the five-foot barrier. They can be spangly, made of exotic leather like ostrich or alligator, but no matter how gaudy, the little cowboy with the big personality stands a mere 4 feet 11 inches above the heels. Little Jimmy Dickens knew he wasn't going to grow any taller, but he also knew he could make it big in country music.

Over more than 50 years, Little Jimmy did that, and more. Sometime in 1948 Roy Acuff heard him singing on the radio and was impressed. He passed the young performer's name on to Columbia Records and the Grand Ole Opry. They were impressed too, and both organizations signed him right up.

From the start, Opry fans ate up Dickens' corny humor. Most of the songs he would release over the years were novelty tunes. But at the Opry he sang all sorts of things. His first hit, "Take an Old Cold 'Tater (and Wait)" earned him the nickname "Tater" from Hank Williams. The name stuck, and soon he had had "Tater" embossed on his guitar strap. When he wasn't hosting the Opry, Little Jimmy belted out songs like "Out Behind the Barn," "I'm Little but I'm Loud," and "Hillbilly Fever." His biggest hit came in 1965, with the release of "May the Bird of Paradise Fly up Your Nose." The song hit it big, thanks to Little Jimmy's usual blend of speedy guitar work and clever word play.

To this day Little Jimmy Dickens still plays up to five shows a week at the Opry. The "Mighty Mouse in his pajamas" can still get out a roar.

GREATEST HITS	
YEAR	SONG
1949	"Take an Old, Cold, 'Tater (and Wait)"
	"Country Boy"
1950	"I'm Little But I'm Loud"
	"A-Sleeping at the Foot of the Bed"
1954	"Out Behind the Barn"
1962	"The Violet and the Rose"
1965	"May the Bird of Paradise Fly Up Your Nose"
1967	"Country Music Lover"
1968	"Raggedy Ann (You've Been Quite a Doll)"

THE 13TH CHILD OF A WEST VIRGINIAN FARMING FAMILY, THE SHORT-STATURED LITTLE JIMMY'S MUSICAL REPUTATION IS 10 FEET TALL.

Nudie, the Cowboy Tailor

In the early '40s, a Ukrainian émigré tailor named Nuta Kotlyarenko decided he'd had enough of dressing showgirls in New York and headed west. In California, Nuta traded in his name for Nudie, shortened the Kotlyarenko to Cohn, and *voilà*, Nudie the Cowboy Tailor was born.

Nudie began designing and manufacturing Western wear such as no real cowboy had ever seen. An early creation was peach-colored, with covered wagons on the back, wagon-wheel details up and down the legs, and spangled with the requisite rhinestones. Nudie brilliantly offered the suit to Porter Wagoner (get it?) for no charge. A huge country star wearing one of his most amazing creations was like a virtual billboard, and that free suit paid Nudie back in spades. Soon everyone who was anyone in country music was wearing Nudie's suits: Little Jimmy Dickens, Dolly Parton, Merle Haggard, Roy Rogers, and Dale Evans. Basically, everybody but Trigger. In 1957, in perhaps the ultimate expression of Nudie's genius, the King himself, Elvis Presley, paid $10,000 for a one-piece gold lamé number. You heard right: THAT suit. That was Nudie.

DIXIE CHICKS

1989–

The Dixie Chicks (from left to right: Emily Robison, Natalie Maines, and Martie Maguire) have weathered political controversy to become more popular than ever.

In the late '80s sisters Emily and Martie Erwin got together with schoolmates Laura Lynch and Robin Macy to form the Dixie Chicks. Martie was an award-winning fiddle master even at that young age, and the girls produced two albums of bluegrass-tinged country. Though the Chicks played local shows in and around Dallas to great acclaim, radio did not pick up on the singles, and they weren't able to produce a hit.

In 1993 Macy left, leaving the Chicks as a trio. They produced another album and managed to procure some high-profile gigs, but commercial success still remained beyond their grasp. When Lynch left the group in 1995, the sisters cast about for a replacement. They had worked with master steel guitar player

"People don't like mouthy women in country music."—Emily Robison

and producer Lloyd Maines on their previous records and at live gigs. Lloyd had a daughter with quite a set of pipes on her, and passed an audition tape to the former Erwin sisters (both had gotten married and changed their names by then). The girls liked what they heard and invited Natalie to audition for them. Nobody told her it was an audition—maybe that's why she sounded so good. Within days Martie Maguire and Emily Robison invited Natalie Maines to join the Dixie Chicks, and the die was cast.

The new lineup got down to work crafting a sound that was modern yet firmly planted in the bluegrass tradition. Natalie was quoted as saying she figured it might appeal to hard-core country fans, and hopefully would get them noticed a bit. Well, *Wide*

Although the Chicks were founded in 1985, when Natalie Maines joined the group in 1995, the band (still intact today) altered its musical direction, creating a new modern/roots hybrid style.

THE CHICKS, PERFORMING ON A TOUR OF EUROPE, GOT INTO HOT WATER WITH THEIR U.S. FAN BASE BUT STOOD THEIR GROUND AND CAME OUT ON TOP.

Open Spaces came out and quickly became the best-selling group album in the history of country music.

Wide Open Spaces, its follow-up, *Fly*, and then *Home* all contained what would become the Chicks' hallmarks: catchy riffs, astonishing musicianship, and harmonies. Oh, the harmonies! Above all else, those Chicks had voices like angels. Natalie's voice could swing from bell-pure to honky-tonk rasp in a heartbeat. The Chicks had chops, but on top of that they had an infectious and irrepressible enthusiasm that sprang out of every song. While in reality they probably spent just about every minute of every day practicing to pull off those finger-busting runs, the whole operation sounded like an improvised, spur-of-the-moment romp. And on top of it all, the Chicks just sounded fun to hang out with, appealing to men and women alike. They were stylish, modern, and put on a helluva show.

Natalie Maines' thrilling soprano draws the listener in, like a jewel in a shop window. Further attention reveals Emily Robison's banjo (or mandolin, guitar, or anything else plucked) lines interwoven with Martie Maguire's soaring fiddle figures. The Chicks' brand of country-rock was immensely popular, and the band dominated not just the country charts, but the rock and pop charts as well. The Dixie Chicks' takeover of popular culture was enshrined when they were invited to sing the national anthem at Super Bowl XXXVII in 2003.

GREATEST HITS

YEAR	SONG
1997	"I Can Love You Better"
1998	"Wide Open Spaces"
1999	"Cowboy Take Me Away"
	"Without You"
2002	"Long Time Gone"
	"Top of the World"
	"Landslide"
2005	"I Hope"
2006	"Not Ready to Make Nice"

Uppity

On stage with the Chicks in London one fine evening in early 2003, Natalie Maines made an offhand comment suggesting that she was ashamed of fellow Texan President George W. Bush. During the run-up to the second Gulf War, American feelings were running high. Maines' comments sparked a media conflagration back home.

Following reports of the comments, radio conglomerates called for a boycott, announcing that they would stop playing the Dixie Chicks' records. Maines backpedaled a bit: "I apologize to President Bush because my remark was disrespectful. Whoever holds that office should be treated with the utmost respect." But she didn't come out in support of the war. The critics continued their indignant howls at all things Chicks. The group couldn't get airplay. Their records stopped selling. And perhaps worst of all, fellow country musicians shunned the band. At the Country Music Association awards that year, not only were the Chicks booed, but they lost out to Toby Keith, a blunt critic who had led the charge against them.

Then the Dixie Chicks got defiant. They appeared naked on the cover of *Entertainment Weekly* (strategically posed to avoid showing the naughty bits), covered in jingoistic slogans. They invited audiences to boo, just to get it over with, but were usually cheered instead. The controversy seemed to mostly dissipate, as the war ground on without an end in sight.

Then came "Not Ready to Make Nice," the first single from 2006's *Taking the Long Way*. The song was a rallying cry for the Dixie Chicks' integrity. The next line is "I'm not ready to back down." Maines may be of small physical stature, but she was clearly feisty and unafraid. Another lyric from the song became the title for the 2006 documentary about the Chicks controversy, *Dixie Chicks: Shut Up and Sing*.

The Dixie Chicks were invited to perform the song at the 2007 Grammy Awards. In addition to burning down the house with their live performance, the Chicks swept the awards, winning Best Album, Best Record, and Best Song. Country audiences sweetened the vindication by pushing the album to #1 on the country charts.

STEVE EARLE

January 17, 1955–

Take a tobacco can full of Texas dirt. Spread it out on a cookie sheet. Dangle your newborn over it, allowing his tiny feet to make their little impressions. The first soil his feet touched was Texan, and so is he, no matter where he's actually born. This technique was first tested on Stephen Fain Earle in 1955. His father was stationed at Fort Monroe, in Hampton, Virginia. Fort Monroe was not actually in Texas, so Earle's grandfather collected and shipped the aforementioned pile of dirt to avoid the indignity of having a non-Texan in the family.

"Sometimes it's fun to be the most radical mother__ in first class." —Steve Earle

Steve Earle grew up in Texas, but a chance encounter with songwriter Townes Van Zandt changed everything. Earle later said of him, "He was a real good teacher and a real bad role model." Van Zandt convinced the young guitar player he could make a go of it as a songwriter, and at age 19 Earle moved to Nashville with the goal of breaking into the music business. While working the oddest of odd jobs to support himself, he gradually found work as a songwriter and began playing as a session musician, all the while honing his own act.

GREATEST HITS

Year	Song
1986	"Guitar Town"
	"Hillbilly Highway"
1987	"Nowhere Road"
	"I Ain't Ever Satisfied"
1988	"Copperhead Road"
	"The Devil's Right Hand"
1990	"Other Kind"
1996	"Ellis Unit One" (on the soundtrack to *Dead Man Walking*)
2004	"The Revolution Starts Now"

Despite the successful musical collaboration between Earle and the Del McCory Band, the relationship didn't last, reportedly due to Earle's propensity for cursing, to which the pious band members objected.

The Write Stuff

Though renowned as a singer and guitar player, Steve Earle first achieved success as a songwriter. In the late '70s he got hired as a staff songwriter for Sunbury Dunbar, a subsidiary of RCA, for the princely sum of $75 a week. Earle looked ready for his first big break when Elvis Presley made plans to record "Mustang Wine," but had to leave the champagne in the fridge when Presley failed to show for the recording session. Carl Perkins later recorded and released the tune. In 1982 Earle had his first hit when Johnny Lee released "When You Fall in Love" (cowritten with John Scott Sherrill) and it climbed to #14 on the country charts.

In 1986 *Guitar Town* took the country and rock worlds by storm. Not so much a crossover album as a reimagining of the power of simple hillbilly music mated with the driving force of rock. The title track rose to #7 on the country charts. Earle found himself embraced by rock critics and audiences as well.

Follow-up albums *Exit 0*, *Copperhead Road*, and *The Hard Way* provided more of the straight-ahead country rock that was becoming Earle's hallmark.

Jailed on drug charges in the late '90s, Earle came out clean and sober. He felt compelled to use the bully pulpit of his music to try to change minds. In particular, his opposition to capital punishment led to the song "Ellis Unit One" being included on the soundtrack to the film *Dead Man Walking*. Earle continues to write, both music and prose.

THE EVERLY BROTHERS

1956–

Harmony never looked so darn cute as it did when the Everly Brothers came along. Don and Phil Everly grew up in country, wound up in rock and roll, and broke plenty of hearts along the way. Building on the close-harmony tradition of singing siblings before them like the Delmores and the Louvins, the Everly Brothers added steel guitar, sharp suits, and a dab of hair pomade, and voilà!—the greatest vocal duo of the '50s was born. The Everlys' heartfelt singing style and their easy country way with a melody bridged the gap between Nashville and the mainstream. They influenced many musicians during the '60s and beyond, from doo-wop to the Fab Four to the folk revival.

It's hard to say just where the Everly Brothers are from: Don was born in Kentucky, Phil in Chicago, they grew up in Iowa, and came of age in Nashville. Their folks were country musicians; Ike and Margaret regularly brought the boys along to their radio appearances. In Nashville the boys met the dynamic husband-wife songwriting team Boudleaux and Felice Bryant, who didn't quite know what to do with a little ditty called "Bye, Bye Love." The Everly Brothers sure did, and the song was a smash. Their popularity rivaled that of Elvis Presley, and the Everly Brothers' wholesome image made them appealing to parents at a time when rock and roll seemed more than a little dangerous.

FROM LEFT: DON AND PHIL EVERLY WERE MUCH MORE SUCCESSFUL SINGING TOGETHER THAN DURING THEIR RESPECTIVE SOLO CAREERS.

GREATEST HITS	
YEAR	SONG
1957	"Bye, Bye Love"
	"Wake Up, Little Susie"
1958	"All I Have to Do is Dream"
	"Bird Dog"
1959	"Till I Kissed You"
1960	"When Will I Be Loved"
	"Cathy's Clown"
1961	"Walk Right Back"
	"Temptation"
1962	"Crying in the Rain"
1965	"The Price of Love"
	"Love Is Strange"

As the '60s waxed into a more complicated decade, the Everly Brothers' popularity waned. A stint together in the Marines, complicated personal lives, and haphazard solo careers broke up the steady stream of hits the brothers enjoyed during their heyday. The Everly Brothers were a key link in the chain of 20th-century American music.

"Phil and I always sang, even when we were apart. That's what we do." —Don Everly

Cain and Abel, Don and Phil

Sibling rivalry goes back a long way, and it was resurrected for a decade-long feud between the Everly Brothers. The harmonies were less than close after a public spat in 1973. Don had hoisted one too many and insulted Phil onstage during a California gig. Phil countered by storming offstage, smashing a guitar, and declaring, "I will never get on a stage with that man again." The rift took years to heal, but in 1983 the Everly Brothers patched things up with an onstage bear hug in London's Royal Albert Hall. There wasn't a dry eye in the house.

FREDDY FENDER

June 4, 1937–October 14, 2006

Baldemar Huerta. Hmm, somehow, you just can't picture rowdy honky-tonk crowds yelling, "Baldemaaaaar!" Yet Huerta wasn't fazed and went right ahead and made records anyway. He sold a few in the late '50s, mostly in Texas and Mexico. But Baldemar saw a new thing coming, from the gringo world. That thing was rockabilly, and Baldemar figured he could take some of the energy and power of the new form and meld it with his beloved conjunto music from Mexico. But first, Baldemar had to go. Freddy Fender was born.

"Hopefully I'll be the first Mexican-American going into Hillbilly Heaven."—Freddy Fender

Freddy promptly had himself a hit, with "Holy One" in 1959, and followed it up with "Wasted Days and Wasted Nights" a year later. Unfortunately, just as his new career was getting going, Fender got busted for marijuana possession and sentenced to five years in Louisiana State Penitentiary, at Angola. After his release Fender migrated to New Orleans, where he became a staple in Bourbon Street's music clubs.

In the early '70s producer Huey P. Meaux saw the potential in Freddy Fender and quickly produced two hits with him. First, he convinced Freddy to rerecord his earlier biographical hit, "Wasted Days and Wasted Nights." Then Meaux talked Freddy into trying something different, too. "Before the Next Teardrop Falls" was a sad slow ballad about a loser at love. Significantly, it had a verse and chorus in Spanish, emphasizing Fender's Mexican roots. A nearly unique Hispanic voice in country music, Fender, with his Tex-Mex touches, was just exotic enough to captivate a wide audience.

Freddy Fender took his last name from the brand of his guitar and choose Freddy because it sounded catchy with Fender.

Texas Tornados

In 1989, four greats of Tex-Mex music got together for a concert in San Francisco, billed as the Tex-Mex Revue. Doug Sahm, Augie Meyers (both previously of the Sir Douglas Quintet), accordion virtuoso Flaco Jimenez, and Freddy Fender realized after that first gig that the whole was greater than the sum of its parts. None of the guys had been touring or recording much. Each had seen some success, some of them decades before. So combining forces seemed natural; their self-titled debut album sold well and got even better reviews. Three more records ensued, and the Tornados continued to play live until Doug Sahm's death in 1999.

Despite several more hits in the '70s, Fender suffered a string of marital, personal, alcohol, and then career problems for more than a decade. He never regained his stride as a solo artist. However, to the surprise of many, Freddy came back to the world of recording in the late '80s via a sort of Tex-Mex super group: The Texas Tornados.

GREATEST HITS

Year	Song
1959	"Holy One"
1960	"Wasted Days and Wasted Nights"
1975	"Before the Next Teardrop Falls"
1976	"Living It Down"
	"Secret Love"
1977	"Feliz Navidad"
1983	"Chokin' Kind"

FLATT & SCRUGGS

1948–1969

Most people think of Bill Monroe as the father of bluegrass. But his prodigal "sons" can certainly be played by Lester Flatt and Earl Scruggs. Lester played lightning-fast guitar and sang with a smooth tenor, Scruggs handled the banjo. And handle it he did, like nobody, before or since. So when Flatt and Scruggs decided to leave Monroe's Blue Grass Boys in 1948, it changed bluegrass history.

Flatt and Scruggs led their new band, the Foggy Mountain Boys, for the next 21 years. Flatt and Scruggs themselves were virtuosos, yet had the foresight to hire equally excellent supporting players nearly as proficient as they. Fiddler Chubby Wise, bass player Cedric Rainwater, and later, Dobro master Buck Graves somehow managed to keep up with their leaders' blistering licks. "Foggy Mountain Breakdown" became the gold standard bluegrass tune, bedeviling the fingers of generations of followers.

Scruggs Picking

Not everybody is good and innovative enough to get an entire style of playing named after them. But not everybody has a name like Scruggs either. Earl Scruggs used three fingers to pick his banjo. The sound was so effective and unique it became synonymous with bluegrass. Those blistering runs of notes, so fast it seems impossible one person could be making so many sounds? "Scruggs picking." Never before had the banjo been so expressive; in Earl Scruggs' hands this antique instrument with ancient African roots was reborn.

Despite much acclaim from performing two bluegrass songs for immensely popular television, (from left) Flatt & Scruggs parted ways when Scruggs wanted to branch out with new material and Flatt desired a more traditional sound.

The Boys played around the South, doing live concerts and radio shows, picking up a sponsor, Martha White Flour. In 1955 they were invited to join the Grand Ole Opry.

By 1962, riding a number of converging waves, Flatt and Scruggs took bluegrass onto the national, and indeed, international stage. The folk revolution just picking up steam in the early '60s set the stage, and urban audiences ate up the formerly old-fashioned sounds of banjo, guitar, and fiddle. At the height of their popularity they played the theme from the *Beverly Hillbillies* television show, "The Ballad of Jed Clampett." Flatt and Scruggs even appeared as themselves in several episodes. The "Theme From Petticoat Junction" followed soon after.

"Foggy Mountain Breakdown" gained further fame in 1968 for the guitar player from Tennessee and the banjo picker from North Carolina when it appeared behind a car chase in *Bonnie and Clyde*. The stylish urban crowd had discovered bluegrass, and liked what they heard.

Their popularity may have ironically helped break them up. By 1969 Earl Scruggs wanted to move the band in new directions. He got them booked into rock venues, and even had them record things like Bob Dylan's "Like a Rolling Stone." Earl Scruggs had enough of that, and they went their separate ways. Each enjoyed solo careers for another decade. Hopes of a planned reunion were dashed when Lester Flatt passed away in 1979.

GREATEST HITS

Year	Song
1949	"Don't Get above Your Raisin'"
	"Foggy Mountain Breakdown"
	"I'll Never Shed Another Tear"
1951	"Come Back Darling"
	"Head over Heels"
	"Till the End of the World Rolls Around"
1952	"'Tis Sweet to Be Remembered"
1962	"Ballad of Jed Clampett"
1963	"Petticoat Junction Theme"
1968	"Like a Rolling Stone"

RED FOLEY

June 17, 1910–September 19, 1968

The postwar years brought America prosperity, a baby boom, and a new, smooth-edged style of country music. Red Foley was among the most popular musicians in this new vein, known for his velvet vocals. Though Foley is often grouped with other crooners of the so-called countrypolitan style, he never became a pop star like his contemporary, Eddy Arnold. His hit song "Chattanoogie Shoe Shine Boy" and a handful of other numbers did top the pop charts, but Foley stayed country through and through, selling 25 million records in the process.

You Ain't Nothing but a Shepherd Dog

"Old Shep" was written and recorded by Red Foley in 1933 and later covered by Hank Snow and Elvis Presley. The sentimental song was indeed about Red's boyhood German shepherd, but the dog's name wasn't Shep, it was Hoover. Depression-era associations with that name weren't the greatest, so the fictional dog got a nonpartisan name. And Red didn't mention that Shep went "where the good doggies go" after being poisoned by a neighbor. Sometimes truth is stranger than a song.

The Foley family musical tradition would continue even after Red's death, with Debby, the daughter of singer Pat Boone, and Red's daughter Shirley, charting both country and pop hits.

Born in Blue Lick, Kentucky, as Clyde Julian Foley, the youngster got his nickname from his red hair. His parents encouraged his singing and even took him to voice lessons. Red won first prize in a talent competition and continued his musical studies at Kentucky's Georgetown College. In 1930 a man came down from Chicago and told Red he wanted to put him on the radio.

That radio station was WLS, and Red became a staple of its Barn Dance show (later called the National Barn Dance), where he performed with producer John Lair's Cumberland Ridge Runners. Red was signed to Decca records in 1941, and the hits started coming. A lot of them were gospel numbers that were the perfect showcase for Red's rich, smooth voice. One of his big, early hits was the patriotic number "Smoke on the Water"—but not the same "Smoke on the Water" you know from Deep Purple. The '40s also saw Red take a stint as host of the Opry's network offering, "The Prince Albert Show," temporarily supplanting Roy Acuff.

During the '50s Red scored big with a number of duets, including some with Ernest Tubb and Kitty Wells, and ventured into rockabilly and boogie-woogie turf. He even went out west for a season to play Fess Parker's Uncle Cooter in the program *Mr. Smith Goes to Washington*. Red was also seen on TV as the host of ABC's *Jubilee USA*. He later returned to Nashville and resumed playing and touring until his death in 1968.

NUGGET: Hank Williams Jr.'s 1968 hit, "I Was with Red Foley (The Night He Passed Away)" was a true story. According to Williams, Red's final words were "I'm awful tired now, Hank, I've got to go to bed." Red died from a heart attack later that night.

GREATEST HITS

Year	Song
1933	"Old Shep"
1944	"Smoke on the Water"
1947	"New Jolie Blonde" (with the Cumberland Valley Boys)
1948	"Tennessee Saturday Night"
1949	"Steal Away"
1950	"Chattanoogie Shoe Shine Boy"
	"Just a Closer Walk with Thee"
	"Sugarfoot Rag"
	"Goodnight Irene" (with Ernest Tubb)
1951	"Peace in the Valley" (with the Sunshine Boys)
1954	"One by One" (with Kitty Wells)

TENNESSEE ERNIE FORD

February 13, 1919–October 17, 1991

Talk about good beginnings. Ernest Jennings Ford was not only blessed with a sonorous, deep baritone voice, but he was born in the birthplace of country music itself—Bristol, Tennessee. He went on to become one of the most popular and beloved crossover country acts during the '50s and '60s. His comical, down-home character, "Tennessee Ernie," was featured on numerous radio and television programs, and Ford hit it big with his cover of Merle Travis' "Sixteen Tons." He also had a way with a spiritual, recording the gold-selling 1956 album *Hymns*, and some 80 more platters of sacred music to boot. Later in life, Ford achieved the highest civilian honor as he was awarded the Presidential Medal of Freedom.

Ford started his career on his hometown station WOPI at the age of 20. He soon traveled to Cincinnati, where he studied voice. During the war Ford served as an Air Force bombardier, flying missions over Japan. Postwar, Ford moved to Los Angeles, where his comical hayseed radio personality was born. "Bless your pea-pickin' heart!" was one of Tennessee Ernie's signature sayings, earning him the nickname "the Ol' Pea-Picker." Soon Ford was installed as a cast member on *Hometown Jamboree*, a country music radio and TV program. After the great success of "Sixteen Tons," the Ford Motor Company invited Tennessee Ernie to host its primetime *The Ford Show*. Other TV appearances included guest stints on *I Love Lucy* as the bumpkin "Cousin Ernie."

The recording industry had a field day with Tennessee Ernie. Capitol Records was the lucky label to sign him, and there he stayed, producing a string of hit records and albums. His voice was equally well suited to moving gospel numbers and rousing boogie-woogie alike.

His good looks, great voice, and comedic cornpone stylings made Ernie Ford popular on both the radio and television. After signing with Capitol in 1948, he stayed with the label for the rest of his life.

GREATEST HITS

Year	Song
1949	"Tennessee Border"
	"Smokey Mountain Boogie"
	"Mule Train"
1950	"I'll Never Be Free" (with Kay Starr)
1951	"Shotgun Boogie"
1952	"Blackberry Boogie"
1955	"Sixteen Tons"
	"The Ballad of Davy Crockett"
1965	"Hicktown"

Speedy and Jimmy

You want fast? Look no further than Speedy West and Jimmy Bryant, the dynamic guitar duo behind Tennessee Ernie Ford during his *Hometown Jamboree* and Capitol years. Speedy played a mean pedal steel guitar, and Jimmy Bryant was often called "the fastest guitar in the country," combining lightning picking with jazzy, bop-influenced runs.

Jimmy Bryant was the first to play Leo Fender's new electric guitar prototype, the Esquire. Adding another pickup, Fender renamed it the Broadcaster, and soon after that it became the Telecaster. Legend has it that in 1950, Fender approached Bryant between sets in a Riverside, California, club with his new solid-body creation. Bryant sat right down on the edge of the stage and started picking. The rest is guitar history.

Speedy and Jimmy were always in demand as session men and cut a fair share of their own sides as well. Some of their best work is on such numbers as "Stratosphere Boogie" and "Flippin' the Lid."

LEFTY FRIZZELL

MARCH 31, 1928–JULY 19, 1975

Sometimes the smallest decisions can have lifelong consequences. William Orville Frizzell could have chosen a right jab perhaps, or maybe a little uppercut to the chin. But William unleashed a left-handed haymaker. That kid never saw the shot coming, the one that decked him, right there at recess. That punch was like nothing that Arkansas schoolyard had ever seen. William not only won the scrape, he earned a new moniker and became forever after "Lefty" Frizzell.

By age 12, young Lefty was playing guitar and singing on the radio, in nightclubs, anywhere he could. By day he was working on oil rigs with his father. A spell in jail cooled his budding career but gave him time to work on his songwriting. When he got out of stir, he got back to singing and playing. In short order he had made a demo of songs at a local recording studio. Nashville producer Don Law heard it, liked it, and by June 1950 Lefty had his first hit record, "If You've Got the Money, Honey."

"When I was 15 years old, I thought Lefty hung the moon. You know . . . I'm not sure he didn't."—Merle Haggard

There was more where that came from; by late October 1951 Frizzell had achieved what no artist had achieved before—four hits in the Top 10, simultaneously. No artist would equal this feat until those upstarts from Liverpool invaded in the '60s.

Frizzell's songs had fairly conventional orchestration. The subject matter wasn't anything to write home about. But Lefty had a unique vocal style that would influence generations of singers to come. Epitomized on "Always Late (With Your Kisses)," Lefty's voice slides up and down within words. "Always" suddenly had three syllables while "late" got bumped up to two. Nobody could express vowels like Lefty Frizzell. That slippery vocal affectation gave his voice a pathos and empathy that belied the happy tinkling of the honky-tonk piano in the background. At the end of "Mom and Dad's Waltz," Lefty tells us how he loves his parents, "I lo-uh-ve them so-oh-oh . . ." With the addition of three little vowel sounds a trite cliché becomes universal truth. Lefty Frizzell at work.

Lefty's Legacy

While Lefty Frizzell wrote and performed his own hits, he is perhaps best remembered for his influence on successive performers. Merle Haggard, Willie Nelson, and Dwight Yoakam all covered Frizzell's songs and freely gave credit for Lefty's influence. And though he didn't write it, he had the first hit with the tragic love tale "Long Black Veil." Over the years, artists as diverse as Johnny Cash, the Band, Joan Baez, Dave Matthews Band, and Bruce Springsteen recorded their versions.

THOUGH HE ONLY MADE IT TO AGE 47, LEFTY FRIZZELL'S LEGACY IS CONTINUED BY MUSICIANS OF RENOWN, INCLUDING WILLIE NELSON, GEORGE JONES, AND RANDY TRAVIS.

NUGGET: Lefty gave an interview right before his untimely death. "When I sing, to me every word has a feeling about it," he said. "I had to linger, had to hold it, I didn't want to let go of it. I want to hold one word through a whole line of melody."

GREATEST HITS

Year	Song
1950	"If You've Got the Money, Honey"
	"I Love You a Thousand Ways"
1951	"I Want to Be with You Always"
	"Always Late (With Your Kisses)"
	"Mom and Dad's Waltz"
	"Travelin' Blues"
1959	"Long Black Veil"
1964	"Saginaw, Michigan"

DON GIBSON

April 3, 1928–November 17, 2003

Don Gibson considered himself a songwriter who happened to sing. And write he did—some of the most famous songs in country music. "Sweet Dreams" was a hit for Gibson and Faron Young before Patsy Cline made the song her own in 1963.

But Gibson was far more than a songwriter; he made his own records, too. While he was working with producer Chet Atkins on "Oh Lonesome Me" in 1957, the two decided to experiment a little bit. In place of the usual steel guitars and fiddles, they changed the orchestration to include piano, guitars, drums, bass, and background singers. This was one of the first records to feature the Nashville Sound, and was a huge #1 hit.

Ten years of hits would follow. "Blue Blue Day," "Who Cares?" "Sea of Heartbreak," and "Rings of Gold" all mined a similar formula: heartbreak and desperation, set against those soothing background vocals and arrangements.

Somehow Gibson's losers were compelling and easy to relate to rather than off-putting. That quality—that ability to imbue tales of loneliness with pathos rather than despair—attracted singers looking for material. In addition to his own recordings, Gibson became most renowned as a songwriter. Patsy Cline, Ray Charles, Roy Orbison, Elvis Presley—well, just about everybody recorded one or another of Gibson's songs, and many had hits with them. Those stories and characters were never far from the truth, as Gibson himself battled the demons of drugs and alcohol abuse throughout the '60s. His second wife, Bobbi, helped him overcome those problems, and he had his last hit in 1972 with "Woman, Sensuous Woman." Later in his career he was gratified to be recognized by being reinducted to the Grand Ole Opry, inducted into the Songwriters Hall of Fame, and finally into the Country Music Hall of Fame in 2001.

A Good Day's Work

Think of your best day ever. Was it that time you were on the championship high school football squad? Maybe the day your first child was born. Even the day you caught that monster bass in the tournament.

Well, humble yourself when you think of Don Gibson's best day ever—one afternoon in 1957 in a trailer park north of Knoxville, Tennessee. For that is the day Gibson wrote "I Can't Stop Loving You." But writing a song that would become a golden standard wasn't enough for Gibson; he grabbed another sheet of staff paper and kept going. Later that same afternoon he composed "Oh, Lonesome Me." How's that for a daily double?

NUGGET: Don Gibson became known as "the Sad Poet" due to his penchant for spinning tragic tales of lost loves and loneliness.

GREATEST HITS

Year	Song
1957	"Oh Lonesome Me"
1958	"Blue Day"
1959	"Who Cares"
	"Don't Tell Me Your Troubles"
1960	"I'd Be a Legend in My Time"
1961	"Sea of Heartbreak"
1969	"Rings of Gold" (with Dottie West)
1970	"There's a Story Goin' Round" (with Dottie West)
1972	"Woman, Sensuous Woman"

"Simple is the only way I can write." —Don Gibson

Though he wrote both on the same day, Gibson much preferred "I Can't Stop Loving You" to "Oh, Lonesome Me." Both titles have been popular covers, but the former outnumbers the latter by about two to one.

VINCE GILL

April 12, 1957–

When not performing, Vince Gill blends his love for country music with his love for golf by hosting the Academy of Country Music Celebrity Golf Classic, an annual charity event.

GREATEST HITS	
Year	Song
1985	"If It Weren't for Him" (with Rosanne Cash)
	"Cinderella"
1990	"When I Call Your Name"
1992	"I Still Believe in You"
	"Don't Let Our Love Start Slippin' Away"
1993	"The Heart Won't Lie" (with Reba McEntire)
	"One More Last Chance"
1994	"Tryin' to Get Over You"
1995	"You Better Think Twice"
1997	"A Little More Love"
1998	"If You Ever Have Forever in Mind"
2000	"Feels Like Love"
2003	"Next Big Thing"
2006	"What You Give Away"

This Oklahoma boy sure did make good. With his sweet tenor and his boy-next-door looks, Vince Gill is known as "the unofficial ambassador of country music." His musical chops, sincere demeanor, and regular-guy charm have helped him sell over 22 million records, win 18 Grammies, and just as many CMA awards.

It started early, Vince learning to play guitar and banjo as a kid and joining a bluegrass band when in high school. Vince's family was musical; "There was always somebody plunking away at an instrument," he says of his home life. Vince went on the road when he was still young, first to Kentucky, where he played with Ricky Scaggs, and then to Los Angeles, where he became lead vocalist for Pure Prairie League. Next it was back-up work for Rosanne Cash in the Cherry Bombs.

During his stint with the Cherry Bombs, Vince met keyboardist Tony Brown. In 1983, Gill moved to Nashville, and Tony Brown, who was also a record executive, signed him to RCA. The songs and albums were good but failed to really break the barrier, until Brown and Gill both moved to MCA; Vince's 1989 album, *When I Call Your Name,* sold a million copies. The '90s continued to be good to Vince, who racked up hit after hit.

Vince Gill is nothing if not versatile. He's equally at home with ballad, bluegrass, or boogie—evidence of his firm grounding in the various roots of country. For his 2006 album *These Days*, Vince paid homage to all those roots. He crafted a 43-song, four-disc masterwork that showcased all his musical talents—and friends—in one big package.

Everybody Loves Vince

The mutual-admiration duet is pretty commonplace in country music. But Vince Gill has made the rounds. First it was Rosanne Cash, and then Reba McEntire. Dolly Parton sang with Vince on "I Will Always Love You." And, of course, Vince has sung with his first wife, Janis Gill, and his current wife, Christian music star Amy Grant.

Beyond the bounds of country, Vince sang with Barbra Streisand on "If You Ever Leave Me." Mark Knopfler of Dire Straits even asked Vince to join the band; he declined, but joined them for "The Bug" on the band's album *On Every Street*.

Vince's latest album, *These Days*, features a gleaming roster of guest vocalists: Phil Everly, Guy Clark, Del McCoury. And the ladies! What ladies! Patty Loveless, Gretchen Wilson, Emmylou Harris, Alison Krauss, Lee Ann Womack, LeAnn Rimes, Bekka Bramlett, Bonnie Raitt, Sheryl Crow, Diana Krall, and his own daughter, Jenny Gill. Whatever Vince has got, he's got a lot of it.

JIMMIE DALE GILMORE

May 6, 1945–

You hear that warbling, plaintive voice? That's the sound of one heart breaking, picking itself up, and starting all over again. In other words, that's Jimmie Dale Gilmore, the sage of West Texas. Raised in Lubbock, and settled now in Austin, Gilmore has traveled a long and dusty road away from the flatlands and back again—older, wiser, and with a gentle humor that shimmers in the quavery strains of that voice. With his long silver hair and his modest, contemplative manner, Gilmore's got a heart as wide and open as Texas.

When he was just 12 years old in Lubbock, Gilmore befriended Butch Hancock, and the two became musical buddies in the town that spawned the likes of Buddy Holly, Waylon Jennings, and of course, their mutual friend Joe Ely. Gilmore and Ely played together and took their show on the road to Austin. Landing back in Lubbock a few years later, they hooked up with Hancock once again, and the three formed the Flatlanders. Aside from one now-legendary eight-track recording from a 1972 Nashville session (finally unearthed and released by Rounder Records in 1990), the three friends went their separate ways for almost 20 years. Gilmore, curious about Eastern mysticism, spent time at an ashram in Colorado, while Ely and Hancock pursued solo careers.

NUGGET: During the '70s Joe Ely played with pedal steel guitar master and music producer Lloyd Maines, who is the father of the Dixie Chicks' Natalie Maines.

When Gilmore re-entered the music scene in the '80s, Joe Ely was on hand to produce his first album. Gilmore loved the old honky-tonk numbers, and the folk stuff, and the blues, and dabbled around a bit. He really hit his stride with his albums of the '90s, finding material better suited to his voice, his guitar style, and his deeply spiritual bent. While he is a gifted songwriter, Gilmore is just as satisfied to interpret contemporary tunes and standards—always with his timeless grace and dignity.

Gilmore recorded his *Come On Back* (2005), a collection of his dad's favorites, in memory of his father, who passed away from Lou Gehrig's Disease.

Hey, Joe

Although Joe Ely may stray, he always comes back to country.

Prolific, personable Joe Ely has had a finger in nearly every musical pot, and always come back to country. After his Flatlanders stint, Joe released his self-titled debut solo album in 1977. Touring London in support of that disc, he hooked up with legendary punk band the Clash. Ely toured with them on both sides of the pond. His ramblings led him back to his roots when he joined the Tex-Mex super group Los Super Seven, whose various members included Freddie Fender, Flaco Jimenez, Doug Sahm, members of Los Lobos, and storied bluesman Clarence Gatemouth Brown.

When Robert Redford asked him to come up with a song for *The Horse Whisperer*, Ely looked up Jimmie Dale and ButchHancock, and the Flatlanders were reunited. That session led to their comeback album, *Now Again*, released in 2002.

GREATEST HITS

Year	Song
1972	"More a Legend Than a Band" (with the Flatlanders)
1988	"Fair and Square"
1989	"Jimmie Dale Gilmore"
1991	"After Awhile"
1993	"Spinning around the Sun"
1996	"Braver Newer World"
2000	"One Endless Night"
2002	"Now Again" (with the Flatlanders)
2004	"Wheels of Fortune" (with the Flatlanders)
2005	"Come On Back"

MERLE HAGGARD

April 6, 1937–

Times were tough in Oildale, California, in the years following the Dust Bowl. James and Flossie Haggard felt themselves fortunate to have come across an abandoned reefer (refrigerated rail car) that could serve as shelter for their family. Which is how Merle Haggard came to spend his first nine years living in a railcar. It actually wasn't a bad setup, a little cooler in summer and warmer in winter, as he would later reminisce. This brilliant iconoclast would change country forever, but he had to survive growing up first. That reefer car was about the only comfort the young Haggard would see

"My second wife, Bonnie Owens, and I worked together after we divorced for a period of maybe 20 years. And I managed to stay friends with another wife. And then there's one that I don't mess with. Everybody's got one of those."—Merle Haggard

for some time. His father died when he was 9, and Merle rebelled, leading to trouble. Like the kind of trouble requiring a stint in the juvenile detention center. More legal troubles followed his release from juvie, and Merle found himself in San Quentin. He raised as much hell in jail as he had outside and ran a still and gambling operation right from his cell. Many stints in solitary confinement ensued, along with many late-night conversations with notorious death row inmate Caryl Chessman. Finally, the young Haggard started to see a way to change his path. Johnny Cash played his series of legendary prison concerts, and Merle was in the audience for several of them. Singing seemed like it might offer Merle a way onto the straight-and-narrow road out of prison.

When he got out, Merle Haggard fairly quickly began performing and recording. Using the many difficult episodes of his rough and tumble life as inspiration, he transformed earlier failures into success. He put together a band and started playing out.

The Nashville Sound was big then—a big lush panoply of strings and backup singers that appealed to city and country folk alike. Haggard pitched his more intense, gritty sound as a counterpoint to the prevailing countrypolitan style. The newly

The Strangers

We all know Merle can sing and play, but did you ever take a listen to his band? The Strangers, that is. From the outset, Merle was smart enough to hire musicians as good or better than he was. This was no easy feat, as he played a mean fiddle and was a veritable master of the Telecaster.

But these were no typical session players. Roy Nichols was a spectacular guitarist of whom Haggard later said, "I've idolized him for 50 years!" And James Burton on lead guitar was unequaled. Steel guitar player Ralph Mooney, pianist Glen Hardin, and Glen Campbell on guitar rounded out the band. Campbell would of course go on to his own fame, but the rest of the Strangers played with Merle for the long haul. Over the years, Haggard strayed from the strictures of country music; he himself once described what he did as "country jazz." He found inspiration in all sorts of places other than the Opry or Music Row in Nashville. The Strangers could play anything he threw at them, and play it well.

No satin and rhinestones for this fellow—Merle Haggard believes in keeping things real. In fact, singing songs about his troubled childhood and stints in prison endeared him to fans.

Merle Haggard's life hasn't been easy. Poverty, the premature death of his father, drinking, jail time, and troubled marriages have all left their marks.

In an onstage group jam, Merle Haggard, Willie Nelson, and Toby Keith make some music in 2004. Haggard's 1983 duet with Willie Nelson of an old Townes Van Zandt composition, the track title of their album *Pancho and Lefty*, garnered them a #1 country hit single.

GREATEST HITS	
Year	Song
1963	"Sing a Sad Song"
1966	"The Bottle Let Me Down"
1968	"The Legend of Bonnie and Clyde"
	"Mama Tried"
1969	"Workin' Man Blues"
	"Okie from Muskogee"
1970	"Fightin' Side of Me"
1972	"It's Not Love (But It's Not Bad)"
1973	"If We Make It Through December"
1977	"Ramblin' Fever"
1978	"I'm Always on a Mountain When I Fall"
1980	"Think I'll Just Sit Here and Drink"
1981	"Big City"
1983	"Pancho and Lefty" (with Willie Nelson)
1988	"Twinkle Twinkle Lucky Star"
2005	"America First"

christened Bakersfield Sound (Oildale was right across the Kern River from Bakersfield, California) gave listeners a rootsy, authentic alternative.

"The Hag" sang with an earnest tenderness that belied his rough themes and subjects. Listeners could relate to tales of everyday, hard-working folk hitting rough patches. Directly confronting and retelling his personal history was a panacea for Haggard. Songs like "Mama Tried," and "Branded Man" were anthems to poor choices in poorer situations. But the heroes always had a certain defiance, a steely grit that would see them stoically accept whatever disaster came next. Or at least get to work the next day. Haggard spent a goodly portion of 20 years charting big with such songs.

In 1969, "Okie from Muskogee" and its sequel "The Fightin' Side of Me" were both huge hits and made explicit the pain of a country being rent by an unpopular war. Despite having acknowledged smoking many a funny cigarette in his day, Haggard proudly declared "We don't smoke marijuana in Muskogee . . ." and proceeded to reject just about every hippie indulgence: LSD, sandals, shaggy hair, and "making a party out of loving." "When you're running down my country, man, you're walking on the fightin' side of me . . ." He drew a line in the sand and dared all those anti-American hippies to step over it. The songs were huge sellers to both the country and pop markets.

Even as Haggard realized what his hard-hat, pro-war anthems (he considered them "spoofs") had wrought, he was working on "Irma Jackson," a song about interracial love. This was a touchy subject in '70s America, and the record company refused to release it.

Whether his pro-American songs had influence we'll never know, but the next year Haggard was granted a pardon for earlier sins by California governor Ronald Reagan. That same year he scored his biggest hit with "If We Make It Through December." More hits followed, and Haggard continued his reign as a country superstar.

By the mid '80s the Hag's grip on the pulse of the record-buying public was starting to slip a bit. He changed record labels several times and recorded some duet albums with people like Willie Nelson and George Jones but was never able to recapture the popularity he'd enjoyed at his peak.

In 2000, continuing his penchant for interesting career moves, Merle signed with a label better known for punk rock than country. He made two well-regarded albums for them, then returned home to his longtime label, EMI. There he made a record of American pop standards, *Unforgettable*, which was well received by critics but didn't sell very well. And in what should have been a surprise to no one, the iconoclastic Haggard reappeared in 2005 with an anti-Iraq war song, "America First." He followed that up in 2006 with a hit duet with Gretchen Wilson on "Politically Incorrect."

The original politically incorrect Hag continues to create music and tour. He claims he writes four or five songs a month but never writes them down. He figures the ones he remembers are the good ones, so he keeps those. And if those are anything like the rest of his oeuvre, they're very good indeed.

The Oildale converted-reefer car is still there, and the highway that runs near it has been rechristened Merle Haggard Drive. The scrappy Okie kid done good over the years, via a twisted and convoluted path worthy of one of his emblematic songs.

MERLE PERFORMING ON A GUITAR WITH HIS TRADEMARK HAND-TOOLED GUITAR STRAP WITH HIS NAME WORKED INTO IT.

MERLE, DURING A BEARDLESS (AND HATLESS) PERIOD, WAS NO LONGER AN EX-CON, THANKS TO HIS 1972 PARDON BY THEN-GOVERNOR RONALD REAGAN, WHO JUDGED THAT MERLE HAD NOT HAD REPRESENTATION DURING HIS TRIAL.

The Saddest Song?

"If We Make It Through December," Merle Haggard's biggest hit, may well be the saddest country song ever recorded. Sure, novelty tunes like Red Sovine's "Teddy Bear's Last Ride" might yank the heartstrings with maudlin tales of crippled children. But Merle's "December" evokes the tragedy in the most mundane and commonplace of situations. Nobody gets shot, no dogs are killed, no barroom brawls—just a man trying to reassure his family that they'll make out despite his loss of a job.

"If we make it through December, everything's gonna be alright, I know . . ." Well, actually, it may not be all right at all. The protagonist's optimism is revealed as desperation and fear, through increasing levels of hardship. By the time he "got laid off down at the factory" in the second verse, we know he's probably not going to make it through December after all. When you throw in the holidays and the stress of not wanting to let down his little girl, well, "If we make it through December, we'll be fine" is revealed by the end of the song to be a futile wish.

EMMYLOU HARRIS

APRIL 2, 1947–

This lovely, lyrical soprano has always shone brightly as her own star but is almost equally renowned as a collaborator. Emmylou Harris has sung duets and trios with a slew of artists from nearly every corner of the music world. From country to folk bluegrass to alternative rock and back again, Emmylou can belt out a number, or blend in gorgeous harmony. Throughout her career Emmylou Harris has always walked just enough off the beaten path to remain true.

Harris' honest artistry has guided her throughout her career. She was country even when it wasn't cool, and when something didn't work, she'd move on to the thing that did. After a childhood in Birmingham and Washington, D.C., she tried the acting route. She soon gravitated back to the guitar, teaching herself folk numbers and warming up those lovely pipes. Moving to New York, she played the Village folk scene, and then she tried her hand in Nashville. The living proved hard, and she returned to D.C. She was discovered in a club there, leading to her move to L.A. to collaborate with the eccentric Gram Parsons.

EMMYLOU CAME INTO HER OWN AS A SONGWRITER LATER IN HER CAREER WITH THE 2000 *RED DIRT GIRL*, WHICH GARNERED HER A 10TH GRAMMY.

GREATEST HITS

YEAR	SONG
1975	"If I Could Only Win Your Love"
	"Coat of Many Colors"
	"The Bottle Let Me Down"
1976	"Together Again"
	"Sweet Dreams"
1978	"Quarter Moon in a Ten Cent Town"
	"Two More Bottles of Wine"
1980	"That Lovin' You Feelin' Again" (with Roy Orbison)
1987	"To Know Him Is to Love Him" (with Dolly Parton and Linda Ronstadt)
1995	"Wrecking Ball"
	"Orphan Girl"
2000	"Red Dirt Girl"

From her first solo album, 1975's *Pieces of the Sky*, through her Grammy-winning 2000 album *Red Dirt Girl*, Emmylou Harris has always had an incredible knack for choosing, and writing, material. Harris has given us songs by country greats like the Louvin Brothers, Buck Owens, Dolly Parton, and Patsy Cline, and later collaborated with Dolly and Linda Ronstadt on their two *Trio* albums. 1995's eclectic *Wrecking Ball* was a surprise hit; Emmylou called it her "weird album," but it won her a Grammy. Harris gained additional exposure with the rootsy soundtrack of *O Brother, Where Art Thou?* Harris seems to intuitively understand that if you nurture the roots, the flower will bloom.

Emmylou's Grievous Angel

Gram Parsons was an unlikely country musician. The scion of a wealthy but troubled Florida family, he studied theology at Harvard and then showed up in flashy Nudie suits. Parsons had an almost mystical attraction to American roots music, taking the Bakersfield Sound and infusing it with the raw energy of rock. A member of the Byrds and the Flying Burrito Brothers, Parsons hung out with the Rolling Stones but was increasingly hobbled by drug use. He cut two solo albums—1973's *GP* and *Grievous Angel*, released the following year. Emmylou Harris was Parsons' muse, and he her mentor, schooling her in country history. They toured together as the Fallen Angels. After Parsons died of an overdose in 1973, Harris determined to carry on his vision of "cosmic American music." Her moving song, "Boulder to Birmingham," is a tribute to Parsons.

FAITH HILL

September 21, 1967–

Faith Hill steps up to the plate. She's completely drop-dead gorgeous, of course. You can see how she got that job filing papers. But she's got pipes on her, too. So you can also see how merely singing along with the radio while filing said papers was enough to get her a backup singing gig. And then that backup singing was good enough to get her signed as a solo artist to Warner Records. And then her debut single, "Wild One," shot straight up to #1 and stayed there four consecutive weeks. Throughout her career, Faith Hill would get into the batter's box on her beauty, but step to the plate and face the pitcher on her talent and hard work. Novelist John Irving says that talent is overrated; perhaps beauty is, too.

"Country music fans are extremely supportive. Once they're with you, they're with you for life."—Faith Hill

Faith herself proclaimed her exasperation at people admiring her looks and overlooking her songs. Double-edged sword, this attractiveness. Ask any 10 people about Faith Hill, and 8 of them will immediately answer, "She's gorgeous!" It's the first and last thing you think of when you hear the words Faith Hill.

There had been beautiful women in country music before. Shania Twain had just recently broken the mold of stand-by-your-man country women. Maybe it shouldn't have been a surprise when Faith Hill went Hollywood. For the video to "Breathe," Hill hired Lili Zanuck, a Hollywood film director. The results were breathtaking and pushed Hill to a level of stardom far beyond the country music world. It was titillating without being dirty, provocative without offending, and full of white billowing fabric. And what wasn't glowing white fabric was Faith: writhing on sparkling white sheets, swaying inside a precariously pinned column of white silk, strutting along atop spike heels in the desert. It was pure Hollywood. Anyone who hadn't heard of her yet got one gander of that lithe body, flawless face, and all that blonde hair, and fell in love. Once in, they might

Not just another pretty face, Faith Hill has a beautiful voice and a generous heart, doing her part to combat adult illiteracy.

FAITH HILL AND HUBBY TIM MCGRAW, THE ULTIMATE COUNTRY-MUSIC POWER COUPLE, ARE RED-CARPET FAVORITES. HERE THEY MAKE THEIR ENTRANCE TO A POST-OSCAR FETE IN 2004.

notice the song, or the particular control and power in the lower registers. The song hit #1 on country and adult contemporary charts and was all over the radio. Hill had arrived. Her beauty may have gotten her up to bat, but she used her talent to knock it out of the park.

That same year, at the 2000 Academy Awards show, Faith again showed her ability to bat a thousand. During Friday night rehearsals for the Sunday night show, Whitney Houston had been forced to withdraw from the performance due to "throat problems." Producers Burt Bacharach and Don Was called Hill Saturday morning. They had already gotten a private plane in the air and they sure hoped she'd be on it. Faith pulled off her gardening gloves, made a quick call to her costumers, and headed for Los Angeles. And 24 hours later, she blew the doors off her musical number in front of a billion viewers. See a pattern? Use her looks to get in the door then—*bam!*—knock 'em dead with the first few notes of that breathy alto.

As one might expect, Faith took advantage of opportunities in the world outside country. She represented Cover Girl cosmetics, acted in a few films and TV shows, and did commercials for the likes of Pepsi. But music is her true calling, and she returned to form (and favor from country audiences) with 2005's *Fireflies*. As radiant as ever, the woman's still striding up to that plate, eyeing the pitcher, and swinging that bat.

NUGGET: Faith Hill and her husband, fellow country star Tim McGraw, have toured together several times. They fell in love on the Spontaneous Combustion tour of 1996, then mounted the Soul2Soul tour in 2000. Soul2Soul2 in 2006 became the highest grossing country music tour in history.

Steep Hill

Not one to forget her humble beginnings, Faith Hill never forgot that her father had dropped out of school to raise her and her 12 siblings. And because of that, he never learned to read. "Around the time I was starting to have a family, I realized what he must have endured and how brave he was. I thought about the fact that others shouldn't have to go through life the same way," said Hill. In 1996 Faith formed the Faith Hill Family Literacy Project. Working with the project, Hill asks fans to bring books to her concerts. These are then collected and donated to try to encourage people to read. A drive on one of her tours collected more than a million books for donation.

GREATEST HITS

YEAR	SONG
1993	"Wild One"
	"Piece of My Heart"
	"Take Me as I Am"
1995	"It Matters to Me"
1998	"This Kiss"
	"Let Me Go"
1999	"Breathe"
	"The Way You Love Me"
2001	"There You'll Be"
2002	"Cry"
2005	"Mississippi Girl"

SONNY JAMES

May 1, 1929–

A gentleman has to sit where it's comfortable. For Sonny James, the #1 spot on the charts suited him just fine. So he stayed. And stayed—57 weeks all together, and the fella wouldn't let it go. James is known as the Southern Gentleman, gaining the moniker for his courtly manners, but also perhaps for the sizable chunk of real estate he owned on the country and pop charts. The late '60s were good to Sonny, and after he'd scored a full 23 songs that hit the #1 mark, things began to slow down, but only a bit. James continued to score hits in the Top 10 for another decade to come. Born to a show-business family by the name of Loden, young Sonny Boy, as he was known in the family act, came to the stage early. Traveling out from their hometown of Hackelburg, Alabama, the Loden Family was soon crisscrossing the southern United States. Sonny's country needed him for a stint in Korea, but that didn't stop the show-biz ball rolling. In fact, it was during his service that Sonny met Chet Atkins, and that was how Capitol Records got ahold of this charming young man with the warm, appealing baritone voice. No mere crooner, Sonny was also a skilled guitarist and prize-winning fiddler.

NUGGET: The Rolling Stones and Donny Osmond don't get mentioned together all that often. But both covered Sonny James' first hit song, "Young Love." The Stones released it in 1964 under the name "Bo and Peep," and Osmond charted big with his1974 version.

GREATEST HITS

Year	Song
1953	"That's Me Without You"
1956	"For Rent (One Empty Heart)"
	"The Cat Came Back"
1957	"Young Love"
1964	"You're the Only World I Know"
1967	"I'll Never Find Another You"
	"Need You"
1968	"When the Snow Is on the Roses"
	"Heaven Says Hello"
	"A World of Our Own"
1969	"Come On In (And Make Yourself at Home)"
	"Since I Met You Baby"
	"Running Bear"
	"Only the Lonely"
1971	"Here Comes Honey Again"
1974	"Is It Wrong (For Loving You)"

In addition to topping the country-music charts, Sonny James performed in such countrified films as *Las Vegas Hillbillies* (1966), *Second Fiddle to a Steel Guitar* (1967), and *Nashville Rebel* (1967).

Sonny's big break came in 1956 with the hit "Young Love," but it wasn't until the late '60s that the big hits really started piling up. Sonny James was ensconced on the country charts, with moderate crossover success. He turned his hand to production, crafting Marie Osmond's million-selling 1973 hit "Paper Roses." The Southern Gentleman was inducted into the Country Music Hall of Fame in 2006.

NUGGET: To the moon! In 1971, Sonny James became the first country artist to record a program for a moon flight. The Apollo 14 crew thanked Sonny by presenting him with an American flag they'd carried to the moon and back.

Who's on First?

Alabama vs. the Southern Gentleman. In a dead heat. Each claims to have had the longest streak of consecutive #1 songs on the country charts. Do the math and it comes out even, except for Alabama's one lapse with their 1982 single "Christmas in Dixie," which never charted above #25. Many critics don't count those holiday tunes, anyway, which are released for their novelty appeal rather than for staying power. So between these two enormously popular acts, the jury is still out. Gentlemen all, they might just call it a draw.

WAYLON JENNINGS

June 15, 1937–February 13, 2002

Though he enjoyed a reputation as a renegade, later in life Waylon Jennings got his high-school equivalency diploma to emphasize the importance of education to his son and others.

Waylon did it his way. No Nashville Sound, no session men, and none of that Music Row business for him. By turning his back on the country music establishment in the early '70s and infusing his music and recording with the raw power and independent spirit of rock, Waylon Jennings probably did more to assure country's survival during those turbulent times than any other musician. The most outlaw of the outlaw movement, Jennings made the hard-luck, hard-living themes of the genre ring true again.

A Texan by birth, Jennings grew up in poverty in the West Texas town of Littlefield. He learned how to play the guitar and became a DJ on the local station while he was barely a teenager. His big break came when he moved to Lubbock and landed a gig playing bass and touring in Buddy Holly's band. Buddy was going on the road in 1959, and he booked a seat for Waylon on the four-seater plane that was to take him and Ritchie Valens to their next gig. The heating system on the tour bus was on the fritz, and Holly was worried about his vocal pipes. Their costar, the Big Bopper (J. P. Richardson), was getting over the flu, so Waylon gave him his seat on the plane. As they were leaving, Buddy joked to Waylon, "I hope your damn bus freezes up again." Waylon responded, "Well, I hope your ol' plane crashes." As most everyone knows, it did. Holly, Valens, Richardson, and their pilot, Roger Peterson, were all killed. Jennings was distraught and guilt-ridden for years. He stopped playing music, turned to the DJ gig again, and drifted to Arizona.

"I may be crazy, but it keeps me from going insane."—Waylon Jennings

When Jennings picked up a guitar again, it was a Telecaster, and the sound was rougher and more rock-oriented. His baritone voice was front-loaded with gravity and urgency. His gigs at a Phoenix bar called J. D.'s attracted the notice of Nashville hit-maker Bobby Bare, who hooked Jennings up with Chet Atkins. Signed to RCA records, Jennings went

GREATEST HITS

Year	Song
1968	"Only Daddy That'll Walk the Line"
1972	"Ladies Love Outlaws"
1974	"This Time"
	"I'm a Ramblin' Man"
	"Rainy Day Woman"
1975	"Are You Sure Hank Done It This Way?"
1977	"Luckenbach, Texas (Back to the Basics of Love)"
1978	"Mammas Don't Let Your Babies Grow Up to Be Cowboys" (with Willie Nelson)
1980	"Theme from 'The Dukes of Hazzard' (Good Ol' Boys)"
1985	"Highwayman" (with Cash, Nelson, and Kristofferson)
1987	"Rose in Paradise"
1990	"Wrong"

into the studio in 1965 with Chet at the controls, and pretty soon Waylon was a star. He was living in Nashville, rooming with Johnny Cash, and cranking out hits the way they liked them.

But the reins were a little too tight for Waylon Jennings. At that time in Nashville, recording meant that you just showed up and delivered the goods. An artist didn't have any say in backup musicians, song selection, production style, or album cover art. Where was the honky-tonk, raw country sound? What was all this smooth, citified pop stuff? Waylon was fed up. When he pulled a pistol on producer Danny Davis during a studio session, the writing was on the wall, and Waylon was dubbed an outlaw.

Two songwriters—Kris Kristofferson and Billy Joe Shaver—gave Waylon the ammunition he needed in the form of gritty, hard-edged songs like Kristofferson's aptly titled "Ladies Love Outlaws." The success of Waylon's self-produced 1973 albums *Honky Tonk Heroes* and *Lonesome, On'ry and Mean* were sweet vindication. Soon a troop of other outlaws gathered around him. These musicians were a raggedy, dangerous bunch to the Nashville establishment. They favored denim and leather over rhinestones, cultivated a biker attitude, and basically hit the nerve of a whole generation. Country music would never be the same.

JENNINGS PLAYING ONE OF HIS HAND-TOOLED LEATHER-COVERED FENDER TELECASTERS, HIS TRADEMARK INSTRUMENT, WITH ITS DETAILED FLORAL LEATHERWORK.

Waylon's commercial success came when he refused to tow the line, but his grandeur was always hobbled by the demon of drugs, which plagued him for over a decade. Nonetheless, during the late '70s and early '80s, he produced some of his best work. The 1976 compilation album *Wanted! The Outlaws* featured mostly Jennings numbers and made him a mainstream superstar. The result was gold record after gold record. *Waylon and Willie* (1978), which paired Nelson's wistful tenor with Jennings' assertive baritone, went multiplatinum.

By the mid-'80s Waylon had quit drugs, cold turkey. He formed a super group, the Highwaymen, with Johnny Cash, Willie Nelson, and Kris Kristofferson. His career was slowed by failing health, and Jennings stopped touring in the '90s. He will be remembered as the man who refused to water down the music; Waylon Jennings liked his country straight up, and straight from the bottle.

JESSI COLTER, HIS WIFE OF MORE THAN 30 YEARS (THEY WERE MARRIED IN 1969 IN A CEREMONY OFFICIATED BY HER MOTHER, A PENTECOSTAL MINISTER), DUETTED WITH JENNINGS ON SUCH HITS AS "SUSPICIOUS MINDS."

The Outlaws

They brought it on themselves. Partly it was that song penned by Kristofferson and made famous by Jennings, "Ladies Love Outlaws," and partly it was the look and the music they favored: all rough around the edges, with a core of heartbroken grit.

In early '70s rebellion was in the air; it was only natural that it would spill over into country music. While Waylon and Willie are the most notorious of the outlaws, Kris Kristofferson and Tompall Glaser are right behind them. And there were women in the posse, too, most notably Jessi Colter, who was also Waylon's wife. Her single "I'm Not Lisa" hit #1 on the country charts in 1975. Sammi Smith was a close second to Colter; her 1971 rendition of Kristofferson's "Help Me Make It Through the Night" became one of country music's best-selling singles of all time.

David Allen Coe: Now there's an outlaw if you ever saw one. The iconoclastic Ohio native first did time at the age of 9. In 1968, the long-haired, bearded, wild man pulled up in front of the Opry's Ryman Auditorium in a hearse, parked it there, and camped out. His album *Penitentiary Blues* gained him a cult following, and his stage antics (roaring onstage on a Harley) didn't hurt. Coe wrote the Johnny Paycheck hit "Take This Job and Shove It."

GEORGE JONES

September 12, 1931–

George Jones was born with a broken arm. Then it was mostly downhill from there. Eventually one of the greatest singers in country music, he sang songs of love gone bad, marriage gone bad, drinking gone bad. But he wasn't content to just sing it; he had to live it. By the time Jones was 24, he'd been married twice, fought with the Marines in Korea, and recorded his first records. And begun what would be decades of alcohol abuse.

"Why Baby Why" was Jones' first hit, in 1955. It was just one of scores of hit records. "Just One More" was next, and was the first of many Jones releases to extol the sins and virtues (and the confusing confluence of the two) of distilled grain products. Recording success never protected Jones from bad choices and bad living and in fact may have contributed to them. Perhaps that hard living informs Jones' singing on "She Thinks I Still Care." The way Jones slurs the words "mist-uh-ake today" or "the happy guy I us-e-d to be-e" gives the songs a depth and complexity belied by the simple lyrics.

A hard drinker like his father before him, Jones had many tales of woe to sing about. His nickname "The Possum" was coined by a coworker who said that he bore a similarity to the animal.

In the early '60s Jones recorded a number of duets with Melba Montgomery. They sounded perfectly matched on record and in fact Jones tried ardently to connect with Montgomery on a personal level, but she rebuffed all advances. "We Must Have Been Out of Our Minds" perfectly matches their voices. It doesn't take much imagination to picture the two as having been together for decades, looking back on that amazing optimism of new love that gets smothered by reality and the dull grind of the years. As with many of his protagonists, "the Possum," as he was known, never got the girl when working with Montgomery. But even more like his protagonists, winning and losing get all twisted up sometimes so you can't tell which is which.

"When people ask me who my favorite country singer is I say 'You mean besides George Jones?'" —Johnny Cash

It wasn't until he met Tammy Wynette that Jones found a musical and personal equal. Like many a house afire, the flames of their passion would singe them and those around them. The two were married in 1969, and they remained so for six years of turbulent private lives and artful public ones. Duets like "The Ceremony" and "Golden Ring" extolled the virtues and benefits of marriage while the two were dealing with their many personal demons behind the scenes. And perhaps worse for

NUGGET: Throughout his career of singing the heartbreaking songs of downwardly mobile losers, Jones showed a playful side. Such near novelty songs as "The Race Is On," "Love Bug," and the supremely clever "I'm a People" were huge hits.

GREATEST HITS	
YEAR	SONG
1955	"Why Baby Why"
1956	"Just One More"
1959	"White Lightning"
1962	"She Thinks I Still Care"
1964	"The Race Is On"
1965	"Love Bug"
1966	"I'm a People"
1967	"Walk Through This World with Me"
1970	"Good Year for the Roses"
1972	"The Ceremony" (with Tammy Wynette)
1976	"Golden Ring" (with Tammy Wynette)
1980	"He Stopped Loving Her Today"
1981	"If Drinking Don't Kill Me (Her Memory Will)"
1985	"Who's Gonna Fill Their Shoes?"

Jones' psyche, when the two divorced in 1975 their record company insisted they continue to record and tour together.

By 1980 when George Jones went on tour to support the surprise smash hit "He Stopped Loving Her Today," the years of abuse were taking their toll. Sometimes you don't get what you want, but what you need. Jones met Nancy Sepulveda on that tour, and after the two were married she helped him conquer his deeply ingrained addictions.

Jones continues to record and tour to this day. Most recently he released *Hits I Missed . . . And One I Didn't* in 2005, a selection of songs he'd originally passed on that had become hits for other artists. And in 2006 he released an album of duets with another grizzled old legend, Merle Haggard. Cleaning up his act hasn't hurt his voice any, this Possum ain't dead yet.

AFTER HIS TRIPLE BYPASS IN 1994, JONES WORKED ON HIS AUTOBIOGRAPHY, *I LIVED TO TELL IT ALL*, WHICH BECAME A BEST-SELLER WHEN IT CAME OUT IN 1996.

Too Sad?

"He Stopped Loving Her Today." Why? Because he died. Right there you have the potential for the saddest song ever. "He said 'I'll love you 'til I die,' She told him, 'you'll forget in time.'" Oh no, he never forgot, never moved on, and only gave it up when he drew his final breath. George Jones himself thought the song far too depressing. At the conclusion of the final recording session Jones said, "I looked [producer] Billy [Sherrill] square in the eye and said, 'Nobody will buy that morbid son of a bitch.' Then I marched out the studio door."

What could have been a schmaltzy novelty tune instead became what many consider the greatest country music song ever produced. Masterful production by Sherrill, and Jones' spectacular voice, produced a huge hit and reminded everyone how formidable a weapon that smoky tenor could still be. The song took Jones back to country superstar status.

Like Mel Tillis' stutter, Jones' drunken slur disappeared when he sang, but was distinctly audible when he spoke. Which became problematic when the culmination of the song is four spoken lines. Jones himself said: "I had been able to sing while drunk all of my life. I'd fooled millions of people. But I could never speak without slurring when drunk. What we needed to complete that song was the narration, but Billy could never catch me sober enough to record four simple spoken lines. It took us about 18 months to record a song that was approximately three minutes long."

The 18-month wait for a window of sobriety was worth it, though, as those four lines still induce chills. "This time, he's over her, for good." Then Jones' soaring singing voice comes back in, augmented by the Jordanaires' vocals, crying steel guitars, and strings. There's little doubt that our poor hero has gone somewhere better and finally found release from his affliction.

THE JUDDS

1983–1990

After Naomi's diagnosis of hepatitis C, the Judds went on a farewell tour to commemorate the retirement of the mother-daughter duo before Wynonna's start of her solo act.

GREATEST HITS	
Year	**Song**
1983	"Had a Dream (for the Heart)"
1984	"Mama He's Crazy"
1985	"Have Mercy"
1986	"Grandpa"
	"Rockin' with the Rhythm of the Rain"
1987	"Don't Be Cruel" (with the Jordanaires)
1988	"Change of Heart"
1989	"Let Me Tell You about Love"
1990	"Love Can Build a Bridge"

Registered nurses work hard. Single mom and RN Naomi Judd was no exception, working hectic all-nighters in the ER. By day there was laundry to fold and floors to wax in their tiny house in Kentucky. Daughter Wynonna would help out, the two of them harmonizing together as they worked. Naomi had an inkling that the two of them sounded pretty good. So one night in 1983, between a triage and an IV drip, she decided to make a break for it. Next day, she packed all their belongings into the old beater, loaded in her daughters Wynonna and Ashley, and headed for Nashville. Nurses can pretty much always find a job, so it was Naomi who found herself tending a music executive's daughter. She slipped him a tape and a copy of her story. The rest is history. Music history.

America went crazy for the beautiful mother with the hard-luck story and her talented daughter. The Judds went on to become the best-selling duo in country music. Their first single rocketed to the top of the charts, and Naomi was able to hang up her sensible shoes and support hose for good. The second single, "Mama He's Crazy" was a music industry phenomenon and led a string of hits that lasted throughout the '80s. The Judds' tight harmonies and laid-back arrangements provided a perfect antidote to the big-city concerns of the day. Their songs about the enduring power of love, with those two spectacular voices intertwining, were sheer magic.

"A dead end street is a good place to turn around."—Naomi Judd

Over the course of the decade, Wynona had matured as an artist and began to forge her own path—a path not in the shadow of her mother. In 1990, Naomi announced that she had been diagnosed with hepatitis C (an unwanted result of the nursing profession). It became clear she would be unable to continue to perform. Wynonna took up the mantle and continued recording and performing as a successful solo artist.

My Wynonna

After her mother's retirement in 1990, Wynonna Judd went solo. Her first record, *Wynonna*, released in 1992, debuted at #1 on the country charts and became the largest-selling country album by a female artist at that time. The album charted four #1 singles, dispelling any doubts that Wynonna might need her mother around to hold her hand. Throughout the '90s and into the '00s, Wynonna produced hit records. Her tours proved to be major moneymakers, and she gave back by performing for U.S. troops overseas with the USO. Wynonna contributed to a number of film soundtracks, and in 2005 she added a star to her tiara by publishing a bestselling autobiography, *Coming Home to Myself*. She continues with her charitable activities and her inspired recording.

NUGGET: The down-home duo surprised everyone in 1990 when they made the first-ever high-tech 3-D music video for the song "Love Can Build a Bridge."

PEE WEE KING

FEB. 18, 1914–MARCH 7, 2000

A POLKA BANDLEADER'S SON, PEE WEE KING (ON LEFT, WITH ACCORDION), SHOWN HERE WITH HIS BAND THE GOLDEN WEST COWBOYS, STOOD ONLY 5 FEET, 6 INCHES TALL (WITHOUT THE 10-GALLON HAT).

GREATEST HITS	
YEAR	SONG
1947	"Ten Gallon Boogie"
	"Kentucky Waltz"
1948	"The Tennessee Waltz"
1949	"Bonaparte's Retreat"
1950	"Get Together Polka"
1951	"Slow Poke"
1952	"Silver and Gold"
	"Busybody"
1954	"Changing Partners"
	"Bimbo"

If we told you that the Tennessee state song was written by a nice Polish boy from way up north in Wisconsin, you'd say, "Aw, come on, now." That is, unless you were familiar with the work of Pee Wee King, born Julius Frank Anthony Kuczynski. Well, you're probably familiar with Pee Wee's work, whether you know it or not. He jotted down a little number on an unfolded matchbox one day, while driving to a gig with his bandmate Redd Stewart. They called their new song "The Tennessee Waltz."

Young Frank, as he was called back in Milwaukee, had saved up his pennies, until at age 14 he had enough money to buy his own accordion and join his father's polka band. The stage name came from a famed bandleader, Wayne King. And the Pee Wee part? Well, that came a little later and was courtesy of Gene Autry himself, who discovered King on radio in the early '30s. King and his band moved down to Louisville to back Autry up. In 1936, King formed a Western swing combo called the Golden West Cowboys.

The Grand Ole Opry invited King's band to join up, and things were never quite the same there after that. First there were the outfits: flashy Western-style Nudie suits. Then there were the tunes: that *oom-pah* polka rhythm instead of the 4/4 time signature of most country, folk, and rock standards. And then there were the wires: Pee Wee King was the first to plug in at the Opry, bringing an electric amp, then a drum kit, and brass, and of course, his mean, rockin' accordion. Jovial and outgoing, King toured with Minnie Pearl, hosted his own TV show for ABC, and appeared in four movies, including Gene Autry's 1938 *Gold Mine in the Sky*.

I Remember the Night

Pee Wee and Redd hit on something strong: that intangible blend of romance and bitterness otherwise known as bittersweet. Their classic song—its lyrics so perfectly suited to the lilting melody, has been sung by many great artists. Patti Page made it a smash crossover hit. And the list goes on: Patsy Cline, Roy Acuff, Elvis Presley, Emmylou Harris, Ella Fitzgerald, James Brown, Leonard Cohen, Tom Jones (with the Chieftans), and Otis Redding, for starters.

Plenty of songs deal in betrayal: the false "friend" who steals the sweetheart. But there's that music—that slow, aching, yearning waltz that just crowds out all other memories. Finally, the music, the betrayal, and the loss are inextricably woven together in the singer's memory. As soothing as a rocking cradle, as lonely as empty arms—that beautiful "Tennessee Waltz."

ALISON KRAUSS

JULY 23, 1971–

ALISON KRAUSS HAS GONE FROM CHILD PRODIGY TO MAINSTREAM MUSIC STAR, GARNERING 20 GRAMMY AWARDS, MORE THAN ANY OTHER WOMAN IN HISTORY.

Child prodigies are a rare breed. It's all about their being preternaturally talented at an unusually young age. But then what? How do you follow winning the Texas State Fiddle Championship at age 12? You enter the Walnut Valley Festival Fiddle Championship and win that at age 13. Then play on a couple of albums (including your brother's) before going on to create and release your first album at the tender age of 16. If you're Alison Krauss, you use that early popularity as a springboard to present and promote the music you love to a broader audience.

Sure, Alison started wowing 'em right out of the gate as a young girl. But unlike many great first acts, she then matured as an artist and went on to nearly single-handedly revive a musical form thought dead by many. When Krauss was invited to join the Grand Ole Opry at age 21, she was the first bluegrass performer so honored in 29 years. Alison Krauss and Union Station would go on to sell more records than any bluegrass act in history. And with guest spots on records by such artists as Vince Gill, Emmylou Harris, Kris Kristofferson, Kenny Rogers, and yes, Phish, Krauss brought the nearly forgotten sounds of bluegrass to audiences who'd never heard anything like it. If "child prodigy" is an incredible rarity, "bluegrass superstar" is an even more evanescent state of being.

All those early awards testified to Krauss' spectacular prowess on the horsehair and catgut, but it became her voice—bell-clear, intimate, breathy—that would electrify millions. Alison got together with her band, Union Station, in 1987, at age 16. She continues to work with them to the present day. Alison may be the star performer, but her band is considered one of the tightest around. In 1998 legendary Dobro player Jerry Douglas joined, and its reputation soared ever higher.

FOR SIMPLICITY'S SAKE, ALISON KRAUSS AND UNION STATION USE THE ACRONYM AKUS FOR THEMSELVES, AND TRAKUS WHEN THEY ARE TOURING WITH CONTEMPORARY BLUEGRASS PIONEER TONY RICE.

NUGGET: Krauss sang several songs on the wildly popular soundtrack for the motion picture *O Brother, Where Art Thou?* She was nine months pregnant during filming, so there was no way she would allow herself on camera. The same fate befell Dan Tyminski, whose voice ended up coming out of George Clooney's mouth when his character sang "I Am a Man of Constant Sorrow" in the film.

Many singers make you want to sing along. Alison Krauss' ravishing voice does the opposite. No matter the catchiness of the tune, any attempt to sing atop that wonder of nature soon falls into embarrassed silence. Not only do you drift into awe at the clarity and control, you quickly feel as if your own pipes are woefully inadequate. Even shower singers just shut up and listen. She's usually singing about love, or more precisely, losing it. Maybe never having it at all. Almost all of her songs are sad, but her voice, oh the voice—you can't pity her, you want to help her. It's not a big voice; it's little, like you're hearing a secret in the corner of the ball. She can belt it when she wants to, but more often it's the restraint and intimate quality that are so extraordinarily compelling. Even from the stage or in front of a camera broadcasting to an audience of millions, that voice draws you in and makes you really feel like you're the only one who can hear. Luckily, though, you're not, and the rest of us can feel the love, too.

GREATEST HITS

Year	Song
1990	"Steel Rails"
1995	"When You Say Nothing at All"
	"Baby Now That I've Found You"
1999	"Forget about It"
	"Stay"
2000	"Buy Me a Rose" (with Kenny Rogers)
	"I Am a Man of Constant Sorrow"
	"Down in the River to Pray"
2002	"The Lucky One"
2004	"Whiskey Lullaby" (with Brad Paisley)
	"The Scarlet Tide" (soundtrack to *Cold Mountain*)
2005	"Restless"
	"If I Didn't Know Any Better"
2006	"Missing You" (with John Waite)

After starting classical violin lessons at age 5, Alison wanted to spice things up a bit, so she tried her hand at bluegrass and country improvisations.

Bluegrass Booster

Bluegrass music has experienced a rebirth recently, in good part due to the efforts of Alison Krauss. In addition to her work with Union Station, Krauss has contributed solo and collaborative efforts to many projects, including film and television soundtracks. Her haunting soprano and nimble fiddle work can be heard in such films as *Twister*, *Eight Crazy Nights*, and *Cold Mountain*.

Krauss brought her bluegrass style to an entirely new audience when she performed on the 2004 Academy Awards with Sting, Elvis Costello, and T-Bone Burnett. Their haunting version of "The Scarlet Tide" left millions of viewers entranced. She has also worked as a producer for such "newgrass" acts as Nickel Creek, the Cox Family, and Reba McEntire. Nickel Creek's 2002 album *This Side* allowed Krauss to add to her burgeoning Grammy collection with a statuette for best producer. She has won 20 Grammy Awards and counting, more than any other female performer in history.

Whether it was working with Def Leppard's video director, performing at Carnegie Hall with the cast of the Grand Ole Opry, or collaborating with the likes of Sting, Krauss has managed to bring bluegrass to a newer, wider audience without compromising its integrity or betraying its authenticity. Some traditionalists would argue that such forays into popular culture somewhat censor the original sources. Krauss has shown with her body of work that the two are not contradictory; that old sounds can come from new places and leave both sides the richer for it.

KRIS KRISTOFFERSON

JUNE 22, 1936–

Just like the overnight sensation pop singer, or the just-discovered football phenomenon, being a genius in several fields is a lot harder than it looks. Kris Kristofferson is the epitome of the guy who can do anything, and succeed magnificently at it. And he's totally handsome. Don't you hate this guy? No, you don't, because despite (or because of) all that, he's cool: grizzled, a little scary, brilliant.

"God protects fools and songwriters."—Kris Kristofferson

His early acceptance of a Rhodes Scholarship gave an inkling of things to come (Bill Clinton was another famous Rhodes recipient). But it was still a surprise when the crazy army kid who landed his helicopter on Johnny Cash's lawn grew up to pen songs that would become part of the American canon. The song he gave Johnny that day was "Sunday Morning Coming Down," which went on to be a huge hit for Cash. "Me and Bobby McGee" was on that first record of Kristofferson's, too, and was a hit for Roger Miller; it became a classic in the hands of Janis Joplin.

GREATEST HITS	
YEAR	SONG
1970	"Me and Bobby McGee"
	"Sunday Morning Coming Down"
1971	"The Pilgrim, Chapter 33"
1972	"Why Me"
1973	"It's All Over, All Over Again"
1974	"I've Got to Have You"
1978	"Love Don't Live Here Anymore"
1981	"Nobody Loves Anybody Anymore"
1982	"Here Comes that Rainbow Again"
1986	"What About Me"
2006	"This Old Road"

AFTER TURNING DOWN AN OFFER TO TEACH AT WEST POINT, THIS RHODES SCHOLAR MOVED TO NASHVILLE, WHERE HE GOT A JOB AS A JANITOR AT COLUMBIA RECORDS, TO TRY TO BREAK IN TO THE MUSIC BUSINESS.

Kris Kristofferson continued writing songs, all the while taking on television and movie roles. His marriage to Rita Coolidge in 1973 produced three albums of music. The two worked out their interpersonal relations through song and hosted a popular TV show together. They were divorced in 1980.

In the mid '80s Kristofferson formed an outlaw country super group, the Highwaymen, with Johnny Cash, Willie Nelson, and Waylon Jennings. Their three albums were huge successes, and the band toured to great fanfare as well.

Kristofferson concentrated on his acting more than music in the '90s, but as the new century dawned, he found himself drawn back to the musical fold. He continues to craft songs and music that resonate with the soul of America.

Gone Hollywood

Not content to have "just" a career creating and performing carefully crafted classic songs, Kristofferson acted in movies on the side. As with most everything he tackled, he was a success from his first role. His 1972 movie *Cisco Pike*, co-starring Gene Hackman and Harry Dean Stanton, was a smash hit. He would go on to star opposite such luminaries as Burt Reynolds, Wesley Snipes, and Ellen Burstyn. And, of course, who could forget his 1976 performance opposite Barbra Streisand in *A Star Is Born*? Kristofferson continued to act throughout the next four decades, appearing in over 150 movies and television shows. Notable roles include a myriad of hard-living cowboy types, grizzled disaffected Vietnam vets, and a vampire hunter in the hugely popular *Blade* series of films.

BRENDA LEE

December 11, 1944–

Four foot, nine inches tall. All of 12 years old. But with a set of pipes on her that could belt a tune like nobody's business. Explosive, you might say. Brenda Lee would be known as Little Miss Dynamite for the remainder of her career. A tiny package, but her powerful voice belied her small stature. Even as she released her first record at age 12, she sounded old enough that her manager created a rumor she was a 32-year-old midget.

A vocal giant, Lee was a kid who grew into a girl and then a woman, all the while singing songs in a voice that revealed no age. It didn't help that by age 16 she was sounding mature enough to be growling and purring about her baby giving her that "special look" in "Sweet Nothin's." But sexy as it was, somehow her girlish lilt left listeners feeling happy and bouncy. You can just hear Brenda grinning in a kind of aural wink, even while she delivers lines full of double entendre.

Lee would go on to have a string of hits in both country and rock markets and in fact is the only woman to be a member of both the Rock and Roll Hall of Fame and the Country Music Hall of Fame. She also had a bit of a side specialty of Christmas songs, and her "Rockin' around the Christmas Tree" has become a holiday standard. Not bad for the pint-sized kid from Georgia.

Baby Miss Dynamite

When Brenda Lee made her first record at age 12, she was already an old pro. She'd won her first talent contest at age five, which put her on the radio for the weekly Borden Star Makers Revue. It didn't pay anything, but talent was allowed all the ice cream they could eat. From there, young Brenda worked a string of radio shows around the South until she was offered $30 to sing on the *Peach Blossom Jamboree* radio show. Brenda demurred in favor of attending the Red Foley show. When Brenda was introduced backstage as a local kid with an amazing voice, Foley insisted she come on stage and sing a song. So she did, and knocked the crowd over with "Jambalaya." As they screamed for more, Brenda sang another, then another. This appearance led to regular stints on various radio and TV shows. Shortly thereafter, Decca records signed her and the rest is history.

NUGGET: In a telling indication of her influence, Brenda Lee is mentioned in Golden Earring's classic rock gem, "Radar Love": "Radio's playing some forgotten song, Brenda Lee's 'Coming On Strong.'"

GREATEST HITS

Year	Song
1956	"Bigelow 6-200"
1957	"Dynamite"
	"One Step at a Time"
1958	"Rockin' around the Christmas Tree"
1959	"Sweet Nothin's"
1960	"I'm Sorry"
1963	"Losing You"
1966	"Coming On Strong"
1973	"Nobody Wins"
	"Sunday Sunrise"
1974	"Big Four Poster Bed"
1975	"Rock on Baby"
	"He's My Rock"
1980	"The Cowboy and the Dandy"
1985	"Hallelujah, I Love Her So" (with George Jones)

The producer of an Augusta, Georgia, TV show suggested that Brenda shorten her last name from Tarpley to Lee, so that it would be easier to remember. She went on to sell 100 million records.

PATTY LOVELESS

JANUARY 4, 1957–

Some overnight sensations happen overnight. Patty Loveless appeared on the country music scene in 1985 and it seemed she'd always been there. In fact, after spending a lot of time on local radio during her teens, Patty had left the business. But when her marriage broke up, she found herself back in Nashville, determined to make it this time. Her husky, rich alto was perfectly suited to traditional-sounding songs about lying, cheating, loving, and losing. She arrived in Nashville just as the New Traditionalist movement was gaining steam, and her songs that harked back to a simpler time put her in company with such artists as Alison Krauss and Dolly Parton.

Loveless released ever more successful singles until her second album *If My Heart Had Windows.* The title song and "A Little Bit in Love" both hit the Top 10 singles chart. But more important to Patty, 1988 was the year she was invited to join the Grand Ole Opry. Patty Loveless was a country star; the Opry made it official.

NUGGET: Patty learned Morse code to be able to communicate after vocal cord surgery. Having mastered the vagaries of the antiquated language, she continues to use it as an avid ham radio enthusiast. She's at call sign KD4WUJ if you want to give her a jingle.

Patty had a number of hit records in the ensuing years, but conflict with her record company convinced her she wasn't being marketed properly. So in 1992 she left MCA for Epic. Just as she was beginning work on an album for her new label, she was devastated to be diagnosed with a career-threatening throat problem in 1992. Emergency surgery was followed by long months of rehabilitation. A year later, Loveless released *Only What I Feel*, followed by *When Fallen Angels Fly* a year later. Both were hugely successful, and each contained multiple hit singles. Let the charts beware: Patty Loveless was back.

GREATEST HITS	
YEAR	SONG
1985	"Lonely Days, Lonely Nights"
1986	"I Did"
1988	"If My Heart Had Windows"
	"A Little Bit in Love"
1989	"Timber, I'm Falling in Love"
1990	"Chains"
1991	"I'm That Kind of Girl"
	"Hurt Me Bad (In a Real Good Way)"
1993	"Blame It on Your Heart"
1994	"How Can I Help You Say Goodbye"
1995	"You Can Feel Bad"
1996	"Lonely Too Long"
1999	"Can't Get Enough"

A COAL MINER'S DAUGHTER, PATRICIA RAMSEY LOVELACE GOT DIVORCED IN 1985 AND CHANGED HER MARRIED NAME, LOVELACE, TO A PERFECT COUNTRY SHOW-BUSINESS NAME, LOVELESS.

Loveless Finds Love

Patty was on her way to a meeting at her record label when she ran into a guy in white painter's overalls in the elevator. Little did she realize that this workman was about to produce her next record, while he remembers thinking, "This mousy little thing is an artist?" Nevertheless, the two fell in love, hard. But Patty didn't want people to think she was being controlled by some sort of Svengali pulling the strings behind the scenes. So they kept it secret as long as possible. But after her switch to a new record label and some success it seemed all right to tell everyone, and the secret was out. Emory Gordy Jr. was already the love of her life; now they were free to work openly together, too. Gordy went on to produce all of Patty's albums. The two seem to relish working together, though they each reserve the right to state that "the office is closed" when they get home at the end of the day.

LYLE LOVETT

November 1, 1957–

Texas native Lyle Lovett has been called "the thinking man's cowboy." With his mop of frizzy hair and a craggy face only Julia Roberts could love, Lovett has been a steady, quirky, and ever-evolving presence in country music for the last two decades. His songs tend toward melancholy tales of lost love, told in language that is equally witty, sophisticated, and simple. Starting off with both feet firmly rooted in country, Lovett took a mid-career venture into an eclectic blend of styles. But his recent albums have come on home to the ranch. The mature Lovett's horizon is as wide and inclusive as the Texas sky, though his gaze remains fixed inward.

"Fortunately, I've never had a job."—Lyle Lovett

Growing up on a ranch in Klein, Texas, Lovett spent more time with the horses than the guitar. He went off to Texas A&M University, and there he started playing in earnest, gigging out at local festivals and honing his insightful style of songwriting. After a stint in Germany, Lovett came back to the U.S. and dove into music, playing the Texas club circuit. His voice—dry, warm, and a little crackled around the edges, added an extra shot of integrity to his wistful songs.

Lovett's 1986 self-titled debut album contained five singles that made the country chart's Top 40, one of them hitting in the Top 10. But clearly there was something different about this guy; his next few albums would confirm this, as Lovett veered over to more alternative, cosmopolitan tastes. He assembled his gospel-jazz-blues inspired Large Band, and then moved out to Los Angeles. In 1993 he surprised the world by becoming Mr. Julia Roberts (the marriage lasted only two years), and he continued dabbling in alternative styles. With 1996's *Road to Ensenada*, Lyle was back in the saddle. He followed with a two-disc cover album, a tribute to fellow Texas songsters (Guy Clark, Townes Van Zandt, Robert Earl Keen, Walter Hyatt), confirming his deep-seated love for his musical roots.

After Lovett received his first guitar at age 7, he performed the song "Long Tall Texan" in a second-grade talent show.

GREATEST HITS

Year	Song
1986	"Cowboy Man"
	"If I Were the Man You Wanted"
1987	"She's No Lady"
	"If I Had a Boat"
1989	"Nobody Knows Me"
	"I Married Her Just Because She Looks Like You"
1992	"I've Been to Memphis"
	"Church"
1994	"Skinny Legs"
	"Moon Over My Shoulder"
	"Blues for Dixie" (with Asleep at the Wheel)
1996	"Don't Touch My Hat"
	"That's Right (You're Not from Texas)"
2003	"San Antonio Girl"

Movie Man

It would take a genius of a director like Robert Altman (*Nashville*) to see the screen potential in Lyle Lovett. Lyle's intelligence and subtle charm are obvious in movies like Altman's *Short Cuts* and *The Player*. You might have seen him in *The New Guy*, or on TV in *Dharma and Greg* or *Mad About You*. Lyle's piercing eyes and cool demeanor make him a natural. He's also had a hand in composing scores for several flicks.

LORETTA LYNN

April 14, 1935–

It's not just the rags-to-riches life story that makes Loretta Lynn an icon, but it sure doesn't hurt. The coal miner's daughter was wed at 13, became a mother at 14, and climbed out of more adversity than a fairytale princess. But the woman is real, the voice is real, and the grace, grit, and sense of humor that helped her weather the storms are as real as they get. A role model for many women, Loretta Lynn stands as the quintessential female country star: tough, smart, and nervy on the inside; charming, lovely and easygoing on the outside.

NUGGET: Patty Loveless, also a Kentucky coal miner's daughter, is Loretta Lynn's third cousin. Coincidentally, Patty also sang with the Wilburn Brothers.

The second of eight children, Loretta Webb was born in a one-room log cabin in Butcher Holler, Kentucky. She sang in church, sang around the house, and made good pies. That is, until she used salt instead of sugar one day in 1948 for a pie she was taking to a pie social. It was there that she met a young man who had just finished serving in the army, a fellow by the name of Oliver "Mooney" Lynn.

Loretta become the first woman to win the Country Music Association's Entertainer of the Year Award, in 1972. She also won in the Vocal Duo of the Year category (with Conway Twitty) every year from 1971 through 1975.

GREATEST HITS

Year	Song
1960	"I'm a Honky Tonk Girl"
1962	"Success"
1966	"You Ain't Woman Enough (To Take My Man)"
	"Don't Come Home a' Drinkin' (With Lovin' on Your Mind)"
1968	"Your Squaw Is on the Warpath"
1969	"Woman of the World (Leave My World Alone)"
1970	"Coal Miner's Daughter"
1971	"After the Fire Is Gone" (with Conway Twitty)
	"Lead Me On" (with Conway Twitty)
1972	"Rated X"
1973	"Louisiana Woman, Mississippi Man" (with Conway Twitty)
1974	"The Pill"
	"As Soon as I Hang Up the Phone" (with Conway Twitty)
2000	"Country in My Genes"

"In the long run, you make your own luck—good, bad, or indifferent." —Loretta Lynn

Moody didn't mind the pie, and he didn't mind Loretta either. The two were married when Loretta was just three months shy of her 14th birthday. It got Loretta out of the cabin, and out of Kentucky; the couple soon traveled to Washington state, where Loretta gave birth to her first child. Three more children followed, and Loretta was the mother of four before she turned 18. Mooney bought her a guitar and encouraged her to sing, so sing she did, all the while wiping noses and making lunches.

Ten years later, when the kids could all tie their own shoes, Loretta won a local singing contest and soon formed her own band. Signed to a small label, Zero Records, she cut her first single, 1960's "I'm a Honky Tonk Girl." Mooney was ambitious, and rightly proud of his wife's talent. The two sent copies to radio stations around the country and then embarked on a cross-country road trip, personally delivering discs and sweet-talking the DJ's into playing the song. The ploy worked, and the tune had moderate success.

NUGGET: Loretta is proudly part Cherokee. In fact, her sister Crystal Gayle was awarded the Cherokee Medal of Honor, the highest honor bestowed by the Cherokee Nation.

In Nashville, one of the doorbells that Mooney and Loretta rang belonged to the Wilburn Brothers, Teddy and Doyle. The Wilburns were established country stars with a publishing, booking, and traveling business. Loretta began to travel and appear on television with the Wilburns, and they helped get her signed to Decca Records. Then her career really took off. Produced by Buck Owens, who had helped Patsy Cline sound her best, Loretta recorded a string of hits that highlighted her honest, honky-tonk sound. As the '60s wore into the '70s, Loretta took on an increasingly independent and hardheaded stance toward her career—unusual for country women. But she always did it with a warm, wise smile on her face. She had earned her right to have a say.

Extricating herself from the Wilburns' influence, Loretta cut her greatest single in 1970, "Coal Miner's Daughter." She used the title for her autobiography, which was published in 1976; in 1980 the book was made into a widely acclaimed and popular movie. Sissy Spacek took home the Oscar for Best Actress for her portrayal of Loretta Lynn.

Continuing to tour and record, Lynn is a perennial fan favorite. In 2004, her artistic album *Van Lear Rose*, produced by Jack White of the White Stripes, won two Grammy Awards. The honky-tonk girl done good.

"You're Lookin' at Country." A member of the Grand Ole Opry since 1962, Loretta was inducted into the Country Music Hall of Fame in 1988.

Crystal's 1977 *We Must Believe in Magic*, featuring her hit single "Don't It Make My Brown Eyes Blue," was the first country album by a female vocalist to ever go platinum.

Sister Crystal

Maybe it's the country in their genes. Or something in the logs of that log cabin. Either way, four out of the eight Webb children went on to become country singers. Loretta, of course, but then there were brother Jay Lee and sister Peggy Sue, who both recorded a portion of songs in their day. But it was Crystal Gayle, Loretta's baby sister, who made the biggest mark on the charts.

Born Brenda Gail Webb, 16 years Loretta's junior, the raven-haired beauty took her stage name to avoid confusion with Brenda Lee, whose label she was on. Driving past a Krystal hamburger restaurant, the two sisters joked that the name had that certain touch of class. But the name stuck. Crystal lived up to her classy moniker, cutting a glamorous figure with her stunning features and floor-length sheet of black hair. But it was the bell-clear voice that kept them coming back for more. Her first hit, 1970's "I've Cried the Blue Right Out of My Eyes" was penned by Loretta. Crystal's mainstream breakthrough came in 1977 with the crossover hit "Don't It Make My Brown Eyes Blue." Crystal Gayle enjoyed a string of hit records, 18 of which hit #1. She was twice named CMA's Female Vocalist of the Year and in 1979 became the first country artist to tour China.

BARBARA MANDRELL

DECEMBER 25, 1948–

IN 1981, BARBARA MANDRELL BECAME THE FIRST PERFORMER TO WIN THE COUNTY MUSIC ASSOCIATION ENTERTAINER OF THE YEAR AWARD FOR TWO CONSECUTIVE YEARS.

Barbara Mandrell was not only country when country wasn't cool, she was playing instruments when the rest of us were spooning baby food onto our heads. So it was that an 11-year-old Mandrell was able to impress none other than Chet Atkins with her skills on the steel guitar. Before long, Barbara was playing as a featured performer on radio, in nightclub shows, and on the road with such country luminaries as Johnny Cash and Red Foley.

NUGGET: Barbara Mandrell was known as the Princess of Steel for her prowess on the steel guitar.

After a brief stint touring as the Mandrell Family, Barbara struck out on her own. It wasn't long before she began having her own hits. She often performed with David Houston, and the two had a number of chart-topping duets as well. Throughout the '70s and the early '80s, Barbara was a queen of country music. Though she promoted a glitzy, rhinestone-studded style, she was self-consciously provincial. Her huge 1981 hit, "I Was Country When Country Wasn't Cool" became her anthem. Mandrell walked a fine line between cosmopolitan production values and old-time mores. Even while Barbara and her sisters starred in their own television show with plenty of glamorous costumes, the sisters made a point of closing each show with a gospel number.

Though forced by health reasons to cancel the show after just two seasons, Mandrell continued making records and touring. A severe car accident in 1984 left Mandrell and her daughters alive, but she required literally years of physical therapy. When Barbara was ready to return to the world of music, she found the New Traditional sound had taken over, and her brand of sequins and sass had fallen by the wayside, dubbed "old fashioned." In 1997, Mandrell gave a farewell concert at the Grand Ole Opry, "The Last Dance." And though she has continued her retirement and focused on acting, astute observers note she never resigned her membership at the Opry.

Listen, Sister

One of the early-'80s' most popular TV shows was *Barbara Mandrell and the Mandrell Sisters*. It featured Louise and Irlene, often making fun of their bossy older sister. Featuring glitzy Las Vegas-style production numbers, a countrified cast of life-sized puppets, and the charming antics of Barbara and her sisters, the show became a smash hit. Barbara showed off her instrumental skill during the regular "guitar pull" segment, where she would play as many as nine different instruments. The recording and performing schedule was brutal, though, and Barbara was forced by exhaustion to retire the show after only two years.

GREATEST HITS

YEAR	SONG
1969	"I've Been Loving You Too Long"
1970	"After Closing Time" (with David Houston)
1973	"The Midnight Oil"
1974	"I Love You, I Love You" (with David Houston)
1977	"Married, But Not to Each Other"
1978	"Sleeping Single in a Double Bed"
1979	"If Loving You Is Wrong (I Don't Want To Be Right)"
1980	"Years"
1981	"I Was Country When Country Wasn't Cool"
1982	"Till You're Gone"
1983	"One of a Kind Pair of Fools"
1984	"Only a Lonely Heart Knows"

KATHY MATTEA

JUNE 21, 1959–

When Kathy Mattea dropped out of college, quit the bluegrass band, and moved to Nashville to make it as a country singer, she did anything she could to make the scene. That included working as a tour guide at the Country Music Hall of Fame, singing backups for Bobby Goldsboro, and singing demos at record companies. Eventually Kathy managed to get signed, and released two well-received if not groundbreaking albums. Third time was the charm, and 1986's *Walk the Way the Wind Blows* was a breakthrough. Sure, it was country, with bluegrass elements, but it also paid homage to the folk tradition. "Love at the Five and Dime" brought Mattea her first hit, and also drew attention to its songwriter, Nanci Griffith. Mattea soon became known as someone who could pick the hit out of an unknown songwriter's demo tape.

Mattea went on to have hit records for the next decade. She sang love songs, trucker songs, and broken-heart songs. Audiences and critics ate it up, and she sold records and won awards galore. "Eighteen Wheels and a Dozen Roses" became her signature hit in 1988, followed by "Come from the Heart," "She Came from Fort Worth," and "Burnin' Old Memories."

For all the country themes, folk music was clearly an influence, too. Ever the musical aesthete, Kathy had always had an interest in bluegrass and older folk forms as well. Trips to Scotland in the early '90s strengthened that connection. In 1991, Mattea released *Time Passes By*, a collaboration with artists such as Emmylou Harris and Scottish singer-songwriter Dougie McLean. Continuing to explore her wide-ranging influences, Mattea released a gospel album, followed by more traditional country albums throughout the '90s.

WHILE SHE DOESN'T CONSIDER HERSELF A POLITICAL ACTIVIST, KATHY MATTEA WILL SPEAK HER MIND ABOUT ISSUES OF CONCERN TO HER, BE IT AIDS OR GLOBAL WARMING.

Saving Planet Earth

In January 2006, Kathy Mattea attended Al Gore's PowerPoint presentation on global warming (which would later be compiled and released as *An Inconvenient Truth*). The material struck her so much that she couldn't sleep for the next two nights. Upon awakening on the third day she resolved to take action.

"I was one of those people who thought that there's nothing a lone person can do to make a difference, and I learned differently," Mattea says. Anthropogenic climate change may be caused by large events, but Kathy believes individuals can help change the world, literally. "Now I want to spread the word of hope to regular people, and help them learn what the huge ripple effect can be when we each make small changes in our daily routines."

GREATEST HITS

YEAR	SONG
1983	"Street Talk"
1985	"He Won't Give In"
1986	"Love at the Five and Dime"
1987	"Goin' Gone"
1988	"Eighteen Wheels and a Dozen Roses"
1989	"Burnin' Old Memories (With a Brand New Flame)"
	"Come from the Heart"
1990	"She Came from Fort Worth"
	"Where've You Been"
1994	"Walking Away a Winner"
1997	"455 Rocket"

NUGGET: Kathy has attracted a solid group of hard-core fans who call themselves "Matteaheads."

MARTINA McBRIDE

JULY 29, 1966–

FOR HER INDUCTION INTO THE GRAND OLE OPRY, MARTINA McBRIDE WOWED THE CROWD WITH A RENDITION OF WILLIE NELSON'S "CRAZY."

Don't let the startling beauty fool you—this lady can sing. She's got good looks, a good heart, and her strong, rich soprano just seals the deal. When she's called the Celine Dion of country music, the reference is to her voice; a Diva she is not. Selling upward of 16 million records, earning four CMA female vocalist awards, and racking up 22 Top-10 singles, McBride has firmly crossed over into the mainstream pop charts, while maintaining her hold on country.

Martina's small-town Kansas upbringing was filled with music. Her father, Daryl Schiff, was leader of a local country band called the Schifters, which became a family affair. Martina joined the band at age 7, going on to play keyboards and sing backup. But that voice didn't belong in anyone's backup section. Martina married John McBride, a sound engineer, and the two moved to Nashville in 1990. Touring with Garth Brooks was the McBrides' first gig there, John working sound, and Martina selling T-shirts. Within two years she was Garth's opening act.

"I'm just the instrument for the song to do whatever it's supposed to do—heal, inspire or encourage." —Martina McBride

Though her honky-tonk-styled first album wasn't the big breakthrough, that came soon enough with 1993's poppier *The Way That I Am*, which yielded her first two hits. "Independence Day" in particular captured the public's attention; McBride's no-holds-barred vocal prowess was set against a moving tale of domestic violence. It has become Martina's theme song, with its refrain "Let freedom ring, let the white dove sing."

After continued success in the '90s, McBride turned her hand to producing, with her album of country classics, 2005's *Timeless*. McBride has forged ahead to new territory with 2007's *Waking Up Laughing*, which she produced and for which she wrote most of the material. The musical direction is more eclectic, showcasing her elegant vocal stylings. Martina McBride was made a member of the Grand Ole Opry in 1995.

GREATEST HITS

YEAR	SONG
1993	"My Baby Loves Me"
1994	"Independence Day"
1995	"Wild Angels"
1997	"Wrong Again"
1998	"Happy Girl"
1999	"I Love You"
2001	"Blessed"
2002	"Concrete Angel"
2003	"This One's for the Girls"
2004	"In My Daughter's Eyes"
	"God's Will"
2005	"Anyway"

Video Made the Country Star

Even in today's image-crazed climate, being telegenic isn't everything, if you haven't got the musical chops to back it up. Martina McBride has both, and something more to boot: an intense and heartfelt social conscience. With her lovely voice and looks, she could just use her videos to play up those assets; instead, McBride has used the medium as a bully pulpit to speak up for the downtrodden. In her award-winning "Independence Day," she shed light on spousal abuse; "Concrete Angel" is a stark portrait of child abuse, and in "God's Will," a disabled child brings spiritual gifts to those who love him.

REBA McENTIRE

March 28, 1955–

Reba. Need we say more? Singer, actress, comedienne, writer, designer, humanitarian. Like other self-made, multitalented women known simply by their first name, Reba McEntire is more than an entertainer; she's practically an institution. Reba has built her empire on warmth, girl-next-door glamour, and a fully loaded set of pipes. The "Queen of Country Music" has sold more than 60 million records, won numerous Grammys, and her 1993 *Greatest Hits Volume 2* sold 5 million copies.

"Be different, stand out, and work your butt off." —Reba McEntire

Reba Nell McEntire grew up on a cattle ranch in Chockie, Oklahoma. Her dad was a champion steer roper; feisty redheaded Reba was discovered while singing the national anthem at the rodeo. Her gutsy, down-home voice had just that touch of sweetness, and the looks didn't hurt, either. But the '70s and '80s yielded only mediocre record sales and tepid charting; no one quite got the potential firebomb waiting to be ignited. Reba finally moved to Nashville, took her song selection, production, and image into her own hands, and in 1984 broke through big. The hits kept coming, and her live shows became major events, with costume changes, lighting, and dancers.

Tragedy struck in 1991 when seven of Reba's band members and her road manager were killed in a plane crash; the singer poured her grief into her bestselling album, *For My Broken Heart*. Three years later, Reba published her autobiography, *Reba: My Story*, followed by the inspirational volume, *Comfort From a Country Quilt*.

Reba is bold, brainy, and beautiful, but her fans also admire her compassion; her braver songs often deal with touchy subjects such as spousal abuse, divorce, immigration, war, even AIDS. And she lends both her talent and her muscle to Habitat for Humanity, raising funds and building homes for the needy.

Stage And Screen

Reba tore up the stage in the 2001 Broadway musical *Annie Get Your Gun*. She ignited the screen opposite Kevin Bacon in *Tremors*. And she held court on her own self-titled sitcom from 2001 to 2007. Add in the TV specials, the lavish road shows, and a lightning bolt of star quality, and you've got Reba.

Reba isn't the only country star to cross over into acting; but she may have been the first to use the small screen as a stepping-stone to the large. Early on, Reba saw the potential in music videos and showcased her acting talent in a string of mini-movies, starring herself and often playing opposite a hunky actor. "Whoever's in New England" started it off in 1986, and "Fancy" built out a three-minute song into a six-minute movie, with back-story, dialogue, epilogue—the works.

GREATEST HITS

Year	Song
1982	"I'm Not That Lonely Yet"
1983	"You're the First Time I've Thought About Leaving"
1985	"How Blue"
1986	"Whoever's in New England"
1987	"What Am I Gonna Do About You"
1988	"New Fool at an Old Game"
1990	"You Lie"
1991	"For My Broken Heart"
1992	"The Heart Won't Lie" (with Vince Gill)
1996	"How Was I to Know"
2001	"I'm a Survivor"
2004	"Somebody"

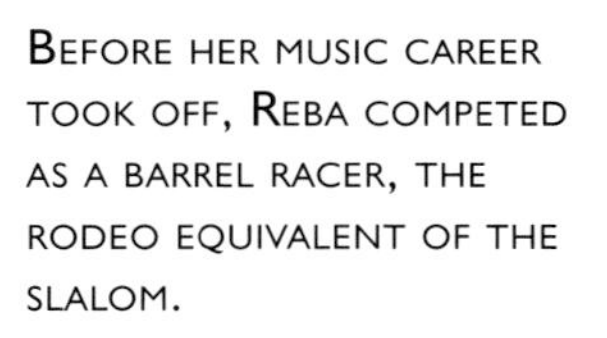

Before her music career took off, Reba competed as a barrel racer, the rodeo equivalent of the slalom.

TIM McGRAW

May 1, 1967–

What's it take to be the guy who's good at everything? Maybe being bad at some things long enough to get good. Tim McGraw's roommates used to hide his guitar to keep him from playing within earshot. But he dug it out from under the bed and got good—and then some. He took on the country music world next and got good at that, too, earning a ton of Top 10 accolades. McGraw has had a #1 song each year since 1994.

Tim wore a big hat, sang songs of cowboys, love, and loss. He sounded a lot like a regular guy, the kind of guy you'd like to have a beer with. Of course, he's a multimillionaire country star married to arguably the most beautiful woman in country, but don't let that bother you. For all those reasons to hate him, Tim McGraw wins you over with his straightforward earnestness. Oh, it's the cowboy in me, the cowboy in you, but most of all " . . . it's just the cowboy in us all."

When Tim romanced and married Faith Hill in 1996, duets seemed a natural, and the two produced some of the most successful ever. Hill's smoky alto played beautifully against McGraw's deadpan growl, and listeners could almost hear the sparks flying between the two.

GREATEST HITS

Year	Song
1994	"Indian Outlaw"
	"Don't Take the Girl"
1996	"She Never Lets It Go to Her Heart"
1997	"It's Your Love" (with Faith Hill)
1999	"My Next Thirty Years"
	"My Best Friend"
	"Something Like That"
2001	"Grown Men Don't Cry"
	"The Cowboy in Me"
2002	"Real Good Man"
2004	"Over and Over" (with Nelly)

Everything and the Girl

When Tim McGraw agreed to tour with the lovely Faith Hill as his opening act in 1996, he had no idea the Spontaneous Combustion tour would change his life. True to the catchy moniker, sparks flew. Tim asked Faith to marry him right as he was running onstage. After what must have been the most jittery show ever, he returned to his bus to find his answer, written on the mirror in lipstick. The two were married in October of 1996 and have three daughters.

When two of the most popular acts in country music marry, it's no surprise they'll work together too. Faith and Tim have sung numerous duets, live and on record. And building on the success of their first, fateful tour together, the pair have mounted several hugely popular Soul2Soul tours. Each plays their own act, then the highlight of the shows is when they sing duets. Lovebirds singing love songs—what could be better?

And again showing his penchant for doing difficult things and doing them well, in 2004 he partnered with the rap star Nelly for the duet "Over and Over." Others had shown what pop crossovers looked like; Tim and Nelly created the first rap crossover. And both of them ended up on the Adult Contemporary charts as well.

Tim McGraw learned at age 11 that the truck driver he called Dad had adopted him. His biological dad was actually famed pitcher Tug McGraw.

Roger Miller

January 2, 1936–October 25, 1992

Miller's "King of the Road" contributed to his six-figure songwriting royalties and to a chain of hotels by the same name in the '70s.

Badoom, boom, boom, baboom, snap, snap, snap, snap, "Trailer for sale or rent…" That's all it takes, those eight beats and five words, and you're instantly immersed in the hobo world of Roger Miller's "King of the Road." Most of us have never swept floors for a night's room, nor will we ever. But Miller's title character is so vividly rendered, we feel what it must have been like. Telling details, like, "I ain't got no cigarettes," or the fact that rooms cost 50 cents brought to life a bygone era, when dropping it all and hitting the rails seemed a viable career choice.

Roger Miller had other hits besides his most famous, of course. He'd originally tried to jump start his music career by stealing a guitar. Filled with remorse, he returned it and joined the military rather than go to jail. When asked where he'd studied, Miller would often answer, "Korea, Clash of '52." Upon his return he hit Nashville, where he would do, or play, anything to get into the music business. When Faron Young asked if he was a drummer, Miller replied, "I'll be a drummer by Monday."

I Love You, Big River

Miller's songs often featured vivid characters in interesting circumstances. So it should have come as no surprise when he created music and lyrics for the 1985 musical *Big River*. Based on *The Adventures of Huckleberry Finn*, the subject matter was perfectly suited to Miller's style. He wrote the music with a country and bluegrass feel befitting the rural settings of Twain's most famous novel. And he apparently had a sure hand on the plow as *Big River* swept the Tony Awards, winning Best Musical, Best Original Score, and other accolades. It won another round of Tony Awards during its 2003 revival.

"Some people walk in the rain; others just get wet."

—Roger Miller

People often said he spoke in songs, and other songwriters would purportedly follow him around picking up verbal scraps. He applied that wit to his own little ditties about goofy lowlifes more often than the serious character studies of "King." More typical Miller fare were songs like "Dang Me," with its carousing new father. He claimed to have written "Dang Me" in four minutes, sitting at a booth at Tootsie's Orchid Lounge.

Miller's brilliant and ebullient personality overflowed into his songs. Sadly, unlike his character in "King of the Road," Miller never ran out of his omnipresent smokes, and in 1992 they finally got the better of him.

NUGGET: In the '70s Miller appeared backed by his most famous song in ads for Monroe shock absorbers. Shocks that were the "King of the Road."

GREATEST HITS

Year	Song
1961	"When Two Worlds Collide"
1964	"Dang Me"
1965	"King of the Road"
	"England Swings"
1966	"Husbands and Wives"
1967	"Walkin' in the Sunshine"
1968	"Little Green Apples"
1971	"Tomorrow Night in Baltimore"
1977	"Baby Me Baby"
1981	"Old Friends" (with Willie Nelson and Ray Price)

RONNIE MILSAP

JANUARY 16, 1944–

With a childhood straight out of a Delta blues song, the affable Ronnie Milsap stands as one of the top country hitmakers of the '70s and '80s. Blending mellow, pop-influenced vocals with serious instrumental prowess, Milsap's style has sometimes been called "country soul." He infused new life and passion into old country and R&B songs, as well as introduced new material that would resonate with a wide audience. Milsap has racked up an impressive total of #1 hits—40—and is the winner of seven Grammy Awards.

NUGGET: A chance meeting in 1970 between Charlie Pride and Milsap's wife, Joyce, in a Los Angeles hotel elevator led to Milsap moving to Nashville, cementing his success.

TRAINED IN CLASSICAL MUSIC FROM A YOUNG AGE, MILSAP CAN PLAY VIRTUALLY ANY WIND OR STRING INSTRUMENT.

Like his hero, Ray Charles, Ronnie Milsap is blind; he was born into poverty, with congenital glaucoma, in rural Robbinsville, North Carolina. His mother believed that the blindness was a mark of God's wrath and passed off her baby to his father and grandfather. When he was only 6, Ronnie was sent to Governor Moorhead School for the Blind in Raleigh. His teachers soon recognized the boy's musical talent and began him on rigorous classical training. Ronnie started on violin and was deemed a virtuoso after only one year; he also became proficient on a number of other instruments, including guitar and the piano, which would become his main instrument.

Hearing rock, country, soul, and blues coming over the airwaves, Ronnie took notice. He formed his own band as a youngster, the Apparitions. Milsap attended college in Atlanta for a short time but declined a full scholarship in favor of becoming a full-time musician. Playing with J. J. Cale, then moving on to session gigs for the likes of Elvis Presley, Milsap recorded a number of minor R&B and pop hits in the '60s and early '70s. When he signed with RCA in 1973 and began working with Charley Pride's producer, Jack D. Johnson, the hits began to come in earnest: Milsap stayed in the Top 10 on the country charts for 15 years. Many of his songs made it to the pop charts and topped the adult contemporary charts as well, making Ronnie Milsap one of the most successful crossover acts in history.

GREATEST HITS

YEAR	SONG
1974	"Please Don't Tell Me How the Story Ends"
1975	"(I'd Be) A Legend in My Time"
1976	"What Goes On When the Sun Goes Down"
1978	"Only One Love in My Life"
1979	"Nobody Likes Sad Songs"
1980	"Cowboys and Clowns"
1981	"Smoky Mountain Rain"
	"(There's) No Gettin' Over Me"
1982	"Any Day Now"
1985	"Lost in the Fifties Tonight (In the Still of the Night)"
1986	"In Love"
1989	"A Woman in Love"

Smoky Mountain Boy

"Smoky Mountain Rain" is probably Ronnie Milsap's best-known song. In an interview on CMT, Milsap tells how he loved songs like "Wichita Lineman" or "Galveston" that cast a place in an almost mythic light. So Milsap asked songwriters Kyle Fleming and Dennis Morgan to pen a tune for his own home region, the hills of Western North Carolina. Milsap put in the "thunder" sounds on the piano, same as he did for Elvis on his "Kentucky Rain."

BILL MONROE

September 13, 1911–September 9, 1996

Bluegrass. It's as old as the hills of Kentucky, as deeply rooted as the turf it's named for, right? Well, sort of. The music itself emerged over centuries, a blend of folk and sacred traditions from the British Isles and Africa. But until Bill Monroe came along, adding his lightning-fast mandolin, his high-lonesome vocals, and his all-string arrangements, the music didn't have a proper name. Known as "the father of bluegrass," Monroe will forever be linked with this musical style, the twangy, energized version of country that is named for his band, the Blue Grass Boys. The band, of course, took its name from Monroe's home state, Kentucky—the Blue Grass State.

> **NUGGET:** Monroe's 1989 win for his *Southern Flavor* album was the first Grammy ever awarded in the Bluegrass category.

Thanks to his uncle, Pendleton Vandiver (the "Uncle Pen" of song), young William Smith Monroe picked up some of the roots music that was floating around his home of Rosine, Kentucky. Uncle Pen,

The youngest of eight, Monroe came from a musical family that included two brothers who played fiddle and two other siblings who played guitar. Bill learned the mandolin at age 10.

After induction into the Country Music Hall of Fame in 1970, Bill Monroe refused to rest on his laurels and still toured extensively for decades.

the brother of Bill's mother, Malissa Vandiver, was a skilled fiddler who taught his nephew to play. It was the mandolin that caught Bill's eye, though, and he developed a virtuosic technique on the instrument when still young. Monroe's father, a prosperous farmer, and his mother had both passed away by the time Bill turned 16 (he was the youngest of eight children), and he headed to Chicago, where some of his brothers had found work at an oil refinery.

Bill and his brothers Birch and Charlie started playing live shows together as the Monroe Brothers, but Birch soon dropped out. Bill and Charlie, who played guitar, continued making music together, working for radio stations in Iowa and Nebraska. They then traveled to Charlotte, North Carolina, where the powerful WBT radio station was based. The brothers hit on some success, recording close to 60 sides for Bluebird Records, before splitting up in 1938. Bill went right on—that mandolin couldn't rest. He assembled a group of players, called them the Blue Grass Boys, and a new musical genre was born.

AFTER BUYING HIS 1923 GIBSON F-5 MANDOLIN (SERIAL NUMBER 73987) IN 1943, BILL PLAYED IT FOR 50 YEARS, THOUGH IT REQUIRED MANY TRIPS BACK TO THE SHOP FOR SOMETIMES EXTENSIVE REPAIRS.

The Opry audition was a turning point for Monroe. He played "Mule Skinner Blues," made famous by Jimmie Rogers. Of course, the Opry's George Hay loved him (Bill had worked for WBT's *Barn Dance* while in Chicago—the show that gave birth to the Opry), and Monroe was made a member of the Grand Ole Opry in 1939. His dynamic stage presence, breathtaking playing, and catchy original songs won over audiences. He briefly traveled with his own tent show, adding comedy routines to season the pot. But the hard-driving music was the wow factor: the rhythm, the standout solos, and something in that voice—high, plaintive, and urgent—that wouldn't let you go.

"I'm a farmer with a mandolin and a high tenor voice." —Bill Monroe

Bill Monroe hit on an instrumental formula that would define the genre of bluegrass: guitar, fiddle, stand-up bass, banjo, and, of course, mandolin. While the personnel of the Blue Grass Boys changed over the years, the early lineup included Stringbean (Dave Akeman) on banjo. His chores were taken on by Earl Scruggs in 1945, whose three-finger picking style became a bluegrass staple. Add guitarist and singer Lester Flatt to the mix, and you've got a hit machine. And hit they did—Bill Monroe and his Blue Grass Boys churned out the sides, in recordings that are now seen as the definitive bluegrass.

Black and Bluegrass

Although bluegrass is pretty much a white Southern tradition, it has roots that reach back to Africa. Bill Monroe was schooled in music by his Uncle Pen, but also by black blues guitarist Arnold Schultz, who sometimes played with Pen. Through him, Monroe may have heard rural African-American dance bands, who used the instruments he would later feature in his Blue Grass Boys. The fiddle, mandolin, and guitar are of European origin, but the banjo is an African-American creation, modeled after several traditional African instruments. The first banjos, made of gourds, were used by slaves in the South. Like all forms of American music, bluegrass is a rich stewpot of ingredients from all over the world.

By the 1950s, country music was changing—a fact that both helped and hurt Bill Monroe. On the one hand, the smoothly produced Nashville Sound took some audience away from his twangy, homegrown acoustic style. On the other hand, his core of loyal fans and followers grew, even as they watched the straight-up traditions of country diluted somewhat. Before he knew it, Monroe was mentor to a passionate and growing breed of bluegrass musicians. Flatt and Scruggs left in 1948 to form their own band, the Foggy Mountain Boys, and more and more combos began to spring up. The bluegrass revival of the '60s cemented Monroe's place as the father of bluegrass, making him a near-cult hero. Not all pioneers are so honored, but during his lifetime Monroe received numerous awards that recognized his unique contribution to country music.

GREATEST HITS

YEAR	SONG
1936	"What Would You Give in Exchange for Your Soul" (as the Monroe Brothers)
1940	"Mule Skinner Blues"
1941	"In the Pines"
1942	"Orange Blossom Special"
1946	"Kentucky Waltz"
	"Footprints in the Snow"
1947	"Blue Moon of Kentucky"
	"Blue Grass Special"
	"Goodbye Old Pal"
1948	"My Rose of Old Kentucky"
1949	"Blue Grass Breakdown"
1950	"Uncle Pen"
1951	"New Mule Skinner Blues"
1952	"Raw Hide"
1953	"I'm on My Way to the Old Home"
1955	"Roanoke"
1957	"Molly and Tenbrooks"

PATSY MONTANA

October 30, 1908–May 3, 1996

Quick! Picture a cowgirl. That image you see—it's probably Patsy Montana. The ebullient, yodeling singer and actress embodied the Hollywood cowgirl image during the Depression years. Montana blazed a trail for women to enter country music sitting high in their own saddles—she was the first female recording artist to ever sell a million records. The fiddling, strumming, yodeling Montana (born Ruby Blevins) hit her mark with the 1935 hit "I Want to Be a Cowboy's Sweetheart."

> **NUGGET:** Among the members of Patsy's backing band for a 1964 live album was young guitarist Waylon Jennings.

Blame it on the 1933 Chicago World's Fair. Rubye (she added the sophisticated "e" at age 17) traveled there from her home in Hope, Arkansas, with two of her 10 brothers. The boys wanted to enter a prize watermelon in the fair, and Rubye wanted to meet up with her pen pals, the Girls of the Golden West (Millie and Dolly Good). While in Chicago Rubye auditioned for the WLS National Barn Dance. She had already seen some success after winning a talent contest in California; in fact, she'd recorded some, thanks to a connection with Jimmie Davis. But the influential National Barn Dance was the big time, and Rubye won a gig singing with the group the Prairie Ramblers. Changing her name to Patsy Montana, she was ready to ride.

The 1935 recording that made Patsy a star was followed by many more, always heavy on the virtuoso fiddling and guitar playing of the Prairie Ramblers (and Patsy herself). The Montana sound was always energetic and upbeat. Patsy toured extensively, first with the Ramblers, then as a solo act, and did a stint on the radio show *Louisiana Hayride*. She toured and recorded as long as she could sit up in the saddle.

GREATEST HITS

Year	Song
1933	"When the Flowers of Montana Are Blooming"
1933	"Montana Plains"
1935	"I Want to Be a Cowboy's Sweetheart"
1936	"The She Buckaroo"
	"Sweetheart of the Saddle"
1937	"My Poncho Pony"
1938	"Cowboy Rhythm"
1939	"I Wanna Be a Western Cowgirl"
	"A Rip-Snortin' Two-Gun Gal"
1940	"Goodnight Soldier"

Patsy Montana thought she'd be done performing by the time she hit 40, but she kept on well into her 80s, saying, "As long as they want to hear my songs, I'll keep singing."

Celluloid Sweetheart

Patsy not only sang about being a cowboy's sweetheart, she also played one in the movies. Her film debut was opposite Gene Autry in the 1939 *Colorado Sunset*. Depression-era Americans loved the image of the cheerful, adventurous cowgirl with the can-do spirit. Decked out in fringed and embroidered Western gear, with her cowboy hat titled back at a jaunty angle, Patsy became an American icon. And girls now had another career choice . . . nurse, teacher, *and* cowgirl!

> **NUGGET:** "Sixteen Pounds" was Patsy's feminist answer to "Sixteen Tons," with lyrics like "You gain sixteen pounds and whaddaya get? Another dirty look from your old man, yet, St. Peter don't you call me cause I can't go, I'm gettin' too heavy to pass through the door."

WILLIE NELSON

APRIL 30, 1933–

Many Native American tribes share an ancient legend of the Trickster. This sacred, profane, wily being is often depicted as a coyote. The Trickster embodies the creative force—by turns amusing, scandalizing, infuriating, and fascinating. He sows creativity via mischief-making; one has to have some chaos to give birth to order. Over nearly a half century of creating and performing, Willie Nelson has matured into the role of the Trickster of country music. Whether outlaw, cowboy, wild man, or mystic sage, Willie, with his vast creativity, talent, and heart, has produced one of the most compelling bodies of work in music.

Willie didn't start out to become the resident coyote of country music. He originally came to Nashville's attention as a songwriter, and a good one. One of his first attempts was a little ditty called "Crazy"—you might have heard Patsy Cline singing it. After cleaning up on the charts, the song went on to become a classic in the American canon. Nelson wrote several other hit songs for others to sing, but he decided he wanted to perform his own work.

No one-trick pony, Willie has shown his range by performing and recording various genres of music, including country, gospel, blues, and standards.

Toward that end, Willie moved to Austin, Texas, in the early '70s. He found the burgeoning progressive country scene percolating there and fit right in. The clean-cut country look was traded in for jeans, long locks of unkempt hair, and what would become his trademark bandanna. When Willie appeared with Waylon Jennings and Jessi Colter on *Wanted! The Outlaws*, the movement had a name, and Willie was a charter member. While many took the Outlaw movement to be a throwback to Western myth, others saw in it the relationship artists had with their corporate overseers. Nashville insiders were used to record companies and producers calling the shots. These new outlaws, among other things, insisted on retaining creative control over the recording process.

NUGGET: Willie Nelson thought so much of the idea of vegetable-based diesel fuel that he invested in a company to manufacture the stuff. Today BioWillie brand biodiesel is available at truck stops all across the land.

Willie used this control to create a masterpiece that his record company didn't even want to release. *Red Headed Stranger* was a straightforward concept album, stripped of the countrypolitan production that Nelson was trying to escape. "Blue Eyes Crying in the Rain" became his first #1 hit. Willie was authentically country, but his outlaw act had rock audiences tuning in too.

Continuing his transition from whiskey river–swimming cowboy to Zen trickster, Willie released *Stardust* in 1978. Wait—what happened to the country cowboy guy? This was an album of jazz standards, songs your parents probably sang to each other. Country audiences often don't approve of their artists taking stylistic or creative leaps of faith. But fans loved it, even country aficionados. *Stardust* remained on the charts for 10 years, introducing legions of fans to the classic American songbook.

Nelson is president of Farm Aid, a nonprofit organization that has held annual concerts to help preserve American family farms since 1985, raising more than $29 million.

Willie performing at the 2006 Farm Aid concert with his trusty Trigger. When asked why he named his guitar that, Nelson replied, "Roy Rogers had a horse named Trigger. I figured: This is my horse!"

Trigger

In 1969, Willie Nelson played an OK guitar. And then some knucklehead went and stepped on it at a particularly rowdy honky-tonk gig. Willie took it to his fix-it guy, who declined to even try to save it. But he did offer Willie a substitute that he had lying around, a Martin N-20 classical guitar. What kind of country musician would want to play a nylon-stringed classical ax? Willie Nelson, that's who. He knew from the first strum that this was his guitar. He later named it Trigger (see Roy Rogers) and declared that he would give it all up when the guitar did.

Almost 40 years later Willie is still going strong, but Trigger is having a bit of trouble keeping up. Classical guitars are used to being lovingly stroked, with bare fingers. Willie's vigorous strumming and picking has worn a hole clear through the soundboard. But that's not the worst of it. Years of buses, airplanes, and honky-tonks have taken their toll. For 25 years, Willie refused to even let anyone near the guitar. But at a certain point it became clear he'd have to retire or give up his promise because the instrument had just about given up the ghost. Technicians from the Martin Guitar company itself performed a unique restoration and repair job which looks to keep Trigger going as long as her master.

One thing they didn't replace is the soundboard. Not only does it help generate that distinctive tone, it's also been signed by more than a hundred friends and esteemed colleagues—everyone from Johnny Cash to Leon Russell, though Roger Miller signed the biggest, right on the front.

Willie isn't the only one counting on old Trigger continuing to remain in this mortal coil. Mickey Rafael, Willie's longtime harmonica player, put it like this: "We would just be replaced. But if Trigger goes, that's it. Game over."

Over the years, Willie repeatedly challenged traditional country fans with his unorthodox lifestyle choices, iconoclastic personality, and Trickster-like habit of choosing "different" material to interpret. What kind of cowboy has twin pigtails going halfway down his back? And sings jazz standards or duets with Bob Dylan? For all his voracious investigations of noncountry musical styles, Willie always made sure to toss out some red meat for the hard-core country fans. When he got together with Waylon Jennings in 1978 and sang "Mammas Don't Let Your Babies Grow Up to Be Cowboys," generations of women wanted to do just that. More conventional country songs like "On the Road Again," "Pancho and Lefty," "Last Thing I Needed First Thing This Morning," and "Me and Paul" complement the more untraditional elements in Nelson's oeuvre. Playing his own songs, reinterpreting classic covers, collaborating with jazz or rock musicians, Willie always brings his astonishing musicianship, and musicality, to the table.

The Trickster both creates order out of chaos and destroys the order that prevents the free expression of artistic and spiritual energies. Like the Trickster coyote of myth, Nelson wields his formidable powers to break the mold of country music strictures, allowing the music to reign supreme. Amusing, scandalizing, infuriating, fascinating—that's our Willie.

Willie is so popular in Germany that his fan site has a link for German readers. Coincidentally, in his youth, Nelson started out playing in German-American Texas polka groups.

NUGGET: Willie's home compound is called "Luck." You're either in Luck or out of Luck.

GREATEST HITS

Year	Song
1962	"Willingly"
1975	"Blue Eyes Crying in the Rain"
	"Last Thing I Needed First Thing This Morning"
1974	"Bloody Mary Morning"
1978	"Whiskey River"
	"Mamas Don't Let Your Babies Grow Up to Be Cowboys" (with Waylon Jennings)
1980	"On the Road Again"
1982	"Always on My Mind"
1984	"City of New Orleans"
1985	"Highwayman" (with Johnny Cash, Waylon Jennings, and Kris Kristofferson)
1989	"A Horse Called Music"
1993	"Maria (Shut Up and Kiss Me)"
1999	"Three Days"
2003	"Beer for My Horses" (with Toby Keith)

After a six-month tour of Europe in 2004, Willie joined up with Bob Dylan for a grueling month-long concert tour of 22 minor-league baseball stadiums.

Two Step

With his first charting single a duet (with then-wife Shirley Collie), maybe it's natural that Willie Nelson has shared so many microphones over the years. Willie has always shown a proclivity for choosing interesting collaborators—more than 80 by one count. His list of duet partners is encyclopedic: Ray Charles, Leon Russell, Webb Pierce, Roger Miller, Dolly Parton, Brenda Lee, Kris Kristofferson, David Allan Coe, Porter Wagoner, Norah Jones, Sheryl Crow, Neil Young, Ryan Adams, to name a few.

Nelson recorded and toured with several country "super groups," most notably the Highwaymen, originally a project with Waylon Jennings. The pair soon invited Kris Kristofferson and Johnny Cash to join them. They produced several hugely popular albums of songs espousing the mythos of the Western outlaw.

Nelson has used the duet form to get even further off the reservation than he could by himself. Though he did plenty of unsurprising duets of traditional songs, he also worked with artists far removed from the Grand Ole Opry. He teamed with rock sensation Sinéad O'Connor for "Don't Give Up," the Peter Gabriel song. And cowrote and sang "Heartland" with Bob Dylan. One of Willie's biggest hits was his duet with Latin heartthrob Julio Iglesias, "To All the Girls I've Loved Before."

Perhaps the oddest collaboration was Willie's work with noted jazz pianist Marian McPartland. In 2002, McPartland invited Willie to perform on her NPR radio show, *Piano Jazz*. Willie and jazz guitarist Jackie King joined McPartland for a few songs: "Crazy," "The Gypsy," and "Heart of a Clown." The two got along so famously that Willie invited McPartland to join him on stage at several subsequent shows.

ROY ORBISON

April 23, 1936–December 6, 1988

When Sam Phillips agreed to let young Roy Orbison audition for his Sun Records label, he liked the sound, but not the band's name. So Orbison and his pals traded in the Wink Westerners for The Teen Kings. They put out a couple records, but it was clear they weren't to be Kings after all. So Roy struck out on his own and had a hit with "Ooby Dooby" in 1956.

Orbison had ambitions beyond cute ditties, though. He hooked up with Joe Melson, a fellow Texan and songwriter. Together they forged a new sound previously unknown in country or rock and roll music. Roy used his powerful voice to tell dramatic stories, full of pathos and yearning. "Only the Lonely" quickly rose to almost the top of the charts. Country had seen balladeers feeling sorry for themselves before, but Roy's chilling voice set atop a deadpan arrangement gave the song an unprecedented power and gravitas.

Roy Orbison was serious about everything but most particularly music. That seriousness was evident and served to make Orbison's music stand out from the glitter and camp of what Nashville was offering those days. Roy's dramatic swoops from resonant lows to falsetto highs emphasized the power and range of his voice. After his first hit, Orbison and Melson achieved a string of successes. "Only the Lonely" was followed with other songs like "Running Scared," until Orbison hit it seriously big with "Oh, Pretty Woman" in 1964. Just mention the title and you can probably hear that eight-note intro in your head. Not merely Orbison's biggest hit, the song was able to knock those lovable mop heads from England out of the #1 spot.

Popular on both sides of the pond, Orbison toured in Great Britain with the Beatles in 1963, who acknowledged him as a big influence.

Despite the huge success of "Oh, Pretty Woman," tastes were changing and Roy had no further chart success until a revival of interest in his career in the '80s. Orbison's duet with Emmylou Harris, "That Lovin' You Feeling Again," drew attention back to the serious guy with the dark shades and killer falsetto. Movie soundtracks, star collaborations, and awards followed. Roy finished out his career as part of the Traveling Wilburys super group, living long enough to record one smash hit record with them.

GREATEST HITS

Year	Song
1956	"Ooby Dooby"
1960	"Only the Lonely"
1961	"Crying"
	"Running Scared"
1962	"Dream Baby"
1963	"In Dreams"
	"Blue Bayou"
1964	"Oh, Pretty Woman"
1980	"That Lovin' You Feeling Again" (with Emmylou Harris)
1988	"You Got It" (with the Traveling Wilburys)

NUGGET: Roy Orbison had vision problems, but he wasn't blind. The huge, dark, wraparound sunglasses became his trademark when he misplaced his regular spectacles before a show in 1963. When he got offstage that night the Beatles told him that he looked cool. That was it—it was dark mysterious shades from then on out.

Lefty Wilbury

During the last few years of his life, Roy Orbison was surprised to find himself in demand, appreciated, and with a huge hit-selling record. George Harrison, Jeff Lynne, and Roy got together at Bob Dylan's home recording studio one fine afternoon and got busy writing and recording. By the time they'd finished they had enough tracks for an album. They were still wondering whether to release a single when record executives heard the tapes and flipped. A single wouldn't be enough, and an entire album was released. The Wilburys were a true super group and each member was given his due. Roy "Lefty Wilbury" Orbison's voice sparkled. It would be the last time that voice was heard—Orbison died shortly after recording that first Wilburys album.

BUCK OWENS

AUGUST 12, 1929–MARCH 25, 2006

Four-year-old Alvin Edgar Owens Jr. marched into his family's farmhouse in Sherman, Texas, one autumn day and announced that if Buck was a good enough name for the mule, it was good enough for him. And so, Buck Owens was born. By the time he was 13, Buck had taught himself guitar and dropped out of school. Several short years later, he and his wife decided to settle in the little town of Bakersfield, California. There he played rough-and-ready honky-tonks that taught him how to handle a crowd in general. In particular, he began figuring out how to get his guitar to make a sound that could pierce the din of those noisy venues. The newly released Fender Telecaster proved perfect for the job. The penetrating sound reached every corner of the dingy dives where Buck Owens and his Buckaroos played.

"I am who I am, I am what I am, I do what I do and I ain't never gonna do it any different. I don't care who likes it and who don't."—Buck Owens

The tone and orchestration Buck developed in those rowdy joints became known as the Bakersfield Sound. It was a distinct contrast with the prevailing Nashville Sound of big strings and smooth vocals. Owens and musical partner Don Rich traded high-harmony vocals and guitar licks on their dueling Telecasters. Unlike most musicians of the era, Buck insisted on recording with his own band instead of session musicians. They took straightforward country arrangements, pushed the drums up in the mix, added a dash of rock and roll, several cups of heavy twangy guitar line, and created a heck of a cake.

Beginning with "Act Naturally" in 1963, Owens had a string of hit singles throughout the '60s. Buck took the lessons he'd learned about sound reinforcement at those Bakersfield dives and used them in recording his hits. Realizing that car radios were becoming a major source of music for listeners, he mixed his records using a set of tiny car speakers. This deemphasized the bass end of the spectrum and highlighted the upper registers, right where those dueling Telecasters of Owens and Rich lived. Their guitar licks seemed to leap right out of the speakers.

NUGGET: Buck Owens and the Buckaroos were the first country band to record outside the U.S. In 1967 they toured Japan and recorded several of the shows. *Made in Japan* was released the next year.

In 1969, Buck was tapped to co-host country's answer to *Laugh-In. Hee Haw* would go on to air for 17 years and make Buck Owens a household name. The show proved to be a double-edged sword though, with its cornpone burlesque of country tics. By the end of *Hee Haw*'s run, the incredible guitarist, singer, and bandleader had been subsumed by the image of the wisecracking picker who complemented Roy Clark's grinner.

Owens enjoyed a late-career comeback in 1988 when Dwight Yoakam teamed with him for a remake of "Streets of Bakersfield." He performed to the end. The night of his death he showed up at his Crystal Palace club to play a gig. After

A sharecropper's son, Buck figured he could make the same five dollars working in a honky-tonk, which he preferred, as he could for a day's work picking cotton.

IN 1951, BUCK REPLACED HIS GIBSON L-7 WITH A YEAR-OLD FENDER TELECASTER, WHICH HE PURCHASED FOR HALF A WEEK'S WAGES, THIRTY-FIVE DOLLARS.

Tele by the Tail

The Fender Telecaster is the coolest guitar ever made. Oh sure, people will talk it down, say it's not as versatile as a Stratocaster or as solid as a Les Paul. But just sit down and listen to Buck Owens and Don Rich playing those dueling Telecasters off each other like chicken and biscuits, and you'll see.

In 1950, Leo Fender designed and built a new guitar, the Broadcaster. The company was soon forced to change the name to Telecaster because of a trademark dispute, after manufacturing only about 30 guitars. But several hundred thousand guitars later, the Telecaster is going strong and has become a legend in its own right.

The Tele was designed with modern production techniques in mind. Traditional acoustic guitars required great skill and expertise to properly manufacture or repair. Fender's new guitar was made of discrete parts that could basically be bolted together. The solid piece of alder or ash that composed its body was easy to cut out and finish with basic woodworking tools. Teles could handle the rigors of touring and being beat up in honky-tonks. Light, tough, and with a pristine tone, Telecasters very quickly grew to be many musicians' essential and beloved tools.

Buck Owens and his musical partner, Don Rich, became identified with the Telecaster. Nonetheless, they're certainly not the only ones to become enamored of the Telecaster's unique sound and feel. Merle Haggard, Waylon Jennings, Dwight Yoakam, James Burton, and too many Nashville studio musicians to count swear by their Teles. Although legions of rock musicians have revered the Telecaster, no genre of musician has embraced it like country players. It doesn't have a huge range of sound like other, more modern guitars, but the tones it makes are unique, recognizable, and critical to the history of country music. Its bright, percussive tone is perfect for cutting through the noise of a rowdy bar or drowning out traffic when coming through the tinny speakers of a car radio.

GREATEST HITS

YEAR	SONG
1959	"Second Fiddle"
1960	"Above and Beyond"
1963	"Act Naturally"
	"Love Doesn't Live Here"
1964	"My Heart Skips a Beat"
1965	"Crying Time"
	"I've Got a Tiger by the Tail"
1966	"Think of Me"
1967	"Sam's Place"
1969	"Tall Dark Stranger"
1972	"Made in Japan"
1988	"Streets of Bakersfield" (with Dwight Yoakam)

eating his favorite chicken-fried steak, he told his band he was tired and would head home instead of playing that night. But on his way out the door he ran into some fans who'd driven all the way from Oregon to see him. He turned around, strapped on the Tele, and played the show. He could still pull out those killer licks, even at the end. Hours later, he died of a heart attack in his own bed.

NUGGET: Buck's band, the Buckaroos, was named by Merle Haggard, who played bass at the time.

BUCK AND THE BUCKAROOS' SOLD-OUT CARNEGIE HALL SHOW IN 1966 SHOWCASED COUNTRY'S MAINSTREAM APPEAL.

BRAD PAISLEY

October 28, 1972–

Not many people go to college to study to become country stars, but Brad Paisley did. In fact he had so much evident talent that ASCAP even awarded him a scholarship to attend Nashville's Belmont University. While there, he met his future producer and songwriting partner.

After graduation, Brad found work in Nashville writing songs and penned hits for several other artists. He put out his first album, *Who Needs Pictures*, and within a year had his own #1 hit, "He Didn't Have to Be." This tearjerker about a man remembering his own stepfather's love to the heart-tugging strains of steel guitar announced that old-time country was back.

Paisley continued what he'd started on his first record, literally, with *Part II*. The fiddle line that ends the last song on *Who Needs Pictures* actually begins *Part II*. The highlight of the album is the humorous "I'm Gonna Miss Her (The Fishing Song)." The video starred Paisley's then girlfriend, Kimberly Williams, as the aggrieved wife who forces her husband to choose between marriage and fishing. Careful what you threaten, ladies, because you might get the answer Brad gives as he bolts out the door heading toward the lake.

Given his first guitar at age 8, Paisley appeared at 12 on the local TV show *Jamboree USA*, for which he soon became a regular.

By his third album, *Mud on the Tires*, Paisley really began stretching his prodigious talents. After the goofy video and subject matter of "I'm Gonna Miss Her," he changed gears with a duet with Alison Krauss. "Whiskey Lullaby" told the tale of a dual suicide enabled by alcoholism. As if to prove his versatility, Paisley released "Alcohol" two years later with a totally different take on the same topic. *Time Well Wasted* served to illuminate yet another facet of this artist's ability. Paisley is clearly just getting started in what promises to be a long career. The country world is looking forward with great interest to see what this young legend will produce in the future.

NUGGET: Brad Paisley plays signature paisley (what else?) Crook Telecasters.

GREATEST HITS

Year	Song
1999	"He Didn't Have to Be"
2000	"We Danced"
2002	"I'm Gonna Miss Her (The Fishin' Song)"
2003	"Celebrity"
2004	"Little Moments"
	"Whiskey Lullaby" (with Alison Krauss)
2005	"Alcohol"
	"When I Get Where I'm Going" (with Dolly Parton)
	"She's Everything"
2007	"Ticks"

Groom of the Bride

Tons of guys watched the 1991 version of *Father of the Bride*. And every one of them had crushes on the incandescent bride, Kimberly Williams. But not every one of them is Brad Paisley. Through his agent, Brad arranged to meet a skeptical Kimberly in 2001. Paisley put on his best charm, and the two hit it off immediately. Williams was swept off her feet, and the couple were married in 2003. Kimberly stays busy with her acting and writing a marriage column for *Redbook* magazine. The couple has a son, William Huckleberry, born in 2007.

DOLLY PARTON

JANUARY 19, 1946–

THOUGH THEY WEREN'T A COUPLE IN REAL LIFE, PORTER WAGONER AND DOLLY PARTON MADE BEAUTIFUL MUSIC TOGETHER AS DUET PARTNERS.

If Dolly Parton were a food, she'd be old-fashioned cotton candy. All pink-and-white spun sugar on the outside, but with a strong inner core that's both firm and resilient. That core has supported the weight of troubles and poverty but has had the flexibility to bend when need be. Blond, buxom, beautiful, brainy, and one of the best singers and songwriters in any genre, period, Dolly Parton is truly country royalty. By most measures the most successful female country artist ever, Dolly sure didn't get where she is today by being a dumb blond. But it didn't hurt that she could play one on TV, and come out laughing.

Dolly was only 13 years old when she made her debut at the Grand Ole Opry. Her uncle, songwriter Bill Owens, gave her that old guitar when she was 7, and she began appearing on radio by age 10. It didn't seem as if she had a choice; music was about all her family had. One of 12 children raised in a one-room shack in Locust Ridge, Tennessee, Dolly has described her family as "dirt poor." Her grandpa, Reverend Jake Owens, was a fiddling preacher and songwriter (he penned the Kitty Wells hit "Singing His Praise"). So from the beginning, music and worship went together, as they often do in the Pentecostal faith. Dolly came along and added something extra.

NUGGET: Eighteen-year-old Dolly met her husband, contractor Carl Dean, at the Wishy-Washy Laundromat on her first day in Nashville. The couple is still married today.

"You'd be surprised how much it costs to look this cheap." —Dolly Parton

Dolly's teens were a shuffle of almost-contracts. After signing to Mercury Records at age 14, Dolly was dropped when her first single failed to chart. But her songwriting talents continued to blossom, and the day after she graduated from high school, she took off for Nashville. There she stayed with Owens, and the two hawked their songs while Dolly took to singing. She finally made the charts in 1967 with her tongue-in-cheek "Dumb Blonde."

Porter Wagoner got an earful—and then an eyeful of Dolly—and invited her onto his television show as a duet partner. The combination of the Nudie-bedecked Nashville-establishment Wagoner and the sweet young thing from the hills was showbiz magic. Their voices blended beautifully, and as duet partners, Parton and Wagoner enjoyed more than 20 Top-10 singles during the ensuing six years. But both artists champed at the bit somewhat; solo success for Dolly would be good for both partners, who held a joint stake in the kitty.

That success finally came in 1971 in the form of "Joshua, " Dolly's first #1 solo single. Next came the autobiographical "Coat of Many Colors," which combined nostalgia for momma, biblical references, and a true picture of Dolly's poverty-stricken childhood. You just had to love her, not because she was deliberately tugging at your heartstrings, but because of the pride and dignity in the lyrics: "Although we had no money, I was rich as I could be, in my coat of many colors that my momma sewed for me." America loves scrappiness, that key

DOLLY LEARNED THE BANJO SOON AFTER LEARNING THE GUITAR AT AGE 7.

Here she comes again. Five-foot-tall Dolly wore high heels and tall hair and quite a bit of Nashville flash to make up for her impoverished childhood as one of 12 siblings.

ingredient in rags-to-riches success; here was a full-blown rose that had sprung from the poorest of soil. Country music had a new sweetheart.

Dolly's next move was to cross over into the pop charts, which she did in 1974 with "Jolene." The song also made her an international star, charting in the Top 10 in the U.K. With its frank woman-to-woman plea, "Please don't take my man," the song has become a trademark. Dolly repeats her rival's name, the pitch rising into a heartrending, minor-key wail. The song's success was no doubt compounded by Dolly's burgeoning image; her hair was getting bigger and blonder, her dresses were getting tighter, and her ebullient nature was becoming impossible to contain. Besides, who would try to take Dolly's man? Only a fool, that's who. Even more to the point, what fool of a man would cheat on Dolly? Feminine sympathies are naturally with a woman wronged; when the woman looks like that, though, the men get on board mighty fast.

Dolly's runaway success of the late '70s and '80s was slightly hampered by a lawsuit with her former duet partner, Porter Wagoner, who was reaping financial rewards from her huge record sales. Finally breaking ties with Wagoner, Dolly soared to superstardom. Her acting debut in 1980's *9 to 5* with Lily Tomlin and Dolly's title song for the film earned her an Academy Award nomination for Best Original Song. More films followed, including *The Best Little Whorehouse in Texas* and *Steel Magnolias*. By the mid-'80s Dolly Parton was a household name; *Sesame Street* even introduced a well-endowed blonde Muppet named "Polly Darton."

As Dolly's fan base grew, her hard-core country audience grew a little skittish. Matters were helped by her collaborations with other great ladies of country—1987 saw the release of her first of two

GREATEST HITS

Year	Song
1967	"The Last Thing on My Mind" (with Porter Wagoner)
1970	"Mule Skinner Blues"
	"Joshua"
1971	"Coat of Many Colors"
1974	"Jolene"
	"I Will Always Love You"
	"Love Is Like a Butterfly"
1975	"The Bargain Store"
1977	"Here You Come Again"
1978	"Two Doors Down"
1980	"Starting Over Again"
1981	"9 to 5"
1983	"Islands in the Stream" (with Kenny Rogers)
1984	"Tennessee Homesick Blues"
1987	"To Know Him Is to Love Him" (with Emmylou Harris and Linda Ronstadt)
1989	"Why'd You Come in Here Lookin' Like That"
	"Yellow Roses"
2005	"When I Get Where I'm Going" (with Brad Paisley)

Hooray for Dollywood

Dollywood is a theme park complete with a steam railroad, blacksmith shop, saloon, and all the wild rides you'd want. In 1986, Dolly became a partner in the operation, which started as Rebel Railroad in 1961, lending it her name and imprimatur. It's only a small part of the business and philanthropic wing of Dolly's empire; the park brings jobs and tourism to the economically depressed Smoky Mountains region where she was born. Parton also spearheads a successful literacy program called Dolly Parton's Imagination Library, which started in her native Sevier County, Tennessee.

acclaimed albums with Emmylou Harris and Linda Ronstadt, *Trio*, followed by *Trio 2* in 1999. In between, she teamed up with Loretta Lynn and Tammy Wynette for *Honky Tonk Angels*. Dolly returned to her roots with several bluegrass albums during the late '90s, including *The Grass Is Blue*, *Little Sparrow*, and *Halos and Horns*.

NUGGET: Dolly the sheep, the first cloned mammal, was named after Dolly Parton. The cells used to clone the animal were taken from a mammary gland.

The new century has seen Dolly branch out with *Those Were the Days*, an album of duets with folk and country artists singing their hits of the '60s and '70s. And on a tribute album, *Just Because I'm a Woman*, female artists from Me'shell Ndegeocello to Sinéad O'Connor cover Dolly's songs. Perhaps the most unusual tribute comes from the White Stripes: "Jolene" has become keystone in the repertoire of the disaffected alt-rock duo. Dolly Parton remains the female country artist to have won the most honors and awards, and continues to reign supreme in the hearts of her many fans around the world.

Kenny Rogers and Dolly Parton's "Islands in the Stream" led to their 1994 collaboration *Once Upon a Christmas*.

NUGGET: When Elvis wanted to record Dolly's "I Will Always Love You," his manager, Colonel Tom Parker, told Dolly she'd have to sign over half the publishing rights to the song. Dolly wisely refused. The song later earned her $6 million just from Whitney Houston's recording alone.

Dolly Parton, a gifted and tough businesswoman, has retained the rights to more than 3,000 songs she's penned that have been performed by other artists.

Go Figure!

Dolly Parton without her famous hourglass figure just wouldn't be Dolly Parton. Even more, Dolly without a sense of humor about her own endowments just wouldn't be our Dolly. She's joked about her breast size, saying, "I wanted to be the first woman to burn her bra, but it would take the fire department four days to put it out." When she trimmed down in the '80s, Dolly frankly admitted to having surgery to bring her bust size back up to her standard proportions. When asked if her breasts were real, Dolly replied with characteristic humor, "Yep, they're mine. Bought and paid for."

WEBB PIERCE

AUGUST 8, 1921–FEBRUARY 24, 1991

Perhaps the most under-heralded country star of the '50s was Webb Pierce. He had more #1 hits than Hank Williams or Lefty Frizzell, but today he remains strangely unknown. Pierce found huge financial success during his lifetime but remained bitter about his lack of greater commercial success. A member of the Grand Ole Opry, he was asked to leave due to conflicts of interest with some of his business ventures. Later in his career he began to act out in more and more extravagant ways. Much as rock stars were beginning to aspire to hellish depths with their consumption of drugs and alcohol, Pierce threw ever-greater sums into esteem boosters disguised as publicity stunts. It started with the guitar-shaped pool, then the twin Pontiac convertibles lined with silver-dollar interiors, and finally Nudie suits of ever-increasing complexity and garishness. As audiences left for rock and roll's rowdier shores, Pierce turned up the volume on the things he'd always done.

When Webb Pierce was starting out in the '50s, cowboys were cowboys. More important, they weren't city slickers. So Webb sung songs like "Wondering" with his reedy tenor voice epitomizing the heartsick yearning of the cowpoke. Another hit, "Backstreet Affair," has the singer chafing against small-town morality. As the '50s wore on, Nashville reacted by producing the countrypolitan sounds of the big city. Pierce continued making his old-time honky-tonk records, as he always had.

His break with the Opry came back to haunt him later. Perhaps due in part to his reportedly abrasive personality, he was never honored with membership in the Country Music Hall of Fame during his lifetime. He was finally inducted into that organization 10 years after his death, on October 5, 2001.

Howdy, Trucker

In 1952, Webb Pierce was so impressed by fellow Louisiana Hayride sensation Red Sovine that he invited him to Nashville. While fronting Pierce's band, Sovine came to the attention of Decca executives and got himself signed. Throughout the late '50s and '60s Red had a number of hits, but his greatest legacy may be his songs about truckers.

"Phantom 309" tells the tale of a ghost driver that haunts the highway where he'd done his last heroic deed. Then, at the peak of the CB radio craze, Sovine hit big with "Teddy Bear." In a performance so over-the-top maudlin as to approach parody, Red nonetheless goes right ahead and provokes tears with his tale of truckers banding together to help make ends meet for a recently orphaned "little cripple boy" and his mother.

NUGGET: Webb Pierce's guitar-shaped swimming pool became such a tourist attraction that neighbor Ray Stevens had to sue to prevent hundreds of visitors a day ruining the peace of his neighborhood.

GREATEST HITS

Year	Song
1952	"Wondering"
	"That Heart Belongs to Me"
	"Back Street Affair"
1953	"There Stands the Glass"
1954	"Slowly"
	"More and More"
1955	"In the Jailhouse Now"
	"Love Love Love"
	"Why Baby Why"
1967	"Fool Fool Fool"
1982	"In the Jailhouse Now" (with Willie Nelson)

THOUGH WEBB PIERCE IS PRACTICALLY UNKNOWN TO THE GENERAL PUBLIC NOW, *EVERY* SINGLE HE PUT OUT FROM 1953 TO 1957 HIT THE COUNTRY TOP 10 LIST.

ELVIS PRESLEY

JANUARY 8, 1935–AUGUST 16, 1977

Ladies and Gentlemen: The King of Rock and Roll, Elvis Aaron Presley. But wait, this is a book on country legends. What kind of country legend was Elvis? Don't make the mistake of being distracted by the karate moves and rock and roll antics of the later years. Look deeper: down, down, through the leaves and branches, down by the roots, down in the muck. That's where Elvis' country heart lived. Beating with memories of mama Gladys, overnight gospel singing jags, the Grand Ole Opry on the radio, the old Negro men from across the tracks playing their cheap guitars. That heart thumped a country beat, don't you forget it.

From that hungry kid with the sultry eyes and loose hips to the bloated rhinestone-encrusted Vegas showman of his later years, Elvis always had a little country in him. His first recordings at Sun Studios were done for his mother, as a belated birthday gift.

WITH HIS CAPTIVATING VOICE AND HIS GOOD LOOKS, ELVIS WOULD GO ON TO STAR IN 33 HIT MOVIES AND HAVE MORE THAN A BILLION RECORDS SOLD.

Sun's owner Sam Phillips heard the recordings and thought perhaps Elvis might be the white man who sang like a black man he'd been looking for. "That's All Right Mama," recorded with guitarist Scottie Moore, bassist Bill Black, and drummer D. J. Fontana, was a hot-running freight train of a song. That and the back of the single, "Blue Moon of Kentucky," were like a shot of adrenaline to the arm of country music. Bill Monroe's old gem had never sounded so energetic and exciting.

In 1956, "Heartbreak Hotel" appeared and changed everything. It was Elvis' first monster hit, rising to #1 on just about every chart. Moore, Black, and Fontana didn't so much follow Elvis as drive him. That beat chugged along inexorably, like a long, slow train. And that train drove Elvis' career to terra incognita. He was clearly the King of Rock and Roll, yet he retained country elements his entire

GREATEST HITS

YEAR	SONG
1954	"That's All Right Mama"
1956	"Blue Moon of Kentucky"
	"Heartbreak Hotel"
	"Blue Suede Shoes"
	"Hound Dog"
	"Don't Be Cruel"
1957	"Mystery Train"
	"All Shook Up"
	"Jailhouse Rock"
	"Teddy Bear"
1958	"King Creole"
1960	"It's Now or Never"
	"Are You Lonesome Tonight?"
1961	"Can't Help Falling in Love"
1962	"Return to Sender"
1964	"Blue Christmas"
1969	"In the Ghetto"
	"Suspicious Minds"

NUGGET: Who among us hasn't shot the television with a high-powered handgun? Well, all right, none of us. But you know you wanted to. Ever pushing the envelope of id, Elvis reputedly filled a string of televisions with hot lead.

Elvis, with Scotty Moore on guitar and Bill Black on bass, first worked at Sam Philips' Sun Studios to produce early hits "Blue Moon of Kentucky" and "Good Rockin' Tonight."

career. From earlier works like "Hound Dog" and "Mystery Train," to later hits like "Kentucky Rain" and "In the Ghetto," Elvis retained country verbal motifs and musical styles while defining a new era—the era of rock and roll. And while he honored and cherished country themes, he was simultaneously authoring country music's replacement in the common culture. For he did have a country heart, and no matter what pop culture antics Elvis got up to before his death, that country heart was fundamental to his success.

"I can guarantee you one thing—we will never again agree on anything as we agreed on Elvis."—Lester Bangs

Testify

Though Elvis achieved renown far and wide for his less savory proclivities, many people forget that he always had an affection for gospel music. Even while helping forge rock and roll amalgam from the ore of country and rockabilly with his Sun recordings, Elvis sang and recorded scores of gospel numbers. He sang all the classics like "Peace in the Valley," "Joshua Fit the Battle," and "Amazing Grace." This mama's boy never forgot his religious roots. And, in fact, a good part of his singing style can be traced both to childhood Sundays in church and the all-night gospel sing-alongs young Elvis attended with his mother.

One has to wonder if the wild African-American influences Elvis adopted came to him via the black gospel tradition of Southern churches. That storied night of December 4, 1956, the "Million Dollar Quartet" of Johnny Cash, Carl Perkins, Jerry Lee Lewis, and Elvis got together to jam. Many later considered that to be the moment rock and roll was born. It was no accident the quartet sang gospel songs that night. Oh, they sang "Blueberry Hill" and whatever pop stuff they could come up with, too. But they rocked those gospel numbers the hardest.

The Jordanaires

The Jordanaires were best known to the public as "Elvis' backup singers." But generations of country fans recognized those smooth harmonies. The Jordanaires had appeared behind such great country voices as Patsy Cline, Eddy Arnold, Merle Haggard, Willie Nelson, Jim Reeves, and George Jones. Quite a trick they pulled off, being famous enough to have a name, yet singing well enough that some of the greatest voices in country music wanted them on their team—unique in country music, in fact. No other act was a backing group yet could (and did) tour and record by themselves. But no other act managed to pull together that trademark rich vocal style. It is estimated that the Jordanaires recorded with 2,500 different artists and have appeared on more Top 10 records than any group in history.

Elvis Presley was a cocky unknown when he first approached the Jordanaires in 1955. They had just gotten offstage backing Eddy Arnold, a superstar at the time. And here was this kid, who didn't even have a record deal, asking them to back him up. Well, a year later Elvis not only had that record deal, he had the clout to break with tradition and give the Jordanaires credit on his album. They went on to sing backup on some of the biggest records of all time, songs like "Don't Be Cruel," and "Jailhouse Rock."

The Jordanaires first recorded with Elvis in 1956. The group performed with him over a 14-year period onstage, in the recording studio, and in 28 movies.

RAY PRICE

January 12, 1926–

Declared an outstanding Texan by governor's decree on his 80th birthday, Ray Price still tours to sellout crowds, performing more than 100 concerts a year.

GREATEST HITS	
Year	Song
1951	"If You're Ever Lonely Darling"
1952	"Talk to Your Heart"
1954	"Release Me"
1958	"City Lights"
1959	"Same Old Me"
	"Heartaches by the Number"
1967	"Danny Boy"
1970	"For the Good Times"
1972	"I Won't Mention It Again"
1973	"She's Got to Be a Saint"

Creating a string of hit singles might be enough for some folks. Mentoring musicians such as Willie Nelson, Johnny Paycheck, and Roger Miller might be seen as quite an accomplishment, too. But if you're Ray Price, you go one better: You invent a beat that comes to define honky-tonk—and still does, more than half a century later.

The "Ray Price Shuffle Beat" can first be heard on "Crazy Arms," released in 1956. This "one two three four" rhythm with just a little bit of swing to it became a classic, heard on scores of honky-tonk records since. Ray himself put his trademark beat to good use on hits such as "City Lights," "Same Old Me," and "Heartaches by the Number." The latter in particular is the perfect honky-tonk song, the absolute pinnacle of the genre. A hot fiddle opens, followed by that trademark shuffle. "Troubles by the score . . ." takes care of the requirement for heartbreak. Right in the middle of the song it all stops, restarted by a steel guitar breakaway that devolves into a duel with the fiddle. All the while that shuffle beat forces listeners to move their feet. Pure honky-tonk persuasion.

Later in the '60s Price began pushing the envelope of the country genre. Just a hint of the Ray Price Shuffle Beat appears in some of his later crossover hits, but just barely. "For the Good Times" bears the slightest clip-clop of Ray's signature beat, but it's buried in the mix behind sounds much more at home in a stylish lounge than a honky-tonk. When country artists cross over into the pop market, they generally hope to broaden their audience, but sometimes their country fans feel left behind. Ray Price was one of the first artists to suffer this fate. The greater his success with pop songs, the less favor he found with country audiences.

Tuxedo Junction

With a middle name like Noble, you'd expect Ray Price to have a certain gravitas. What you might not expect is seeing a certified country star in a tuxedo. Ray wore his share of rhinestone-bespeckled suits, but from the late '60s onward, Price gravitated toward city-slicker togs more suited to James Bond than the Opry. Price began this sartorial statement during the early '60s, to match up with his pop chart success. By 1967, Price had a monster crossover hit with "Danny Boy." This lushly orchestrated number was so sophisticated that only a tux would do.

NUGGET: Early in his career, Ray Price was dubbed the Cherokee Cowboy, although he was neither Cherokee nor a cowboy.

CHARLEY PRIDE

March 18, 1938–

Strumming his cheap guitar on the back of the bus on those endless runs between games, baseball player Charley Pride realized that he probably wasn't going to make the big leagues. So he strummed a little harder and decided to make a go of a music career. Two guys named Red—Foley and Sovine, that is—heard his songs and persuaded him to hang up his cleats and head to Nashville. A short time later, Chet Atkins heard Pride's demo tape and signed him on the spot.

Charley started slow with his first few singles, but the third, "Just Between You and Me," was a huge seller. By this time many fans had bought his album and figured out he was black. A black guy, playing country! It shouldn't have been quite such a surprise, though; much of country music has its roots in the blues, and the banjo was modeled on instruments brought to the New World from Africa. Oh, and the steel guitar? The first recordings were by black musician Blind Lemon Jefferson.

Exception Proves the Rule

Early in his career, Charley Pride took the stage to wild cheers. But the cheers slowly faded as the audience, who'd only heard him on the radio, realized that he was black. When he played the Grand Ole Opry in 1967, Pride was the first black performer since Deford Bailey, 42 years prior. It's not surprising that Charley Pride became the first black country star; his rise to stardom, in the late '60s and '70s, was a time when racial barriers were falling. What is surprising is that there was no rush of talented African Americans ready to follow Pride through the door he cracked open with such difficulty. Charley Pride showed that there could be such a thing as a black country superstar. Forty years later, there still hasn't been another—Cowboy Troy, with his "Hick-Hop" style of country rap, is a notable exception. Whether this tells of Pride's greatness or country music's smallness is hard to say.

"I couldn't remain a faceless voice forever. Most of Nashville realized I was black and word was getting out to the rest of the country as well."—Charley Pride

NUGGET: Charley Pride was not just a pretty face. He shrewdly invested in many businesses over the years, including the Charley Pride Theater, various radio stations, and the First Texas Bank.

GREATEST HITS

Year	Song
1966	"Snakes Crawl at Night"
1967	"Just Between You and Me"
1969	"I'm So Afraid of Losing You Again"
1970	"Is Anybody Goin' to San Antone"
1971	"I'd Rather Love You"
	"Kiss an Angel Good Morning"
1972	"It's Gonna Take a Little Bit Longer"
1973	"Amazing Love"
1975	"Then Who Am I?"
1976	"My Eyes Can Only See as Far as You"
1977	"More to Me"
1981	"Mountain of Love"

Pride's "Kiss An Angel Good Morning" featured a country beat, with steel guitar fills. Nashville-style backup vocals and Pride's smooth baritone gave it a modern feel; in fact, the song was a huge crossover hit in the country and pop markets. Pride made those catchy arrangements—the play between country touches and city-slick productions that became his trademark. Recording with Chet Atkins at RCA, Pride became an exemplar of the Nashville Sound, racking up thirty-six #1 singles over 20 years.

From sharecropper's kid to country-music star, Charley Pride is ranked second in sales for RCA (after Elvis), with more than 70 million albums.

JOHN PRINE

OCTOBER 10, 1946–

Underestimate the class clown at your peril. Sitting in the back of the class, wryly sharpening his verbal barbs, he might be the only one with the courage to speak the truth and the perspicacity to recognize it. John Prine is the clown prince of country music.

Although he is often unknown to those outside the business, Prine's influence is nonetheless huge. Prine never got much popular acclaim as a performer; his voice was called gravelly and worse. But his songs are perfect little gems, encapsulating the whole of human experience with an absolute minimum of words. "There's a hole in Daddy's arm, where all the money goes . . ." is enough to instantly transport the listener to the world of damaged 'Nam vet Sam Stone and give chills doing it. Though he never had a hit of his own, many other musicians covered his songs, notably Bonnie Raitt, who had a huge smash crossover hit with "Angel from Montgomery." Prine was working as a mailman in 1970, gigging at night in Chicago, when he ran into Kris Kristofferson. No slouch as a songwriter himself, Kristofferson would be the first in a long line of songwriters who would appreciate the genius of John Prine. Kris helped Prine get a record deal, and in 1971 John Prine appeared. Every song on the album was a sharply observed snapshot of the underbelly of American life. Prine's characters were vivid and memorable, at once familiar and new. They were by and large losers, flotsam tossed aside by the rising tide, yet in Prine's hands they were treated with respect, even love.

AFTER HE WAS DROPPED BY ASYLUM, PRINE FORMED HIS OWN LABEL, OH BOY RECORDS, WHICH PRODUCED HIS MOST COMMERCIALLY SUCCESSFUL AND CRITICALLY ACCLAIMED ALBUMS.

Prine continues writing songs and releasing albums, trading some of his bitter earlier emotions for lighthearted wordplay. "It's a Big Old Goofy World," "Dear Abby," "Speed of the Sound of Loneliness," and "Some Humans Ain't Human" all share Prine's proclivity for illuminating the big picture with sharply rendered, often humorous details.

"If you're looking at the big picture, you've got to get a really small frame sometimes."—John Prine

GREATEST HITS

YEAR	SONG
1971	"Illegal Smile"
	"Sam Stone"
	"Hello in There"
	"Angel from Montgomery"
1973	"Dear Abby"
	"Christmas in Prison"
1975	"Come Back to Us, Barbara Lewis"
1978	"Sabu Visits the Twin Cities Alone"
1990	"It's a Big Old Goofy World"
1991	"The Missing Years"
1999	"When Two Worlds Collide" (with Tricia Yearwood)
	"(We're Not) The Jet Set" (with Iris Dement)
	"We Must Have Been Out of Our Minds" (with Melba Montgomery)
2005	"Crazy as a Loon"

Johnny's Girls

Though known primarily as a songwriter, in 1999 Prine released *In Spite of Ourselves*, almost entirely composed of classic country covers, in duet with various female greats. Patty Loveless, Iris Dement, Emmylou Harris, Melba Montgomery, and others joined with John in reviving forgotten country chestnuts. The album features everything from Merle Haggard's "(We're Not) The Jet Set" sung with Iris Dement to Charley Pride's heartbreaking "I Know One," delivered with the proper angst in duet with Emmylou Harris. Just about every tragic couple in country is represented, along with their respective ways of building, or more often mourning, a marriage.

RASCAL FLATTS

2000–

THE MEMBERS OF RASCAL FLATTS (FROM LEFT: GARY LEVOX, JOE DON ROONEY, AND JAY DEMARCUS) CITE POP, R&B, BLUEGRASS, COUNTRY, AND GOSPEL AS INFLUENCES.

It had to happen—country music needed a boy band of its own, and Rascal Flatts burst forth to fill the void. With their blend of country, pop, and R&B sensibilities, these three guys—Jay DeMarcus, Gary LeVox, and Joe Don Rooney—are delivering a new kind of country music to a young, image-conscious audience. They're kinda cute. They dress hip. They hire progressive, arty videographers. But the truth is that they can really play and can sing some tight harmonies. So, boy band, or this generation's Alabama? You decide.

"When you come see us live, you see we're anything but a boy band."—Jay DeMarcus

Rascal Flatts came together in Nashville, but two of the three are from Columbus, Ohio. Bass player and pianist Jay DeMarcus made the trek to Music City first and then convinced his second cousin, singer Gary LeVox, to join. DeMarcus found work playing in Chely Wright's band, where he met Oklahoma boy Joe Don Rooney. Meanwhile, the cousins were playing regular gigs at the Nashville club Printer's Alley. One night their guitar player had to bow out, and Rooney came around to fill his spot. The three clicked, and Rascal Flatts was born. The name was suggested by a piano player friend of Joe Don's but was rejected by the others at first, who feared "Little Rascals" references to Alfalfa and Buckwheat. But they couldn't fight the pull of the cool, odd image that "Rascal Flatts" conjures up. As their record sales attest, the name worked.

NUGGET: Breaking news! Guys dig hot chicks! Joe Don Rooney is married to Playmate of the Year Tiffany Fallon, and Jay DeMarcus took Allison Alderson, former Miss Tennessee, as his bride.

Moonie Rooney

A little controversy never hurt any entertainer's career, as long as it's the right kind of controversy. The Dixie Chicks nearly went under from their antiwar message that some took to be unpatriotic. But the Rascal Flatts controversy was the regular old risqué kind. On the video for their song "I Melt," the camera catches a glimpse of band member Joe Don Rooney's bare backside during a love scene with model Christina Auria (Don is the blond one and the only one who was single at the time). Some viewers objected, and CMT pulled the video until the Rascals could offer up a clean-cut version of the video, which they obligingly did.

The trio has won a number of high honors in its short career, including four CMAs for Vocal Group of the Year. Rascal Flatts has achieved much crossover success with their appealing, catchy singles; "Bless the Broken Road" held on to the #1 spot for five weeks and won a Grammy for the songwriters. Thank God they're country boys!

GREATEST HITS

Year	Song
2000	"Prayin' for Daylight"
2001	"I'm Movin' On"
2002	"These Days"
2003	"Love You Out Loud"
	"I Melt"
2004	"Mayberry"
	"Bless the Broken Road"
	"Skin (Sarabeth)"
2005	"Fast Cars and Freedom"
2006	"What Hurts the Most"
	"Me and My Gang"
	"Life Is a Highway"
	"My Wish"
2007	"Stand"

JIM REEVES

August 20, 1923–July 31, 1964

To someone accustomed to belting out a tune that could be heard above the din of the honky-tonk, it was natural to just yell one's heart out. Jim Reeves made a couple of records that way and released them to an indifferent public. It wasn't until Reeves hooked up with legendary producer Chet Atkins at RCA records that he realized that he didn't have to play to the cheap seats when in a modern recording studio. That big microphone would grab every sound made within an inch of it. The merest whisper could be captured, and the finest nuances recorded. And if you caressed that microphone, almost kissed it—well, that intimacy came right through the speakers. When Bing Crosby or Dean Martin did it, they called it crooning. When Gentleman Jim Reeves did it, they called it history.

Croon River

Working with Chet Atkins and other producers at RCA records, Jim Reeves became one of the prime exemplars of the Nashville Sound. He certainly had the pipes, but the way he used them, and the way they were recorded, made all the difference. Literally something as small as the distance from the singer's lips to the microphone could make the difference between smooth and harsh. And the Nashville Sound was all about smooth. Smooth vocals, smooth strings, and insouciant piano brought a suavity and worldliness that was in direct conflict with traditional country sounds. Gentleman Jim Reeves was one of the first to doff the cowboy duds for a modern suit and tie. Reeves had a string of #1 hits until his untimely death at the height of his popularity.

"If I, a lowly singer, dry one tear, or soothe one humble human heart in pain, then my homely verse to God is dear, and not one stanza has been sung in vain." —Jim Reeves' epitaph

NUGGET: The same flight instructor had trained both Reeves and the pilot of Patsy Cline's ill-fated last flight.

"Four Walls," released in 1957, was Reeves' first big country hit. But it did something unusual for a country song: It appealed to pop audiences, too. Reeves' first hit was also his first big crossover. Producers at RCA had cooked up that production, later known as the Nashville Sound, specifically to broaden the appeal of country music. And boy did they, ever. Reeves went on to a succession of hits, in both the country and pop markets.

That velvety baritone and debonair style charmed listeners the world over. But in 1964, at the height of his popularity, Gentleman Jim was killed when the small plane he was piloting crashed. His records continued to sell big, both in the United States and abroad.

GREATEST HITS

Year	Song
1957	"Four Walls"
1958	"Anna Marie"
	"Home"
1959	"Billy Bayou"
1960	"He'll Have to Go"
1962	"Adios Amigo"
	"I'm Gonna Change Everything"
1963	"Is This Me?"
1964	"I Guess I'm Crazy"
	"Welcome to My World"
1965	"This Is It"
1966	"Blue Side of Lonesome"
	"Distant Drums"
	"I Won't Come in While He's There"

Before making it in the music business, Reeves played with the St. Louis Cardinals for three years, until an ankle injury curtailed his baseball career.

CHARLIE RICH

DECEMBER 14, 1942–JULY 25, 1995

RICH GOT HIS NICKNAME SILVER FOX IN 1971, WHEN A WOMAN IN ALASKA CALLED HIM THAT ONE NIGHT IN A BAR. IT WOULD BECOME THE NAME OF HIS 1974 ALBUM.

GREATEST HITS	
YEAR	SONG
1960	"Lonely Weekends"
1965	"Big Boss Man"
1972	"I Take It on Home"
1973	"Behind Closed Doors"
	"The Most Beautiful Girl in the World"
1974	"There Won't Be Anymore"
	"She Called Me Baby"
	"A Very Special Love Song"
	"I Don't See Me in Your Eyes Anymore"
1976	"Since I Fell for You"
1977	"Rollin' with the Flow"
1979	"Spanish Eyes"

In country music it's quite possible to be too cool for the room. People like their music the way they like it, and they don't take kindly to folks messing around too much. Just new enough is generally the way Nashville prefers things. Charlie Rich was always a critical darling, but he had trouble reaching commercial heights as dizzying as his reviews. He melded elements of jazz, rhythm and blues, and rockabilly into his country. But his audience just didn't seem to want to follow him there.

"At first I didn't dig country."—Charlie Rich

In 1973, Rich released the album *Behind Closed Doors*. The title song was a country smash, but an even bigger crossover hit. That Nashville Sound sure did appeal to pop audiences. Rich's mellow voice brought a worldliness to country; he sounded as if he were standing there at the bar, gesturing you in and offering a drink. At the end of "Behind Closed Doors" he sings, "She makes me glad that I'm a man." Shocking sentiments for a country song.

One Drink, and then Another

Like many entertainers, Charlie Rich had some problems with alcohol. Unfortunately for his career, he displayed many of those problems publicly. Most notoriously, when presenting at the 1975 Country Music Awards, a visibly intoxicated Rich lit the envelope containing John Denver's name afire. The audience, chock-full of musicians and industry suits, was scandalized. Indeed, it would be years before Rich would have another country hit.

Rich's songs all seemed to involve love gone bad. When he played a character, it was the saddest guy in the world. True to his name, Charlie's rich baritone somehow made listeners empathize and identify with, rather than pity, the protagonist. "The Most Beautiful Girl in the World," the second single off that amazing album, established him as a star. Right from that first "Hey," he had us. That one syllable embodied the vocal mastery that Charlie brought to the table. In Rich's songs, everybody has either courted, divorced, or been the most beautiful girl in the world. Whether we lost the girl or not, we were there with him as his voice caught. Hey, was that a tear I heard?

Rich had a string of hits through the mid '70s, but by the advent of the '80s, frustrated with his lack of additional success, he retired. He put out a final album in 1992, and true to form, it was applauded by critics but largely ignored by audiences.

LEANN RIMES

AUGUST 28, 1982–

Already an old hand at performing, LeAnn Rimes had been playing in talent shows for seven years when she hit the country music scene like a bomb in 1996 with "Blue." The song had been written for Patsy Cline, and it showed. That throaty alto voice with the knowing slide off the note into blues territory was like nothing anybody had heard in years. But this voice was coming out of a kid, all of 13 years old!

No flash in the pan, Rimes followed that first single with "One Way Ticket," a perky little number that raced right to the top of the country charts. Then a year later, in 1997 LeAnn released *You Light Up My Life: Inspirational Songs*. The album contained the hit "How Do I Live," which went on to be the best-selling country single to date. LeAnn had proven she was more than just a kid with a few good songs in her—she was a star.

"I needed to become something besides the star everybody had built me up to be."—LeAnn Rimes

GREATEST HITS	
YEAR	SONG
1996	"Blue"
	"One Way Ticket"
1997	"How Do I Live"
	"You Light Up My Life"
1998	"Looking Through Your Eyes"
1999	"Written in the Stars" (with Elton John)
2000	"Can't Fight the Moonlight"
2002	"Life Goes On"
2004	"Rockin' Around the Christmas Tree"
2005	"Nothin' 'bout Love Makes Sense"
2006	"Something's Gotta Give"

LEANN'S SECOND ALBUM, *YOU LIGHT UP MY LIFE: INSPIRATIONAL SONGS*, HIT SIMULTANEOUSLY AS #1 ON THE COUNTRY, POP, AND CONTEMPORARY CHRISTIAN CHARTS FOR ITS 1997 RELEASE.

NUGGET: In 2005 LeAnn was chosen to sing the song "Remember When" in celebration of Disneyland's 50th anniversary.

As is the case with many child stars, Rimes felt hemmed in by her squeaky-clean status. Twenty-year-old LeAnn appeared in the video to "Life Goes On" in 2002 wearing the skimpiest of shifts. Shot in New Orleans in a dreamy, rock-influenced style, the steamy imagery raised temperatures throughout the country. Though neither the critics nor fans seemed to appreciate seeing their little girl "all growed up," the videos and pictures had served their purpose. LeAnn returned to critics' and fans' favor with the more traditionally country-sounding *This Woman* in 2005.

Catfight

Country Music Awards 2006. Cameras are on all the nominees. Carrie Underwood's name is announced as winner, and Faith Hill freaks out. She honestly looks completely shocked, and not just a little miffed. Well, no big deal—we've all made faux pas like that; Hill was just unlucky enough to get hers caught on camera. Right?

Wrong. Fans freaked out, calling Hill ungrateful and a sore loser. The newly popular Internet contributed to the imbroglio; the video of the event itself remained online to be endlessly savored or pouted over, depending on one's affiliation. Then LeAnn got involved, posting on her own Web site that she was on Faith's side, and that Carrie Underwood was being uppity for such a young star (an interesting position to take for someone who had swept the awards shows at the tender young age of 15). Then LeAnn took it all back, Faith apologized and praised Carrie Underwood to the stars, and finally Carrie said it was all just a big misunderstanding. Ladies, please!

TEX RITTER

JANUARY 12, 1905–JANUARY 2, 1974

One of the great singing cowboys, Tex Ritter had sharpened his spurs playing Western types on stage and radio. He sang a recurring role in the first New York radio Western, *The Lone Star Rangers,* and starred in the predecessor to *Oklahoma!* on Broadway. So it was natural for him to take his deadpan baritone to Hollywood. He found success starring as a singing cowboy in B-grade Westerns, and he made some 40 of them during the late '30s and early '40s. On his horse, White Flash, he would invariably ride to the rescue and vanquish the bad guys, generally singing a song or two along the way.

"I grew up skinny and creepy, and I made friends by doing Tex Ritter imitations."—Patti Smith

TEX, BORN WOODWORD MAURICE RITTER, HELPED TO CREATE THE COUNTRY MUSIC ASSOCIATION, OF WHICH HE WAS PRESIDENT FROM 1964 TO 1965.

Tex achieved even greater success as a recording artist. In 1942 he became the first artist signed by the then newborn Capitol Records. His first release, "Jingle, Jangle, Jingle," went on to not only be a huge seller but also become a country classic. His cowboy persona worked even better on record than film, and Tex began a long run of chart-topping hits.

Tex developed another innovation during this period: the country record album. Songs from the *Western Screen* contained just what it said, tunes previously heard only in movies. Country songs had heretofore been released as just that, single songs, until this innovation. Tex saw the advantages of the long-playing format and began creating albums that contained thematically related songs. Cowboy songs, hymns, patriotic songs, all were grist for the album mill.

NUGGET: To this day, Tex Ritter is the voice of "Big Al," the fattest bear in Walt Disney World's Country Bear Jamboree attraction. "Big Al" sings "Blood on the Saddle" to the general merriment and mocking of the other ursine animatronic creatures.

Tex Ritter was always a supporter of country music's establishment as a legimate musical genre. He helped found the Country Music Association in 1958, was inducted into the Country Music Hall of Fame in 1964, and was made a lifetime member of the Grand Ole Opry in 1965.

NUGGET: Tex Ritter's son John grew up to be an actor and enjoyed a long and successful career until his sudden death in 2003.

Oscar!

Tex Ritter was the nexus for a number of firsts that star-studded night in 1953, for that was the night of the first television broadcast of the Academy Awards. Tex was all over the production. First, he had sung the theme for the Grace Kelly and Gary Cooper film classic, *High Noon*. And not just the theme: Tex's tune had been used throughout the movie, in a narrative role.

Then, Tex was invited to sing the song on stage that night, alongside all the movie stars and in front of a first-time national audience. Capping off the evening, the song won the Oscar for Best Song in a Film. Not a bad night for a kid from Beaumont, Texas.

GREATEST HITS

YEAR	SONG
1933	"Goodbye Old Paint"
1943	"Jingle, Jangle, Jingle"
1944	"Jealous Heart"
1945	"Boll Weevil"
1946	"You Two-Timed Me One Time Too Often"
	"You Are My Sunshine"
1948	"Rye Whisky"
1950	"Daddy's Last Letter"
1952	"High Noon (Do Not Forsake Me, Oh My Darlin')"
1955	"Remember the Alamo"
1961	"(I Dreamed of a) Hillbilly Heaven"

MARTY ROBBINS

September 26, 1925–December 8, 1982

He didn't start out to be the gunfighter ballad singer. No, Marty Robbins started out playing more traditional country on programs like the Grand Ole Opry. He even had a number of hit singles in the early '50s. But Marty was always looking around for something new to try. "White Sport Coat" was kind of a teen pop number. Then, in 1959 Marty released *Gunfighter Ballads and Trail Songs*. This album contained both "El Paso" and "Big Iron." They widely surpassed all of his previous successes: "El Paso" was a #1 hit on both pop and country charts. Robbins would mine the lode of the heroic and tragic lone gunfighter for the next 20 years.

NUGGET: In 1959, Robbins won the first country Grammy ever awarded, for "El Paso."

A brilliant and unconventional spirit, Robbins was involved in numerous creative and business ventures. He recorded and released albums of rockabilly and traditional Hawaiian music, started a booking and talent agency, and released the first country record to feature a fuzz-toned guitar effect (which came from a "broken" studio amplifier). He even starred in films, notably *Ballad of a Gunfighter*, which was based on his album of the same name.

GREATEST HITS	
YEAR	SONG
1953	"I'll Go on Alone"
1956	"Knee Deep in the Blues"
1957	"White Sport Coat"
1959	"El Paso"
1960	"Big Iron"
1962	"Devil Woman"
1965	"Ribbon of Darkness"
1968	"I Walk Alone"
1970	"My Woman, My Woman, My Wife"
1976	"El Paso City"

Vroom

All the great country legends have been top race-car drivers as well. Yeah, right! Marty Robbins alone bore that distinction. He would regularly compete in NASCAR races at the Nashville Fairground, and then race across town to be on stage at the Grand Ole Opry for Saturday night's live radio show.

Though he had a killer instinct, he was a gentleman competitor. In 1972, Robbins was driving his Dodge Charger in the Winston 500 race at Talladega Raceway. He couldn't believe how fast he was going and was clocked at 188 miles per hour, much faster than his usual pace. After the race- he immediately asked race officials to check his carburetor. It was indeed found to be illegal, and he was disqualified, forfeiting the purse he'd won. "It was worth it," he later said. "In fact, I'd have paid that much money for a picture of those boys' faces when I passed them."

"I'm in this business because I despise honest labor."—Marty Robbins

In 1970 Robbins had another enormous hit, with the plaintive "My Woman, My Woman, My Wife." What could have been a completely over-the-top exercise in kitsch was sung so convincingly that both pop and country audiences responded, and the song was a smash. They say to write what you know, and Marty did so: He and his wife, Marizona, were happily married for 38 years, until his death in 1982.

Martin David Robertson first used the stage name Jack Robinson to hide his performing from his disapproving mother; he later settled on Marty Robbins.

JIMMIE RODGERS

SEPTEMBER 8, 1897–MAY 26, 1933

AN AUTOGRAPHED PICTURE OF THE SINGING BRAKEMAN; IN HIS SIX YEARS OF FAME, BETWEEN TOURING AND PERFORMING ON THE RADIO, RODGERS RECORDED 127 SONGS.

What a difference a day makes. The day was August 4, 1927, and the difference was country music. That's the day that Jimmie Rodgers, "the father of country music," wandered into a warehouse in Bristol, Tennessee. The Victor Talking Machine Company had set up some contraption there to record local musicians. A field recording, they called it. One of those musicians was Jimmie Rodgers. The Carter Family happened to be there, too. Ralph Peer was the man in charge, and the recordings he made that day came to be known as "the Bristol sessions," considered the birth date of country music. Jimmie Rodgers may have left Bristol $100 richer, but the world was left richer still—with "treasures untold," to paraphrase one of Rodgers' early songs. American music would never be the same now that country was born.

There was music before Jimmie Rodgers, sure—some that we'd even today call country. But Jimmie did for country music what bluesman Robert Johnson did for early rock and roll: He took all those threads of American roots music—folk, hillbilly, gospel, work chants, string bands, jazz, and especially blues—and wove them seamlessly together into a new idiom. When listeners heard Rodgers' plaintive voice, singing their own troubles, they immediately recognized this music as their own.

Rodgers' childhood reads like the stuff of legend. Born in Meridian, Mississippi, he was left motherless at a young age and was sent to live with an aunt. He was a restless boy, and when sent back to his father at age 11, he began to drift to the seamy side, frequenting pool halls and dives. He ran away at age 13 to join a traveling medicine show. Finally his father, a railroad foreman, caught up with him and put him to work on the rails. Rodgers worked a variety of jobs on the railroad and traveled around the South. Along the way he picked up musical influences, from the chants of work crews to the African-American blues.

But Rodgers had been bitten by the music and performing bug and couldn't shake it off. In 1927, he traveled to Asheville, North Carolina, where he made his radio debut. Later that year he hooked

NUGGET: For 1930's "Blue Yodel # 9," Rodgers called on his friend Louis Armstrong to back him on trumpet. Satchmo's wife, Lillian, sat in on piano.

up with the string band the Tenneva Ramblers, and with them he traveled to Bristol. On the eve of the famous recording session, an argument over who would get top billing led to a breakup of that alliance. Rodgers decided to record solo, backed only by his guitar. Those recordings had enough

I Hear the Train A' Comin'

Country music has more trains than the Southern Pacific. Three words help to explain the phenomenon: rhythm, romance, and work. First there's that *chukka-chuk* train rhythm, heard in everyone's songs from DeFord Bailey to Johnny Cash. Then there's the romance of riding the rails—hopping on board that freight like a hobo drifter, sleeping in a boxcar, and tumbling off in some dusty whistle stop. And finally there's work—the railroads employed millions throughout the first half of the 20th century. For Jimmie Rodgers, it was personal. Son of a railman and a railroad worker himself, the Singing Brakeman had the locomotive in his soul.

GREATEST HITS	
YEAR	**SONG**
1927	"The Soldier's Sweetheart"
	"Sleep Baby, Sleep"
	"Blue Yodel (T for Texas)"
1928	"Waiting for a Train"
	"Brakeman's Blues"
	"In the Jailhouse Now"
	"My Old Pal"
	"My Carolina Sunshine Girl"
1929	"Frankie and Johnny"
	"Train Whistle Blues"
1930	"Pistol Packin' Papa"
	"Blue Yodel #8 (Mule Skinner Blues)"
	"Blue Yodel #9 (Standin' on a Corner)"
1931	"T.B. Blues"
	"My Blue-Eyed Jane"
1932	"Peach-Pickin' Time in Georgia"
1933	"Mississippi Delta Blues"
	"Years Ago"

After the 1927 success of "Blue Yodel (T for Texas)," Rodgers relocated to Kerrville, Texas, for the mild weather and to perform on a weekly radio show in nearby San Antonio.

moderate success that Rodgers was emboldened to travel to New York, find Ralph Peer, and convince him to record some more songs. Out of this second session came his breakthrough side, "Blue Yodel (T for Texas)." The song sold half a million copies, and the Singing Brakeman's career was launched.

Plagued by tuberculosis, which he'd contracted at age 24, Rodgers eventually had to quit working the rails. Luckily, the period from 1928 to 1931 was fruitful for him. He recorded many songs and toured to great popular acclaim. But the Depression wasn't good for entertainers: Concert tickets and record prices were beyond most families' budgets, and Rodgers' income and his health both took a turn for the worse.

Rodgers' last recording session is as legendary as his first. Realizing that he was near death, he traveled to New York City in May 1933 for one last session. He was so ill, he had to rest on a cot between takes. His last recorded song, "Years Ago," was done solo, just like his first. No session men, just Jimmie and his guitar. Rodgers died three days later, at age 35.

Yodel-Lay-Ee-O!

What do the Swiss Alps and the American plains have in common? The yodel—that low-to-high cry that's made to carry over a long distance, such as from one mountain peak to another, or from one lonesome cowboy to his pardner. There's even Hawaiian yodeling—sounds like a slide guitar. Jimmie Rodgers incorporated yodeling into many of his songs, issuing a series of 13 "Blue Yodels." Surprisingly adaptable in the hands of Rodgers, his yodels could either be mournful or joyful, a wail or a chuckle, depending on the mood of the song. Other notable country yodelers were Slim Clark, Elton Britt, Wilf Carter, Patsy Montana, and Gene Autry.

KENNY ROGERS

August 21, 1938–

Knowing when to hold 'em, Rogers has charted in each of the last five decades. His greatest hits album sold 12 million domestically and another 12 million internationally.

GREATEST HITS	
Year	Song
1969	"Ruby, Don't Take Your Love to Town" (as a member of the First Edition)
1977	"Lucille"
	"Daytime Friends"
1978	"Every Time Two Fools Collide" (with Dottie West)
	"The Gambler"
1979	"She Believes in Me"
	"Coward of the County"
1980	"Lady"
1981	"Through the Years"
1983	"We've Got Tonight" (with Sheena Easton)
	"Islands in the Stream" (with Dolly Parton)
1984	"Crazy"
1987	"Make No Mistake, She's Mine" (with Ronnie Milsap)
2000	"Buy Me a Rose"
	"Years Ago"

A star during the '70s, Kenny Rogers made the jump to outright superstar in the '80s. He'd been a member of the New Christy Minstrels in the '60s and then the First Edition. Kenny Rogers and the First Edition (as they became known) had enjoyed some fairly major hits, such as "Reuben James" and "Ruby, Don't Take Your Love to Town." Vivid characterizations and heart-tugging stories combined to create compelling songs. Kenny's gruff-yet-friendly voice and smooth orchestrations defined a new genre: middle-of-the-road country. It was when he went solo in the late '70s, however, that Rogers' career really took off.

"Don't be afraid to give up the good for the great." —Kenny Rogers

Kenny had a few minor solo hits, and then 1977's "Lucille" blew the doors off his career, sending him into the stratosphere of pop culture. A simple song, really, but Rogers' gritty voice draws the listener in to the story. The catch in his voice right there in the beginning clues in the audience that this tale might not be a love song after all. The new gravel in his voice suited Rogers well. Led by the single "Lucille," he went on to break records and hit #1 in 12 countries outside the United States. Turned out that listeners overseas were just as seduced by this troubadour and his sandpaper voice of hard knocks.

If "Lucille" was a huge, career-making hit, the follow-up album, *The Gambler* was unprecedented. The title song became Rogers' signature tune. And over the years Kenny would reinforce the image of himself as "the Gambler" through film and television. The lyrics were so catchy, so sensible that they sounded like received wisdom, rather than a tune somebody had written: "You got to know when to hold 'em, know when to fold 'em. Know when to walk away, know when to run . . ." Deep thoughts, in the form of a parable of a grizzled Old West gambler, who coincidentally has a white beard, just like Rogers himself. "Coward of the County" followed a similar formula and received similar television treatment. Rogers had again exercised his aptitude for expanding a simple song's story into an entire universe of character and action.

NUGGET: In 2000, Kenny Rogers had another #1 single, "Buy Me a Rose." At 61 years young, this made him the oldest musician ever to top the country charts. At 59, Hank Snow had reached the summit of the charts, 26 years prior.

During the '80s Kenny also began a tradition that would serve him well over the years: duets with female singers. He had known singer Dottie West for years, and when she suggested that they do an album together it seemed a natural idea. And indeed it was: West and Rogers made three highly regarded (and hugely appealing) albums together and were seen on tour and enjoyed by millions. "Every Time Two Fools Collide," "Anyone Who Isn't Me Tonight," and "What Are We Doing in Love" were popular enough to take eventual spots as country standards. Rogers was at her bedside in 1991 when West expired from injuries received in a car accident.

In addition to West, Rogers collaborated often with other musicians over the years. He sang a number of duets with fellow legend Dolly Parton. "Islands in the Stream" was yet another huge crossover and international hit. As was becoming his habit, Rogers took such typical country elements as his gravelly voice and locations like barrooms and poker halls and forged them into something new. Not just new, but something that appealed to entire swaths of the music-listening population that had never before considered country.

Rogers continued to have hits well into the '90s, though he never recaptured the precipitous commercial heights he enjoyed in the previous decade. He did have yet another monster hit in the year 2000, "Buy Me a Rose," with legend Alison Krauss. Heading into a new century, Rogers may well yet still have some surprises in store.

Before performing with the First Edition in 1967, Rogers (second from left) performed with the Rockabilly Scholars, the Bobby Doyle Trio, Kirby Stone Four, and the New Christy Minstrels.

The fourth of eight children born into humble circumstances, Kenny has achieved success with his writing, singing, producing, acting, charitable works, and business enterprises.

Kenny Rogers™

Country artists have often been identified with the characters they sing about. Kenny Rogers took that to the next level by actually producing movies based on his hit songs. He didn't just appear in a video, he became "The Gambler." Through five full-length television movies, Rogers explored the world and characters suggested by his signature song. Country artists had played cowboys on film for decades. Rogers was the first, and so far the only artist to use a single song as a springboard to a whole world of characters and intrigue. By starring in these projects himself, he cemented his spot in the popular culture. Nobody, before or since, had ever created an entire mythos around one song. He had created a brand, and the brand was Kenny Rogers. "Coward of the County" received similar treatment. Cinematic and illustrative lyrics lent themselves to being filmed, and as the star, Kenny just reinforced his character in the public eye. In the process he became a major pop culture icon of the '80s.

Then, in the '90s, Rogers expanded his branding with the creation of Kenny Rogers Roasters, a chain of chicken restaurants to which Kenny contributed his name and a spicy recipe. Meanwhile Rogers continued to record, published three photography books (*Kenny Rogers' America* and *Kenny Rogers: Your Friends and Mine*, and *This Is My Country*), and starred in several movies and television shows. Brand Kenny™ is going strong and showing no sign of fading buyer interest, even into the 21st century.

RICKY SKAGGS

JULY 18, 1954–

INDUCTED INTO THE GRAND OLE OPRY IN 1982, SKAGGS HAS BEEN A MAJOR FORCE IN REVITALIZING THE BLUEGRASS TRADITION.

When you're from Kentucky, you're issued a bluegrass seal of approval at birth. At least that's what a glance at the career of prolific, multitalented Ricky Skaggs would lead you to believe. The homegrown music just seems to run through his veins. A child prodigy on the mandolin, Skaggs was on stage at age 5 with Bill Monroe, the father of bluegrass himself. For more than 30 years, Skaggs has maintained a level of musicianship and chart success that has won him fans, honors, and professional esteem. For his dedication and contributions to the form, 12-time Grammy winner Skaggs has been called "the ambassador of bluegrass."

"Country rocks, but bluegrass rules!"—Ricky Skaggs

Where do you go after appearing with Bill Monroe at age 5? Onward to Flatt & Scruggs, of course. Ricky pulled off that coup by age 7, appearing with them on television. At 16, he became a member of Ralph Stanley's band, the Clinch Mountain Boys, along with his friend, the late Keith Whitley. The two young musicians later released a few albums together during the '70s, while Ricky also appeared with such progressive bluegrass outfits as J. D. Crowe and the New South. Fronting his own band, Boone Creek, for a spell, Skaggs then went on to join Emmylou Harris in her Hot Band. Harris has called Skaggs "an encyclopedia of bluegrass."

Good Friends, Good Music

Part of the bluegrass tradition is that everyone gets 15 seconds of fame (bluegrass is fast) in the form of a solo. Well, that kind of playing well with others leads to strong musical friendships, and Ricky Skaggs is a prime example. He has played with such greats as Doc Watson, Alison Krauss, David Grisman, Emmylou Harris, and Dobro master Jerry Douglas. Skaggs teamed with guitarist Tony Rice for several albums and in 2007 released a collaborative effort with Bruce Hornsby.

Skaggs finally recorded his first solo album in 1981; its success helped him land a contract with Epic Records. Who woulda thunk it? A rootsy bluegrass tenor with lightning-quick picking style, turning out hit records during the age of country pop? Well, selling was believing, and largely due to Ricky Skaggs' efforts, the New Traditionalist movement was born. In fact, Chet Atkins credited Skaggs with "single-handedly saving country music." Ricky took a little detour into straight country during the early '90s, but his heart and soul were in bluegrass. His return to the form, with the virtuosic band Kentucky Thunder, was the Grammy-winning 1997 *Bluegrass Rules!* His fans would no doubt agree that Ricky Skaggs rules bluegrass.

NUGGET: Ricky's 2006 Grammy trophy was courtesy of Mr. Rogers. Skaggs was a contributor to *Songs from the Neighborhood: The Music of Mr. Rogers*, which won Best Musical Album for Children.

GREATEST HITS

YEAR	SONG
1981	"Don't Get above Your Raisin'"
	"You May See Me Walkin'"
1982	"Cryin' My Heart Out Over You"
	"I Don't Care"
	"Heartbroke"
1983	"I Wouldn't Change You If I Could"
	"Highway 40 Blues"
	"Don't Cheat in Our Hometown"
	"Honey (Open That Door)"
	"Uncle Pen"
1984	"Country Boy"
1985	"Cajun Moon"
2000	"Soldier of the Cross"
2003	"A Simple Life

CARL SMITH

March 15, 1927–

You don't get to be Mister Country by cleaning windows or sweeping floors. No, you gain that moniker by playing country music anywhere you can, to anyone who will listen. That's how Carl Smith did it. He played radio shows all over the South before landing a regular gig at country radio giant WSM in 1950: mornings six days a week, and the Grand Ole Opry once a month. That regular radio exposure got him a record deal, and before long he had his first hit single. Smith would go on to have more than 30 Top 10 country hits throughout the '50s and '60s.

NUGGET: Smith earned the money to buy his first guitar by selling flower seeds door to door.

His first hits were fairly standard honky-tonk fare. Smith's talent for smoothing some of the rough edges off that hard-core country served him well. He sang love songs mostly, the sad ones where the guy lost the girl and we all know he ain't getting her back. His gentle singing voice, paired with such traditional country instrumentation as steel guitars and tinkly piano fills, gave a reassuring aspect to his work. Fans reacted strongly to Smith's presentation, and for several years there, every single he released went immediately into the Top 20.

Born in Maynardsville, Tennessee, Carl Smith gained fame in country music and married one of Ma Maybelle's daughters. Here he is with Carlene Carter (his daughter by first wife, June).

GREATEST HITS	
Year	Song
1951	"Let's Live a Little"
	"If Teardrops Were Pennies"
1952	"Let Old Mother Nature Have Her Way"
	"Don't Just Stand There"
	"Are You Teasing Me"
1953	"It's a Lovely Lovely World"
	"Just Wait 'Til I Get You Alone"
	"Hey Joe"
1954	"Back Up Buddy"
1955	"Loose Talk"
	"Don't Tease Me"
1957	"You Are the One"
1959	"Ten Thousand Drums"

Smith courted (and subsequently married) June Carter backstage at the Opry and the two sang frequent duets on the radio and on recordings such as "Time's a Wastin'." Ironically, considering his usual mellow style, Carl Smith was the first person to bring a drum set on the stage of the Opry. Despite the scoffing of traditionalists, he used the additional percussion to raise the energy level of his performances. With that propulsive beat anchoring the other instruments in the band, listeners' toes set to tapping and hands to clapping that much faster.

Mister Country moved out of radio and got into television late in the '50s, to great success. His handsome looks, invisible to radio audiences, made him a favorite of viewers. Smith both hosted his own *Country Music Hall* program and performed frequently as a guest on others' shows. He retired in the '70s.

True Love

Mister Country met the adorable June Carter backstage at the Opry in 1951. The two stars fell hard for each other and were soon married. They had one daughter, Carlene, who went on to be a country singing star in her own right. Carl and June divorced in 1956.

A year later, another fellow Opry star, Goldie Hill, the Golden Hillbilly, caught Carl's eye. This time it was true love—they have just celebrated their 50th anniversary. The two currently raise horses on their spread south of Nashville.

HANK SNOW

May 9, 1914–December 20, 1999

The radio made hoboes of us all. Hank Snow was a nice boy from Brooklyn . . . Brooklyn, Nova Scotia, that is. Way up there in the chilly maritime provinces, young Snow could turn a knob on the dial and hear Jimmie Rodgers singing about dusty rail lines and peach-pickin' time in Georgia. How the young Canadian (born Clarence Eugene Snow) found his way onto the Opry stage to become an influential and prolific country star sounds like a tall tale. That old-time country music exerted some kind of pull, as Hank Snow's journey to Nashville attests.

The rambling of his youth became the centerpiece of Snow's musical subject matter. He was known for traveling songs—his two biggest hits were his breakthrough "I'm Movin' On" and his great "I've Been Everywhere," a catalog of American cities delivered like a fast-talking auctioneer. Hank's "The Last Ride" was a hobo elegy for a rail-riding pal.

In addition to popularizing country music in the States, this Canadian developed an international following in such places as Great Britain, Australia, Germany, and Japan.

Snow's rambling started young. At age 12, he ran away from an abusive home to work on a North Atlantic fishing trawler. Back home for a spell, young Clarence saved up to buy a mail-order $5.95 guitar, learned some Rodgers-style yodels, and hit the road again. His first stop was Halifax, where he played in clubs and then landed a gig on CHNS, billed as the Blue Yodeler. The radio men suggested that Clarence change his name to Hank—sounded more country. Heading south, Hank befriended Ernest Tubb at the Big D Jamboree in Dallas, and the Texas Troubadour wrangled his new buddy onto the Opry stage.

NUGGET: Hank and his trick pony, Shawnee, performed onstage in Hollywood when Hank was trying to break into the U.S. market.

In Nashville, Hank changed his nickname to the Yodelling Ranger. Fired by his love of country roots music, Snow seemed to embody the spirit of Jimmie Rodgers, preserving both his style and the substance of his music. Hank did branch out and incorporate some boogie and rhumba and even made a stab at rockabilly. But when you sing what you know and love, it shows; Hank Snow's rambling days stayed with him until he took "his long last ride."

GREATEST HITS

Year	Song
1950	"I'm Movin' On"
	"Golden Rocket"
1951	"The Rhumba Boogie"
1952	"A Fool Such as I"
1954	"I Don't Hurt Anymore"
1958	"Big Wheels"
1960	"Miller's Cave"
1961	"Beggar to a King"
1962	"I've Been Everywhere"
1963	"Ninety Miles an Hour (Down a Dead End Street)"
1974	"Hello Love"

The Ranger and the Colonel

When Elvis Presley played the Opry in 1954, his one and only time, it was to open for the Yodelling Ranger, Hank Snow. Hank had talked the Opry into giving the young singer a chance. Earlier that same year, Snow had formed a short-lived management partnership with Colonel Tom Parker, and Elvis was one of their clients. While Hank was pushing Elvis toward the country fold, Colonel Tom was pulling the other direction, into that newfangled rock and roll. We all know who won the tug-of-war.

SONS OF THE PIONEERS

1934–

THE SONS OF THE PIONEERS WOULD GO THROUGH MANY INCARNATIONS, WITH A VERITABLE WAGON TRAIN–LOAD OF PARTICIPANTS, SOME OF WHOM STILL CARRY ON.

Scene: a long dusty main street, way out in the Old West. A tumbleweed tumbles across the dirt road, which is scarred with the tracks of wagon wheels. Suddenly, we hear thundering hoofbeats, and a cowpoke rides in, with spurs that jingle jangle jingle. There's a saloon in town, but it's full of whiskey and wild, wild women. That cowhand just wants some cool, cool water. But he hears the call of the blue prairie and the echoes from the hills. Time to follow that tumbleweed trail, into the everlasting hills of Oklahoma.

NUGGET: Willie Nelson's famously beat-up guitar, Trigger, is named for Roy Roger's horse.

The Sons of the Pioneers: Their song titles alone add up to a picture of the West that is as deeply embedded in our American imagination as the wagon ruts in that dusty main street. The definitive Western combo is also the longest-running country vocal group. With their full harmonies, evocative lyrics, and easygoing melodies, the Sons of the Pioneers hold a unique place in American music. In 1977, the Smithsonian Institution designated the group as "national treasures." Their cheerful, infectious songs—both on records and in Western movies—make you sit up a little taller in the saddle and smile the cowboy way.

The Sons of the Pioneers were formed in Los Angeles, in the midst of the Great Depression. Their upbeat musical Americana arrived as a welcome ray of

GREATEST HITS

YEAR	SONG
1934	"Tumbling Tumbleweeds"
	"Way Out There"
	"Moonlight on the Prairie"
	"Ridin' Home"
1940s	"Blue Prairie"
	"Happy Rovin' Cowboy"
	"Cigareetes, Whusky, and Wild, Wild, Women"
1948	"Cool Water"
	"The Everlasting Hills of Oklahoma"
1949	"(Ghost) Riders in the Sky"
	"Room Full of Roses"
	"My Best to You"
1950	"Wagons West"

ROY ROGERS INTRODUCED MANY SONGS TO THE AMERICAN PUBLIC. IN 1944, HE AND THE SONS OF THE PIONEERS WERE THE FIRST TO POPULARIZE COLE PORTER'S "DON'T FENCE ME IN."

Roy Rogers, King of the Cowboys

Roy Rogers (Born Leonard Franklin Slye, 1911–1998) was a whole lot more than a TV cowboy; he embodied the brave, forthright, and good-natured hero of mid-century America. With his trusty sidekick played by Gabby Hayes, and mounted on his golden palomino, Trigger, Roy galloped into the hearts of a generation of American children. His image was slapped on everything from cereal boxes to lunch pails to dime-store pistols. He made over 50 movies, his radio show ran for nine years, and his television program aired from 1951 to 1964. Rogers was inducted into the Country Music Hall of Fame twice, once as a founding member of the Sons of the Pioneers, and once as an individual country singer.

In 1945, Roy was cast opposite a young starlet and singer known as Dale Evans (her given name was Frances Octavia Smith). The two clicked right away on screen. A year later, Roy's wife, Arline, died in childbirth; Roy and Dale married in 1947. The two remained together, on screen and off, for the rest of their lives. Dale was known as the "Queen of the West" and wrote "Happy Trails," the famous Roy Rogers Show theme song. "Happy trails to you, until we meet again," sang Evans, atop her buckskin horse, Buttermilk. You bet those kids tuned in next week.

sunlight for a gloomy populace. A fellow from Cincinnati, Leonard Slye (later known as Roy Rogers), teamed up with Tim Spencer and Bob Nolan; the three called themselves the Pioneer Trio. During their radio debut, the announcer dubbed them the "sons of the pioneers," seeing as how they were too young to have been pioneers themselves. The name stuck. Besides, they were no longer a trio; they'd recently added fiddler Hugh Farr, whose guitarist brother Karl was soon to join the group as well.

This original lineup, which swapped Spencer out for Lloyd Perryman in 1936, was considered the true heart of the Sons of the Pioneers. Nolan's tunes, such as "Tumbling Tumbleweeds" and "Cool Water," have become classics. You know, the song with the liquid echo: "Cool (water) clear (water) water (water)." You're thirsting before the song is over. Perryman would become the longest-running member of the group, performing until his death in 1977.

A new little outfit called Decca Records signed up the Sons in 1934 (on the same day as Bing Crosby, in fact). Soon audiences got even more of a taste for these singing cowboys through the medium of movies. The Sons of the Pioneers were featured in several Gene Autry movies. When the Singing Cowboy found himself in a contract dispute with the studio, Leonard Slye auditioned for his role, using the stage name Roy Rogers. He got the part, and an American icon was born. But his newfound movie success meant that Slye was forced to leave the Pioneers, due to contractual conflicts; he was replaced with his friend Pat Brady. The group maintained friendly ties with their old founder Slye, and they were often featured as backup musicians in his films.

Through the '40s, the Sons of the Pioneers continued with screen and recording success; these are seen as their golden years. The great Western director John Ford used their songs in several of his movies. A group still performs under the name of the Sons of the Pioneers, its current members having overlapped with original personnel, now all passed away. Their legacy can still be heard in so much country music—just listen for that thundering-hoofbeat rhythm, those keen harmonies, and that optimistic cowboy twang.

A RADIO ANNOUNCER INTRODUCED THE GROUP AS THE SONS OF THE PIONEERS RATHER THAN THE PIONEERS, BECAUSE NONE OF THE MEMBERS WERE OLD ENOUGH TO BE PIONEERS. THE NAME STUCK.

THE STATLER BROTHERS

1955–2002

The Delmore Brothers. The Louvin Brothers. The Everly Brothers. The Statler Brothers. One of these things is not like the others. You guessed it—the Statlers. They are neither Statlers nor brothers. To be fair, there is a sibling pair among the quartet, but the name came on a whim, cadged from a box of facial tissues. Inspiration is like that, sometimes.

Inspired is what the Statlers' fans mostly feel about them. Sometimes likened to a barbershop quartet (from the play between the super-low basso profundo and the three middle voices), the Statlers saw harmony as a calling. Starting off as a church vocal trio in Virginia, the three founding members were bass Harold Reid, baritone Phil Balsley, and tenor Lew DeWitt. When Harold's younger brother Don joined the group, they were on their way, calling themselves the Kingsmen. Their strong suits were complex four-part harmonies and great comic patter between songs. Johnny Cash heard them and invited them on tour. The name was changed, and the Statler Brothers opened for the Man in Black from 1963 to 1971. They had spiritual authenticity, amazing musicality, and the rare ability to not take themselves too seriously.

From left to right: Phil Balsley, Jimmy Fortune, Don Reid, and Harold Reid. Tenor Jimmy Fortune replaced Lew DeWitt in the '80s after ill health forced DeWitt to retire.

NUGGET: "Flowers on the Wall," the Statlers' first big hit, was used in Quentin Tarantino's 1994 Academy Award–winning movie *Pulp Fiction*.

The Statler's first hit, 1965's "Flowers on the Wall" was an immediate country and pop crossover hit. It had the great harmonies, acoustic guitar, and dash of tambourine that mainstream listeners associated with the folk-rock acts of the day. During the '70s the group regularly held the top slots on the charts. DeWitt was forced by illness to bow out in 1983 and was replaced by Jimmy Fortune. The hits kept coming through the '80s, including the group's #1 song "Elizabeth," an homage to La Liz. After nearly 50 years together, the Statlers hung up their traveling shoes in 2002.

GREATEST HITS

Year	Song
1965	"Flowers on the Wall"
1970	"Bed of Roses"
1972	"Do You Remember These?"
	"The Class of '57"
1973	"Carry Me Back"
1975	"I'll Go to My Grave Loving You"
1978	"Do You Know You Are My Sunshine?"
1980	"Charlotte's Web"
1983	"Elizabeth"
1984	"My Only Love"
1985	"Too Much on My Heart"
1987	"Forever"
1989	"More Than a Name on a Wall"

The Holy Bible

Eight years in the making isn't much, considering how long it took to assemble the original. The Statler Brothers' two-record set, *The Holy Bible*, was released in 1974, after years of planning. One disc for the Old Testament, one for the New, the records tell Bible stories in catchy, concise little two-minute songs—ideal for kids' (and adults') short attention spans. The vocal range of the four men lends itself to the varied moods in the Book, from the up-tempo, scoldy "Eve" ("He gave you the world, what were you thinkin', girl?") to the reverent "The Lord's Prayer" (you know the words) to the stately "The King Is Coming," which closes out both discs. Whether enjoyed from a sacred or secular perspective, this great collection of songs is a reminder of country music's deep gospel roots.

GEORGE STRAIT

May 18, 1952–

Here's the straight dope on George Strait: the guy is a country superstar because he deserves to be. An affable, handsome Texas rancher with a deep, mellow voice, Strait has had more hit records than any other country artist, topping out at fifty-three #1s. In record sales he's right behind Elvis and the Beatles. He sings and plays and what the heck more do you need?

George is pure country, straight up. His image is no-frills—just a Resistol hat, a clean shirt, a polished belt buckle, and a winning smile. His early '80s success gave birth to a generation of neo-traditionalist "hat acts," notably Garth Brooks, Dwight Yoakam, and Clint Black. But Strait was there first, and his good taste, consistency, and vocal chops were hard for the younger fellows to match. Any one of them would tip their hat to King George, as Strait is affectionately known.

George Strait performs at the Country Music Awards. Strait was inducted into the Country Music Hall of Fame in 2006.

GREATEST HITS

Year	Song
1981	"Unwound"
1982	"Fool Hearted Memory"
1983	"Elizabeth"
1984	"Right or Wrong"
	"My Only Love"
1985	"Does Fort Worth Ever Cross Your Mind"
	"The Chair"
	"Too Much on My Heart"
1986	"Nobody in His Right Mind Would've Left Her"
1987	"Am I Blue"
	"Forever"
1989	"More Than a Name on a Wall"
1990	"Love Without End, Amen"
1992	"Heartland"
1995	"Check Yes or No"
1997	"Carrying Your Love with Me"
1999	"Write This Down"
2002	"She'll Leave You with a Smile"
2004	"I Hate Everything"
2006	"Give It Away"
	"It Just Comes Natural"

NUGGET: Shopping for jeans? Try the Wrangler style called the "George Strait Cowboy Cut," for a double dose of cowboy authenticity. Available in original or relaxed fit.

"It Just Comes Natural," the title of one of Strait's recent hits, pretty much describes his own career. He has a Midas way with a song—nearly every number Strait touches turns to gold. Partly this is because he's always picked the right tunes. His tastes run to honky-tonk and Western swing, and it just happens that his pipes do, too. He perfected that cool swoop down onto the notes like George Jones. Most of Strait's songs have to do with lost love, but he's smart enough to choose the ones with the witty lyrics and the clap-along beat, like "Write This Down" or "All My Ex's Live in Texas." "And that's why I hang my hat in Tennessee" continues the lyric.

"I'm a country singer. I don't want to be in the middle of the road. A fella could get run over out there."—George Strait

George Strait has had his share of tragedy. His mother left the family when he was just a boy, taking his sister with her. Strait and his brother, Buddy, were raised by his dad, a math teacher, spending weekends working on the 2,000-acre ranch that had been in their family for a century. After high school, George married his sweetheart, Norma. They welcomed two children into the world, but tragedy struck again when daughter Jenifer was killed in a car accident at age 13.

Strangely, George wasn't a country fan from the start. As a teenager, he'd admired old '60s British Invasion groups and had played guitar in a couple of garage bands. When he enlisted in the army in 1971 and was stationed in Hawaii, George really got country. The no-doubt homesick Texan heard classic sounds coming in over the airwaves, and he got bit by the country bug, big time, in the form of Hank Williams, George Jones, and Merle Haggard. Strait was especially impressed by Merle's tribute album to Bob Wills. "Right or Wrong," the great Wills Western swing tune (also covered by Merle) has become one of George Strait's standards.

When he was discharged, George headed right back to Texas and formed his own band, Ace in the Hole. With its great instrumentalists and swingin' beats, the band nonetheless failed to break through the slick pop sensibilities that dominated country in the late '70s. Finally, striking up a friendship with Erv Woolsey, a former MCA man, George got a break. Some of the guys from Music Row took a side trip to Texas and went home with a contract signed by George Strait.

One hit record after another, one award after another. Movie-star looks, rodeo credentials, a fabulous home, and lovely family. No chance occurrence that Strait chose to record Merle Haggard's "My Life's Been Grand." And here's another thing: He's loyal. How many superstars have stuck with their original, college-era band? Well, George Strait continues to tour and record with his Ace in the Hole musicians, because they're tight, they're good, they know all those great songs, and what the heck more do you need?

Not a songwriter himself, Strait has worked with, among others, Dean Dillon, Whitey Shafer, Aaron Barker, and Jim Lauderdale.

Admired by fans for his cowboy bona fides, Strait enjoys steer-roping, fishing, and hunting.

Rope 'Em!

Cowboy singer means what exactly? Singers who croon about the lone prairie and git along little doggies? Don't get us wrong; we love 'em—who doesn't? But how many singers are there who are actually real cowboys on top of it? Like, who could survive at a rodeo for two seconds without getting booed or thrown or gored? George Strait, for one.

Not only is Strait a member of the Professional Rodeo Cowboys Association (PRCA), but 2007 saw the 25th Annual George Strait Team Roping Classic. He doesn't just host the event, or lend his name; Strait competes against the top team ropers in the country, often partnered with his son Bubba or his brother, Buddy.

A fourth-generation rancher, Strait also makes it his business to perform at the Houston Livestock Show and Rodeo. His 2002 performance at the Astrodome, the last time that venue hosted the event, set attendance records and produced Strait's album *For the Last Time: Live from the Astrodome*. The video for his early hit "Amarillo by Morning" set the stage for Strait's regular use of rodeo imagery in his videos and photos. He's the real deal.

HANK THOMPSON

September 3, 1925–

Hank Thompson was trained as a radioman in World War II. When not on duty, he'd strum a guitar to pass the time during those long, lonely nights at sea. When he returned stateside after the war, the G.I. Bill allowed him to attend Princeton, where he studied electrical engineering, capitalizing on the skills he'd learned in the radio shack of that destroyer. Right about graduation time, Hank realized that he'd much prefer to use the guitar skills he'd honed lying alone on his bunk.

"Time wounds all heels."—Hank Thompson

Hank set about putting together a band. Hank Thompson and his Brazos Valley Boys played Western swing, a jazzy, syncopated branch of country. Their first single was a song Hank had written while on that ship, "Whoa Sailor." The song became a hit, and Hank knew he'd chosen the right career.

Hank Thompson is still a figure on the world stage, performing near to 120 shows a year. He was elected to the Country Music Hall of Fame in 1989.

Honky-Tonk Angel

Hank Thompson had a huge hit with "The Wild Side of Life." That song contained the line, "I didn't know God made honky-tonk angels." The phrase refers to a girl who is led astray by a honky-tonk lothario. Kitty Wells and her songwriter J. D. Miller heard that song and came up with "God Didn't Make Honky Tonk Angels," Wells' "answer song." Kitty explained that God didn't make those women stray, their men's poor behavior did. And even though country music was quite conservative in those days, Wells' song still ended up being an even bigger hit than Thompson's. In fact, it sold so well that Kitty Wells became the first female country singer to sell a million records.

The success of "Whoa Sailor" showed them they were doing something right and encouraged them to do more. Which they did: Hank went on to have a string of hit songs during the '50s, '60s, and even into the '70s.

Always a showman, Hank did what he could to distinguish himself from the plethora of cowboys vying for the public's attention. He started out wearing wild outfits, but soon realized that he could use his electrical engineering experience in a way that would benefit his performing side. He was one of the first musicians of any kind, and certainly the first country musician, to bring a sound and light system along to gigs so that they could be assured of looking and sounding great. To the same end, Thompson was also the first to record in high-fidelity stereo.

When the '70s came around, Hank found himself selling fewer records as tastes changed and Western swing was supplanted by the Nashville and Bakersfield sounds. He continued to tour and play gigs through the '80s.

NUGGET: In 1961, Thompson released the first country album to be recorded live. *At the Golden Nugget* was an instant classic and a huge seller.

GREATEST HITS

Year	Song
1946	"Whoa Sailor"
	"Swing Wide Your Gate of Love"
1949	"Humpty Dumpty Heart"
1952	"Wild Side of Life"
1960	"This Broken Heart of Mine"
1962	"Squaws Along the Yukon"
1966	"A Six Pack to Go"
1969	"New Wine in Old Bottles"
1976	"Sting in This Ol' Bee"

FLOYD TILLMAN

December 8, 1914–August 22, 2003

It's nice to think that Western swing sprang fully formed from the sawdust on some cowboy dancehall floor. It's also nice to think that Willie Nelson's distinctive vocal style just emanated forth, a pure, quavery stream of pathos. But the answer to both of those wishful-thinking scenarios is Floyd Tillman. Along with Bob Wills, Tillman was one of the earliest creators of Western swing during the '30s and '40s. His singing style, his songwriting, and his musical versatility make Tillman one of the most influential artists in country music history.

The son of a sharecropper in the town of Post, Texas, Floyd had his first gigs playing mandolin with his brothers at local dances. Pretty soon Floyd had mastered the guitar as well. Moving to San Antonio, Tillman hooked up with bandleader Adolph Hofner, who was trying out some of that jazzy new Western swing style. Tillman began writing songs and then moved to Houston, where he worked with a number of dance bands. By 1938, Tillman had come into his own, with his first songwriting hit, "It Makes No Difference Now." Bing Crosby latched on to that one and took it to the top the following year.

At the height of his career Tillman retired from life on the road. He continued to record and write songs and at his death had composed more than 1,000 tunes.

You know a lot of Floyd Tillman songs—you just don't realize it. The numbers he penned have been recorded by the likes of Ernest Tubb, Ray Charles, Glen Campbell, and even Burl Ives. Tillman did his part during the war as a radio operator, but also with his sentimental "Each Night at Nine," in which a soldier overseas begs his wife to "tell the kiddies I'm doing fine, give them my love, dear, each night at nine." Tillman also wrote the first country "cheatin'" song, the much-covered "Slippin' Around."

GREATEST HITS

Year	Song
1938	"It Makes No Difference Now"
1940	"Daisy May"
1942	"They Took the Stars out of Heaven"
1944	"Each Night at Nine"
	"G.I. Blues"
1946	"Drivin' Nails in My Coffin"
1948	"I Love You So Much It Hurts"
1949	"Slippin' Around"
1950	"I'll Never Slip Around Again"
1960	"It Just Tears Me Up"

NUGGET: Jimmie Davis, the Singing Governor, paid $300 for the rights to Floyd's 1938 songwriting hit, "It Makes No Difference Now." Twenty-eight years later, Floyd won back the rights to his song.

The Influence

Shortly before he died in 2003, Tillman was honored in a way that usually doesn't happen until an artist is a memory: a tribute album called *The Influence*. And this wasn't just any tribute with any old artists. This had Floyd singing his original songs with Dolly Parton, Merle Haggard, Hank Thompson, Leona Williams, Mel Tillis, and, of course, his great champion, Willie Nelson. Floyd's style of singing a lyric just a split second after the beat, giving a languid feeling to even the perkiest of numbers, has become a signature sound of Nelson's as well. In fact, Willie called him the Original Outlaw, for Tillman's ability to think outside the box in an era when people liked their music in its proper place.

MERLE TRAVIS

NOVEMBER 29, 1917–OCTOBER 20, 1983

Oh, he had his own hit records, but Merle Travis became a legend mainly due to his guitar playing and writing more than the actual records that he released. His unique style of picking the guitar with fingers and thumb was picked up from banjo-playing neighbors of his family in Muhlenberg County, Kentucky, where Travis grew up. This stylistic innovation enabled him to play the bass line with his thumb and the melody with his fingers. This made it sound as if two people were playing when only one was working the fretboard.

In 1946, Travis released *Folk Songs of the Hills*, interpretations and reimaginings of the songs he remembered hearing during his youth in Kentucky. Although the collection would have made a perfect LP, it was released as four 78-rpm records instead and sold poorly. Poor sales aside, the collection included "Sixteen Tons," "Dark as a Dungeon," and "Smoke, Smoke, Smoke that Cigarette." All three would go on to be hits years later, notably the former, which, performed by Tennessee Ernie Ford, would be a monster crossover hit in 1955.

In addition to his writing and performing work, Travis acted on the silver screen. He appeared in the smash 1953 movie *From Here to Eternity*, singing his own song, "Re-Enlistment Blues." Yet, for all his obvious talents, Travis remained a tragic figure in country music. Though his ax handling never seemed to suffer, a number of public incidents of out-of-control drunken behavior handicapped his attempts to achieve the commercial heights of many of his associates.

Finger and Thumb

Merle Travis was never able to achieve the commercial success of many of his contemporaries and friends. But his finger-and-thumb style of guitar playing was so distinctive that he was imitated by legions of country artists for years to come, including Chet Atkins, whose smooth playing style would be heard on so many Nashville Sound recordings. Or Scotty Moore, Elvis Presley's longtime guitarist, who picked up his licks from hunkering over a radio, listening to Travis play on those early radio gigs at WLW in Cincinnati.

He wasn't just a brilliant stylist; he was a technician, too. Merle was the first to play a solid-body electric guitar, and the model he developed with Leo Fender went on to be the basis of the sound for the bulk of country and rock and roll records to come. For the guitar Fender came up with was known as the Broadcaster, later rechristened the Fender Telecaster.

"The saddest songs are written when a person is happy." —Merle Travis

GREATEST HITS	
YEAR	SONG
1946	"No Vacancy"
	"Cincinnati Lou"
1947	"Sixteen Tons"
	"Dark as a Dungeon"
	"Over by Number Nine"
	"Nine Pound Hammer"
1948	"Divorce Me C.O.D."
	"So Round So Firm So Fully Packed"
	"Three Times Seven"
1953	"Re-Enlistment Blues"

SON OF A FARMER IN KENTUCKY COAL COUNTRY, MERLE TRAVIS PENNED THE CLASSIC "SIXTEEN TONS," ABOUT THE LIFE OF A HARDSCRABBLE, DEBT-RIDDEN BUT INDOMITABLE MINER.

RANDY TRAVIS

May 4, 1959–

When the charming former delinquent Randy Travis was cooking the meals and washing dishes at the Nashville Palace in the early '80s, he'd hear whistling and shouts from the dining room. He'd strip off his greasy apron, throw a little water on his face, grab his guitar, and jump on stage. Food was forgotten, the conversations stopped, and forks laid down as soon as Randy's sonorous baritone rang out. After a song or two, he'd thank the audience for its applause, then strap that apron right back on and try to catch up on the dishes. He did this enough times to get a demo tape out of it and then managed to get it to some executives at Warner Brothers Records, who promptly signed him.

In the manner of long-struggling overnight successes everywhere, Randy hit big with his first album, *Storms of Life*. It came out in 1986 and took right off. The first single, "1982," was a Top 10 hit. The next single, "On the Other Hand," did even better and rocketed to #1. Travis was in the first wave of New Traditionalists just hitting Nashville.

GREATEST HITS

Year	Song
1986	"1982"
	"On the Other Hand"
1987	"Forever and Ever, Amen"
	"I Won't Need You Anymore"
1988	"Honky Tonk Moon"
1989	"It's Just a Matter of Time"
1990	"A Few Ole Country Boys" (with George Jones)
1991	"Forever Together"
1992	"Better Class of Losers"
	"She Got the Rhythm and I Got the Blues" (with Alan Jackson)
	"If I Didn't Have You"
1994	"Whisper My Name"
1998	"Out of My Bones"
2002	"Three Wooden Crosses"

Randy Travis on stage at Wembley Stadium in 1989. Hoping his son would become a country singer, Randy's father filled the house with the sounds of Hank Williams and Stonewall Jackson.

"It's not what you take when you leave this world behind you. It's what you leave behind you when you go." —Randy Travis

Just as mainstream country was modernizing with rock and pop influences, Travis and his cohorts Ricky Skaggs and George Strait made music that harked back to older, more traditional country styles.

Travis continued to have hits throughout the '80s and into the '90s. By the latter half of the decade it appeared that Randy's smooth baritone and straight arrangements were losing ground to more modern stylists like Garth Brooks and Shania Twain. Travis continued to record but spent more of his creative energy on acting. He appeared in several major motion pictures, including Francis Ford Coppola's *The Rainmaker*.

Inspiration

Though he had never been shy about his faith, Randy had not recorded any overtly religious music. That changed in the year 2000 when he recorded and released *Inspirational Journey*, an album of contemporary gospel. The album sold pretty well, so Travis continued mining the gospel vein with *Rise and Shine*. Its first single, "Three Wooden Crosses," crossed over from gospel into the country charts and surprised nearly everyone by topping at #1. Travis was understandably thrilled with this genre change that felt like a second career and has continued to create and release inspirational music.

TRAVIS TRITT

February 9, 1963–

"The sound of outlaw music sets me free," growls Tritt. Despite his rebellious image, Tritt has a strong family life with a wife of 10 years and three children.

Timing isn't everything. Otherwise, Travis Tritt wouldn't have made the huge splash he did in the early '90s. And he wouldn't have gone on to be one of the most successful new country acts in the last two decades. In an era dominated by such clean-cut hat guys as Garth Brooks, along came another kind of New Traditionalist. Longhaired, hard-rocking, and a little scruffy around the edges, Travis was hewing to a different tradition—the one laid out by the '70s outlaws, Waylon Jennings and company.

"If you're gonna sing, sing loud."—Travis Tritt

When Tritt's first album, *Country Club*, came out in 1990, the title song got the message across loud and clear: This one's for you. With lyrics like "I drive an old Ford pickup truck, I do my drinkin' from a Dixie cup," done in amped-up honky-tonk style, complete with fiddle breaks, Tritt made blue-collar pride cool again, the way George and Tammy did with "We're Not the Jet Set." Later songs like "Lord Have Mercy on the Working Man," showed Travis was on the side of the rednecks and good ol' boys, the regular guys he grew up with in Georgia. And the regular guys rewarded him by buying his records—lots of them. His second album, *It's All About to Change*, went multiplatinum.

Although Travis Tritt is anything but a Nashville player, that hasn't stopped him from forming some tight bonds with other musicians. He's a great collaborator, and his 1994 album, *My Honky Tonk History*, includes appearances by Gretchen Wilson, John Mellencamp, and Béla Fleck. One of Tritt's career highlights was a tribute to Ray Charles, when he and Brother Ray performed together on CMT's *Crossroads*. Travis' voice has matured into a deep, full-bodied sound; you can hear him on cuts by a long list of greats, including Johnny Cash, George Jones, and his outlaw hero, Waylon Jennings.

NUGGET: The O'Reilly Factor set to music? Travis Tritt and John Mellencamp teamed up for the duet "What Say You," a catchphrase of the garrulous TV commentator Bill O'Reilly. But is the lyric "I'm not afraid to speak my mind" talking back to O'Reilly, or backing him up? What say you?

Whiskey + Women + Music = Honky-Tonk

Travis Tritt's trifecta of T-R-O-U-B-L-E comes in the Southern version of wine, women, and song. When "the whiskey ain't workin' anymore" there's a "woman warm and willing" to take its place. It's all part of the honky-tonk antihero that Travis portrays on so many of his songs. Broken, boozy, and just this side of bitter, his song characters use the bottle to feel "10 feet tall and bulletproof," but there's always that rival who's packing kryptonite. We all know the feeling—when you can't get an even break, and you know there's only you to blame. Travis makes you feel like you're not alone as you knock back just one more in the mythical, magical honky-tonk of his songs.

GREATEST HITS

Year	Song
1989	"Country Club"
1990	"Help Me Hold On"
1991	"Anymore"
	"Here's a Quarter (Call Someone Who Cares)"
1992	"The Whiskey Ain't Workin'" (with Marty Stuart)
1993	"Can I Trust You with My Heart"
	"T-R-O-U-B-L-E"
1994	"Foolish Pride"
1996	"More Than You'll Ever Know"
2000	"Best of Intentions"
2001	"Love of a Woman"
2004	"What Say You" (with John Mellencamp)

ERNEST TUBB

January 9, 1914–September 6, 1984

No tonsils, no yodel. So along with his ice cream, Ernest Tubb had a whole bowlful of doubt to help his recovery from throat surgery. He'd spent years teaching himself to yodel like his idol Jimmie Rodgers. Now, any hope of a career yodeling the blues was gone with his tonsils. He would also have to abandon the Rodgers song repertoire he'd perfected.

For every door that closes, another opens. Forced to abandon the yodel, Tubb had to develop a new vocal style and write a whole new set of songs to accommodate it. That flat, twangy baritone with a tenuous grasp on the key would gain Ernest fame and fortune.

"You're different, you sound different, you act different, you look different; if that's the way you honestly feel it, then that's the way you want to do it, and don't let anybody change you." —Ernest Tubb

"Walking the Floor over You" was Tubb's first and biggest hit. "Waltz across Texas" was another Tubb tune that would become an instant classic. Both songs featured the relaxed, laid-back style that would become Tubb's trademark. They also showcased another long-running theme of Ernest's: He would call the soloists out from his band by name. When Ernest blithely directed attention, "All right now, Buddy Emmons . . ." or "Here we go, Leon Rhodes . . ." listeners knew a flawless steel guitar melody or impossibly nimble lick would follow. Tubb's band, the Texas Troubadours, became renowned for showcasing some of the finest musicians in country music. Such virtuoso players as Owen Bradley, Billy Byrd, and Tommy "Butterball" Page passed through the Troubadours over the years.

For decades Ernest Tubb was the dean of country musicians. He helped expand the popularity of country music by bringing the Opry to New York's Carnegie Hall in 1947. His incredible musicianship, generous support of fellow musicians, and affable style earned Tubb legions of fans on both sides of the stage door.

Aw, Shucks

Tubb was self-deprecating to a degree unusual in a country star and didn't think much of his own voice. He often told interviewers that, "If a man pointed at a jukebox playing one of my songs and said to his girlfriend, 'I can sing better than that guy,' 95 percent of them would be right." Another time duet partner Red Foley was sitting in the control room while Ernest was recording his part of "You Don't Have to Be a Baby to Cry." A visitor commented to Red, "I'll bet you wish you could hit that low note." Foley quipped, "I bet Ernest wishes he could hit that low note!"

As a 19-year-old radio singer in San Antonio at the height of the Great Depression, Tubbs made ends meet by digging ditches for the WPA.

GREATEST HITS

Year	Song
1940	"Blue Eyed Elaine"
1941	"Walking the Floor over You"
1944	"Soldier's Last Letter"
1945	"Tomorrow Never Comes"
	"It's Been So Long Darling"
1946	"Rainbow at Midnight"
	"Filipino Baby"
1948	"Blue Christmas"
1949	"You Don't Have to Be a Baby to Cry"
1965	"Waltz Across Texas"

TANYA TUCKER

October 10, 1958–

Tucker is also known as the "Texas Tornado." *Cosmopolitan* magazine described her voice as having the "kind of restless intensity that stays in your mind."

GREATEST HITS	
Year	**Song**
1972	"Delta Dawn"
	"Love's the Answer"
1973	"Blood Red and Goin' Down"
	"What's Your Mama's Name, Child"
1974	"Would You Lay with Me (In a Field of Stone)"
1975	"Lizzie and the Rainman"
1976	"Here's Some Love"
1980	"Dream Lover" (with Glen Campbell)
1987	"Love Me Like You Used To"
1988	"If It Don't Come Easy"
	"Strong Enough to Bend"
1992	"Two Sparrows in a Hurricane"

Talk about precocious! Tanya Tucker released her first record when she was a mere filly of 13. "Delta Dawn" was a hit right out of the box. Tanya's scratchy alto already sounded like she'd soaked a lifetime of hard living into her pipes. All the more remarkable that a mere girl could sound like this. What would become the trademark Tucker sass is evident already, but also a world-weariness that belied her youth. Right from the get-go, Tanya Tucker was a star; she proceeded to have five #1 singles over the next 18 months. Two in particular showed the range this kid possessed: "Blood Red and Going Down" told the tale of a child watching her father kill her cheating mother, and "Would You Lay with Me" was a love song for grownups. Thirteen, sure, but Tanya was no kid.

Shame!

When 13-year-old Tanya Tucker showed up on the country scene, she was adorable—people loved her for her spunk. But in 1978, 19-year-old Tanya released *TNT*. Boom! Back then, album covers were the size of dinner plates, 12 inches across. And Tanya filled a good portion of that 12 inches with pure sexual magnetism. Nashville was Not Amused. Oh, but she looked hot—red nails and lips, posed provocatively against a box of high explosives.

But the thing that most riled people up was the pants. Shiny, black, and stretched to within an inch of their life, those pants probably still have people upset. It wasn't just that people were shocked to see their former little girl all grown up—*TNT* looked like a contemporary rock cover. Nashville starched shirts were in an uproar, yet audiences didn't seem to care, and the album reached #2 on the country charts and crossed over into the pop market as well.

NUGGET: Tanya Tucker is a serious competitor on the cutting-horse circuit.

Right through the '70s and into the '80s Tucker scored hits. She seemed to attract controversy from the beginning. First there was the preternaturally mature child singing adult-themed songs. Later, her switch to more rocklike styles, musically and sartorially, alienated hard-core country fans even as it broadened her appeal. Offstage antics bemused the traditionally staid world of country, too: When in her 20s, Tucker scandalized Nashville by conducting a public affair with the then 40-something Glen Campbell.

Yet through all, Tanya continued to create compelling music. By the turn of the century, Tucker was semiretired until starring in *Tuckerville*, her own reality show, on cable television.

SHANIA TWAIN

August 28, 1965–

Shania Twain performs on a Nashville stage in 1995. At 22 years old, Twain lost her mother and adoptive father to a car accident. She put her music career on hold to raise her three younger siblings.

Remember the first time you laid eyes on Shania Twain? Thought so. When you snapped yourself out of it you had one thought: Shania Twain is a stone-cold fox. She may certainly be described as a perceptive songwriter and a singer with an extraordinary and formidable set of pipes. All that aside, the first, last, and middle impression people have of her is, "Wow!" Women think she's beautiful, what with her glowing skin, radiant dark mane of hair, and sparkling eyes; men generally just stare, mouths agape.

Shania's beauty is both her most formidable weapon and her cross to bear. Country music had seen beauties before, but never had people seen such a radiantly sexy woman. More, a woman who confidently displayed her charms with every bit of lighting and styling that MTV had to offer. Shania brought an incredible glow and empowerment to the table—she was incredibly sexy without being dirty.

NUGGET: In 2005 Twain was awarded the Order of Canada, her native country's highest civilian honor, given to those who "make a major difference to Canada."

Shania herself recognized early on the value of promoting herself via video and channeled her creative energy into producing amazing visual imagery at the expense of touring. She was the first country star to employ modern film techniques—long lenses, beauty lighting, and over-the-top styling—and it was just plain traffic-

GREATEST HITS	
Year	Song
1995	"Whose Bed Have Your Boots Been Under"
	"Any Man of Mine"
	"No One Needs to Know"
1997	"Come on Over"
1998	"You're Still the One"
	"From This Moment On"
1999	"Man! I Feel Like a Woman"
	"That Don't Impress Me Much"
2002	"I'm Gonna Getcha Good!"
	"Up!"
2003	"Forever and for Always"
	"She's Not Just a Pretty Face"
2004	"Party for Two" (with Billy Currington)

Says Twain about her producer: "Mutt was able to bring out a presence in my voice that I usually only use when I'm songwriting with my acoustic guitar."

In the Dog House

The epitome of a reclusive genius, Robert "Mutt" Lange produced some of the greatest heavy-metal albums of all time. Things like AC/DC's *Highway to Hell* and Def Leppard's *Pyromania*. After a decade of producing monster metal, Mutt heard Shania's first album and felt the same way she did—it seemed a poor reflection of her talent and potential. Mutt wrote Shania a letter explaining this and explaining how he would like to remedy that. Six months of hours-long phone calls ensued. When the two finally met in person, the proverbial sparks flew. After love came marriage, and then they released the album they'd been working on, *The Woman in Me*, and changed country music forever.

Shania's records are indeed collaborations with Mutt. Though her name is on the marquee, Mutt is doing far more than twiddling knobs. He and Shania write all the songs together, and he plays various instruments as well. But it is his production that really shines. Shania's playful and sexy voice is brought front and center, of course, but Mutt manipulates the instruments and effects to give her records a unique sound. Even Shania's voice gets the occasional effect added—to startling effect—on songs such as "I'm Gonna Getcha Good."

Mutt is notoriously publicity shy; the couple live in a chalet in Switzerland, and they're reportedly moving to a sheep station in New Zealand. His musical connection with Shania continues, and the couple show no sign of ceasing to create groundbreaking country music for the foreseeable future.

stopping. If she wasn't slinking around a beach in a barely-there cover-up, she was prancing around the desert dressed head to toe in leopard print or perhaps zooming around on a set reminiscent of *Tron*. Old-timers and hidebound critics complained that Shania was cheapening country with all her navel-baring antics. Audiences cared not a whit for what those old-fogie critics thought. They went ahead and made Shania an international superstar and an emblematic country act of the '90s.

Of course, all this talk about Shania's looks belies the fact that the records she makes with her husband and producer, Mutt Lange, are full of great songs. Twain and Lange built up the image of a feisty, confident woman, unafraid of her own sexuality or the man's world in which she swims. "That Don't Impress Me Much" opens with a purr and then devolves to Shania's laughingly delivered denunciations of macho suitors. Mutt's guitars and production fillips are there too, underscoring and contrasting Shania's sassy attitude. "Man, I Feel Like a Woman" lets Twain stake a claim to her prerogative to "have a little fun." That video had a band of "himbos" backing up Shania in an affectionate homage to Robert Palmer's seminal "Addicted to Love" video.

When she did get around to touring, Shania put together a great-sounding band that could translate the studio perfection of Mutt's production into a live show. Any rumors that Shania didn't tour because she couldn't perform live were laid to rest in 1998. The "Come on Over" international tour broke box office records and was considered hugely successful on all scores.

In 2002, after a two-year hiatus, Shania came roaring back with *Up!* "Forever and Always" showed that Twain and Lange could still come up with the goods. This perky love song showcased Shania's appealingly packaged vocals playing against and around Lange's catchy guitar breaks and effects tricks.

The door that Shania busted open won't be shut again. Following her success, other country women embraced their sexuality and weren't afraid to flaunt it on video. Faith Hill, Martina McBride, and even a look-who's-grown-up-now LeAnn Rimes produced hugely successful videos showcasing their looks alongside their talent.

A Canadian who lives in a Swiss chalet, Twain has no down-home country image. Still, she is a global superstar on the country music scene.

CONWAY TWITTY

SEPTEMBER 1, 1933–JUNE 5, 1993

Conway Twitty was the greatest hit-maker in country during his lifetime. He had the soulful, deep voice, the emotionally charged phrasing, and the heartthrob looks that were the makings of a teen idol. And that's what he was, until he tired of rock and roll and found his true calling in country. Throughout the '60s and '70s, it was a no-brainer. Where's Conway Twitty? Oh, there he is—hogging #1, as usual. A great singer who was a first-rate interpreter of others' songs, Twitty was a respected songwriter as well: He penned 11 of his forty #1 hits. His smooth delivery and sophisticated subject matter helped make country music appealing to an adult audience.

NUGGET: The teen-idol character of "Conrad Birdie" in the musical *Bye Bye Birdie* is based on Conway Twitty.

GREATEST HITS

YEAR	SONG
1958	"It's Only Make Believe"
1959	"Danny Boy"
1960	"Lonely Blue Boy"
	"What Am I Living For"
1961	"C'est Ci Bon"
1968	"The Image of Me"
	"Next in Line"
1970	"Hello, Darlin'"
1971	"How Much More Can She Stand"
1973	"Baby's Gone"
	"You've Never Been This Far Before"
1975	"Linda on My Mind"
1980	"I'd Love to Lay You Down"
1981	"Tight Fittin' Jeans"
1986	"Desperado Love"

Conway Twitty's name is an amalgam of Conway, Arkansas, and Twitty, Texas. Harold Lloyd Jenkins doesn't have that country ring to it. Twitty originally planned on a career in baseball—he was even offered a spot on the Phillies. A tour of duty in Korea sidelined the sports career. Then, when Twitty heard Elvis, he headed straight for Memphis, where Sam Phillips was impressed enough to give him a chance at Sun Records. A few years of struggling later, Twitty hit the jackpot with "It's Only Make Believe," which features the Jordanaires on backup. But Twitty's country career was unstoppable once it started up in the mid-'60s, thanks in part to producer Owen Bradley's influence.

HIS FATHER WAS A MISSISSIPPI FERRYBOAT CAPTAIN, AND HIS GRANDFATHER TAUGHT HIM TO PLAY GUITAR. AT 12 YEARS OLD CONWAY TWITTY WAS PLAYING ON AN ARKANSAS RADIO STATION.

For a solid 10 years, Loretta Lynn was Twitty's constant duet partner. Starting in 1971, they performed together and recorded an album of duets a year. The two enjoyed 14 Top 10 hits, while both continued solo careers. Twitty was a good businessman, too, investing in property and opening an amusement park called Twitty City. But Twitty's sultry, earnest, and masterly way with a song will always be his greatest legacy.

Is It Hot in Here?

The sexiest man in country? A lot of his fans would say that was Conway Twitty. Many of his songs had an overtone of sensuality, and when he sidled right up close to the mic and dropped his voice down low, hearts beat a little faster. His "You've Never Been This Far Before," with its suggestion of an imminent deflowering, was banned by several radio stations. He kept things pretty clean on his duets with Loretta Lynn—they had great chemistry, but she was a respectable married woman, after all. Twitty saved his steamiest songs for his solo efforts, like "I'd Love to Lay You Down" and his smoky version of the Pointer Sisters' "Slow Hand."

PORTER WAGONER

August 12, 1927–

Born in Missouri's music-rich Ozark Mountains, Wagoner grew up on a farm. TV viewers came to know him by his rhinestone-covered clothes and blond pompadour.

No overnight success for Porter Wagoner, no sir. The tall skinny kid from Missouri worked his way up from playing between broom sessions at the local market to hosting at the Grand Ole Opry, and then starring in his own television show. Along the way, Wagoner always mixed the traditional and the modern. His blend of honky-tonk, hard country, and sentimental tearjerkers was a moderate success. Which is how he came to showcase old-time country on the newest high-tech medium of the time: television.

"Porter Wagoner's music is timeless and truly a piece of America's musical tapestry." —Marty Stuart

The Porter Wagoner Show

Porter already had plenty of stage experience when he was offered his own television show in 1960. He'd been a member of the Opry for four years and had clocked hours and hours of local radio before that. So *The Porter Wagoner Show* seemed a natural for the lanky Missourian. And oh, what a natural! The show would run for 21 years and ultimately be viewed in more than 100 markets. Before *Hee Haw* or Country Music Television, *The Porter Wagoner Show* was where America got its country. And the look and feel of the show, from Wagoner's flashy Nudie suits to the easy banter between musicians, colored the way America viewed country for decades.

The show was already doing quite well when Wagoner found he needed a new singer to replace the departing Norma Jean. A tiny little gal with an hourglass figure and huge hair was tapped for the role. Young Dolly Parton was completely unknown at the time—a condition that was corrected the moment she opened her mouth. Audiences were enthralled, and Wagoner recognized a good thing when he saw it. Dolly became his costar, and the pair sang regular duets. They complemented each other perfectly. Like Fred and Ginger, he gave her class, and she gave him sex appeal. Their first single together, "The Last Thing on My Mind," rocketed up the charts even as they continued to perform regularly together on TV. Seven years of Top 10 hits would follow.

In 1975, amid much acrimony, Dolly left both the show and her partnership with Wagoner. They later resolved their differences and continued to occasionally duet into the '80s. She went on to unparalleled acclaim as a solo artist, while Wagoner continued to film his TV show and sporadically record. But none of his solo work was as successful as the duets with Dolly.

GREATEST HITS

Year	Song
1954	"Company's Comin'"
1955	"A Satisfied Mind"
1956	"Eat Drink and Be Merry (Tomorrow You'll Cry)"
1962	"Misery Loves Company"
1965	"Green, Green Grass of Home"
1966	"Skid Row Joe"
1967	"The Last Thing on My Mind" (with Dolly Parton)
1969	"Just Someone I Used to Know" (with Dolly Parton)
1975	"Say Forever You'll Be Mine" (with Dolly Parton)
1976	"Is Forever Longer than Always" (with Dolly Parton)
1980	"Making Plans" (with Dolly Parton)

KITTY WELLS

AUGUST 30, 1918–

Naughty boys! Kitty Wells' first career move was to dole out a slap on the wrist, in the form of a song. The song was "It Wasn't God Who Made Honky Tonk Angels," and the wrist was Hank Thompson's. Wells' 1952 hit was an "answer song" to Thompson's "The Wild Side of Life," which contained the line "I didn't know God made honky-tonk angels." Kitty answered that God didn't make good girls go wrong—men did. Cheating men, to be specific. Her stance was controversial. To defend fallen women by blaming their philandering husbands was a mite irregular, and some radio stations refused to even air the tune. As the Dixie Chicks can tell you, though, controversy sells. And this song sold big—to the tune of 800,000 copies.

NUGGET: Kitty followed her 1952 success with another rebuke. Her 1953 "Paying for That Back Street Affair" was an answer to Webb Pierce's "Back Street Affair."

Kitty Wells had been gigging around her native Nashville for some time before her big hit. Born Muriel Ellen Deason, she changed her name at the suggestion of her husband, musician Johnnie Wright. It was borrowed from the traditional folksong "I'm Going to Marry Kitty Wells." During her bountiful career, Wells played a reverse game of the "lady in the drawing room, hellcat in the bedroom" routine. In her private life, Kitty was a homemaker, faithful wife, and devoted mother. On stage, while maintaining her gingham-and-lace ladylike demeanor, she told the poignant tales of women sinning, spurned, or caught in impossible, bittersweet love affairs.

HER MOTHER WAS A GOSPEL SINGER, HER UNCLE AND FATHER COUNTRY MUSICIANS. MUSIC WAS IN WELLS' BLOOD, AND HER FIRST RADIO PERFORMANCES WERE WITH HER SISTERS AND A COUSIN.

The effect of Wells' success can't be overestimated. Kitty opened the doors for many great female artists to come, from Patsy Cline to Loretta Lynn to Dolly Parton. During the 1991 Grammy Awards, Kitty Wells became the first female country artist to receive a Lifetime Achievement Award. The same night, Wells was awarded for her collaboration with k.d. lang, Loretta Lynn, and Brenda Lee on a medley called—what else? "Honky Tonk Angels."

GREATEST HITS

YEAR	SONG
1952	"It Wasn't God Who Made Honky Tonk Angels"
1953	"Paying for That Back Street Affair"
1954	"Release Me"
1955	"As Long as I Live" (with Red Foley)
	"Making Believe"
1958	"She's No Angel"
	"I Can't Stop Loving You"
1962	"Heartbreak USA"
	"Will Your Lawyer Talk to God?"
1968	"My Big Truck Drivin' Man"

Name That Tune

You can sure get a lot of mileage out of a good tune. Such is the case with Kitty Wells' "It Wasn't God Who Made Honky Tonk Angels," written by J. D. Miller. The melody duplicated Hank Thompson's "The Wild Side of Life." But Hank, in his turn, had slightly modified Roy Acuff's "The Great Speckled Bird." Well, hold on a minute, now. Seems that Acuff tune (written by Reverend Guy Smith) was lifted from the Carter Family's "I Am Thinking Tonight of My Blue Eyes." And the buck stops there—though who knows whether A. P. Carter himself didn't pay a nickel to some hillbilly for the tune, as was his wont. Imitation is the sincerest form of flattery.

HANK WILLIAMS

SEPTEMBER 17, 1923–JANUARY 1, 1953

You owe Hank Williams. Without him you'd have no Willie, no Johnny, no Merle—heck, no Elvis, no Dylan, no Springsteen. Hank started it all. His rough-hewn performing style, direct emotional connection with the songs, and energetic vocal delivery made him a star. But it was the songs themselves that made him a legend. Hank's timeless lyrics, unforgettable tunes, and heartfelt delivery have become as indigenous to the American landscape as the hills of Alabama where he was born. Hank Williams' life and lyrics combine to form a mythic figure who stands taller than any other in country.

"If a song can't be written in 20 minutes, it ain't worth writing." —Hank Williams

And he recorded for only six years! In those six brief years, Williams produced a body of work that defined country music and set the stage for nearly all popular music to come. One can't help but wonder what he might have done had he lived longer, but like many legends, he flamed out at the height of his popularity. No coincidence that "I'll Never Get Out of This World Alive" was his last single.

Hank was an enigma to most who knew him or worked with him. Born with a congenital spine condition, probably spina bifida, young Hank was in near-constant pain. He got used to bearing his pain in silence, watching others, separate and alone. That pain accompanied him his entire life. That stoic silence followed him his whole life too—even those closest to him claimed not to know him. He was a taciturn cipher to most who encountered him. The only way to know Hank was through his music.

Hank Williams got his start as "that singing kid" in the late '30s on local radio in Alabama. He was successful enough to be able to subsidize musicians to be his Drifting Cowboys. Drift they did, touring the South with Williams' mom, Lillie, booking gigs. The War Department intervened in Hank's nascent career by drafting every one of the Cowboys. And in a sign of things to come, the radio station fired him for repeatedly showing up drunk for the show.

His brilliance and his self-destructive tendencies would fight within him for the whole of his short career. The brilliance began to show itself in 1947, when Hank recorded "Move It on Over," his first

GEORGE HAMILTON PLAYS WILLIAMS IN MGM'S 1964 FILM. THE MOVIE WAS TITLED FOR A SONG THAT HAS BEEN COVERED BY LOUIS ARMSTRONG, PATSY CLINE, ELVIS PRESLEY, AND RAY CHARLES.

GREATEST HITS

Year	Song
1947	"Move It on Over"
1948	"Honky Tonkin'"
	"I Saw the Light"
1949	"Lovesick Blues"
	"I'm So Lonesome I Could Cry"
1950	"Why Don't You Love Me"
1951	"Cold Cold Heart"
	"Hey Good Lookin'"
1952	"Jambalaya"
	"Settin' the Woods on Fire"
	"You Win Again"
	"I'll Never Get Out of This World Alive"
1953	"Your Cheatin' Heart"
1989	"There's a Tear in My Beer" (dubbed recording with Hank Williams Jr.)

THROUGH THE PHYSICAL DETERIORATION, ALCOHOLISM, AND MARITAL WOES, WILLIAMS WAS CONSISTENTLY RED HOT IN THE STUDIO. HE RECORDED TOP 10 HITS RIGHT UP UNTIL HIS DEATH.

Book of Luke

Superman's got Clark Kent, Jekyll had Hyde, and Hank Williams had Luke the Drifter. In contrast to Hank's drunken, womanizing lout, the alter ego he created was the preacher man, traveling the country saving souls. Hank would be honky-tonkin' all night, carousing 'til the cows came home. But Luke was the kind of character who would show up in church the next morning, collar stiff, nails clean, ready to denounce the high life. Hank's "Luke the Drifter" recordings, released after his death as *Hank Williams Sings Luke the Drifter*, had similar instrumentation to Hank's "real" records. These songs were long tone poems, however, with Hank—er, Luke—delivering stories that ended up sounding a lot more like sermons. He didn't sing, he testified. And when he sang it was more like gospel than that high lonesome that folks were used to.

While Hank's tunes were about drinking Saturday night, Luke was beyond days of the week. He was worried about your soul. "Be Careful of Stones That You Throw" told a tale of a girl shunned by self-righteous parents. Parents whose daughter is later saved by, you guessed it, the outcast. Or "Picture of Life's Other Side," which offered various vignettes of bad-living folk getting their just desserts.

Luke the Drifter was a fascinating diversion for an artist of Hank's larger-than-life appetites and talents. Luke could well have been created at the behest of the record company, worried that fans couldn't deal with this moralistic side of their normally fun-loving star. Hank Williams was notoriously difficult to know in any way other than his songs. How curious that when he took off the Superman costume, he found a sanctimonious preacher lurking underneath. Williams' star burned so bright and hot, he was described as writing songs "compulsively." Perhaps Luke became a vessel for Hank's remorse at his louche behavior. Or not. Maybe he just woke up on Sunday, determined to put down the bottle, behave better, and get some savin.' But of course, Saturday night comes around soon enough, and a little of that 'shine might taste mighty fine right about now . . .

huge hit. This tragicomic tale of a hapless husband forced to negotiate bed space with the family pooch set the standard for what would be a string of rapid-fire hits. "Lovesick Blues," "I'm So Lonesome I Could Cry," "Why Don't You Love Me," and "Cold Cold Heart" followed in quick succession.

Yet the more successful Williams became, the worse his troubles became. He drank, cheated, drank, was cheated on, and drank some more. Yet through it all, he wrote some of our greatest songs. The list is long, but the fact that they were created in just a few years is astonishing. Hank died in the back of a Cadillac limo on the way to a New Year's Day gig; the probable cause was an overdose of morphine. Hank was trying to leave the bottle behind and control his pain any way he could. America grieved the loss of this flash of brightness—his funeral was one of the largest Alabama had ever seen.

WILLIAMS' SONGS CROSSED GENRE BOUNDARIES. WHEN TONY BENNETT COVERED "COLD COLD HEART" IN 1951, HE BECAME REGARDED AS ONE OF AMERICA'S GREAT POPULAR TUNESMITHS.

SMILING FOR THE CAMERAS, AUDREY AND HANK WILLIAMS SHARE A RARE PEACEFUL MOMENT IN THEIR OTHERWISE TUMULTUOUS AND TROUBLED MARRIAGE.

Miss Audrey

Crash! Bam! Clatter! Oh, don't mind the noise. That's just Hank and Audrey at it with the dishes again. Wait, Audrey! Not the teapot!

Behind every great man there's a great woman. Behind Hank there was a great deal of trouble and strife—"rocky marriage" doesn't begin to describe it. Hank Williams and Audrey Mae Sheppard were married at a gas station on the outskirts of Andalusia, Alabama. The 1944 wedding was officiated by a justice of the peace, and that was the last domestic peace that Hank ever knew. Married twice and divorced twice (they split for good in 1952), Hank and Audrey had one of the most acrimonious relationships in show business history.

By all accounts Audrey was a hectoring, pesky backstage presence. And when she stepped onto the stage itself, matters were even worse. Audrey frequently invited herself onstage with Hank to play double bass and exercise her vocal pipes (to call it "singing" would be charitable). One critic likened Audrey's dulcet tones to "fingernails scraping down a blackboard."

Now granted, the woman was living with a hard-drinking man. No one knows what goes on behind closed doors, et cetera. But there's another reason to look past the marital strife: the songs. Hank channeled all that fussin' and fightin' into his songwriting, giving us such classics of conjugal bliss as "Move It on Over" (spoken to the dog, who has to make room in the doghouse for the beleaguered husband) and "Your Cheatin' Heart." Faithfulness, it seems, wasn't at the top of the Williamses' list of virtues. So let's tip our hat to Audrey for giving Hank the material for his dozens of brilliant songs of misery.

HANK WILLIAMS JR.

MAY 26, 1949–

Though Hank Williams Jr. was only 3 years old when his famous father died, by the age of 11 he was up on stage singing Hank Sr.'s songs in a nearly identical voice. Hank Jr.'s first single, at age 14, was "Long Gone Lonesome Blues," a virtual Hank Sr. imitation. Two years later Hank Jr. did the soundtrack to *Your Cheating Heart*, a documentary on his father's career. Hank even took on the nickname Bocephus, his daddy's pet name for him.

But having thoroughly tilled the soil of imitation, Hank had grown sick of just being a doppelganger of his famous father. He found his own path, leaving behind the high-lonesome sound for the allure of country rock and Southern boogie. In the song "Family Tradition," he came to terms with his legacy. Williams explicitly and musically staked a claim to his own style while acknowledging his roots. The song was a huge success, and Williams moved into the ranks of country superstars. In the '80s alone he scored 35 Top 10 singles. His unrepentantly rowdy, fun-loving persona came across in songs and videos so strongly that even the Nashville establishment had to acknowledge his talent.

"I've been around a long time, and life still has a whole lot of surprises for me." —Hank Williams Jr.

In 1989, Hank Jr. came full circle by recording "There's a Tear in My Beer," his father's old honky-tonk song. Using modern recording and video technology, Hank Jr. appeared to sing and play along with Sr., with all the makings of a bona fide family reunion.

NUGGET: The beard, scraggly hair, dark shades, and big ol' hat on Hank Jr. aren't affectations. In 1975 a serious mountaineering accident in Montana left Williams with a shattered skull and face. After nine surgeries to put him back together, he needs all those props to cover the scars.

GREATEST HITS

YEAR	SONG
1964	"Long Gone Lonesome Blues"
1965	"Mule Skinner Blues" (with Connie Francis)
1968	"It's All Over but the Crying"
1979	"Family Tradition"
1981	"All My Rowdy Friends Have Settled Down"
1982	"A Country Boy Can Survive"
1984	"All My Rowdy Friends Are Coming over Tonight"
1989	"If the South Woulda Won"
	"There's a Tear in My Beer" (with Hank Williams Sr.)
1990	"Ain't Nobody's Business"
1992	"Come On Over to the Country"
1995	"Hog Wild"

HE LEARNED PIANO FROM JERRY LEE LEWIS AND GUITAR FROM JOHNNY CASH. WITH A VOICE LIKE HIS FATHER'S AND AN ARSENAL OF SONGS, HANK JR. WAS BOUND FOR STARDOM.

Are You Ready for Some Football?

In 1991, executives from *Monday Night Football* heard Williams' "All My Rowdy Friends Are Coming over Tonight" and thought it fit with the image *MNF* wanted to project. Indeed, with a reworked lyric "All My Rowdy Friends Are Here on Monday Night" the song was a total smash as the theme for the popular sports program. Four years in a row Williams won Emmy awards for his work on the opening montage. Some 16 years later the theme is still popular, and Williams reworks it every few years. For 2006, when *Monday Night Football* switched networks from ABC to ESPN, Hank redid the theme yet again, this time with an all-star band. Little Richard, Steven Van Zandt, Bootsy Collins, and Charlie Daniels joined Williams to jam on this now-classic anthem.

LUCINDA WILLIAMS

JANUARY 26, 1953–

Lucinda Williams takes all the heartache and yearning of her country sisters before her and raises them one. But she does it in a thoroughly modern way. From her early indie albums to her 1998 breakthrough *Car Wheels on a Gravel Road* to her most recent *West*, Williams is a poet, provocateur, and a disarmingly passionate singer. Her self-penned songs describe the drunken angels and broken hearts of her predecessors like Loretta and Kitty, but she allows the complexity and nuance of modern love to shimmer between the lines. In her dry, crackled voice, she traces the outlines of love and loss in its many forms: broken relationships, mourning, loneliness. And then she kicks it all out with a sexy, joyful number like "Right in Time."

People have puzzled over Lucinda; it was never clear just how to peg her. Was she folk? Rock? Country? Cajun? Blues? How about all of the above? She's a native of Lake Charles, Louisiana, but her dad was an English professor. The only convenient category was the catch-all "roots music." Williams' roots go back to her early love of music as diverse as the Delta blues, Hank Williams (no relation), and Leonard Cohen. The simple answer is that Lucinda Williams is an original. She's often tagged as a singer-songwriter, but she's cut from the same bittersweet cloth as Willie Nelson, Bob Dylan, and John Prine. Williams' sultry, croaky twang is uniquely her own.

Two things Lucinda Williams has no shortage of: great songs and ardent fans, many of them her fellow musicians. Her songs have been covered by Emmylou Harris, Mary Chapin Carpenter, Patty Loveless, and Tom Petty, among others. Lucinda's 2007 release, *West*, is an elegiac set of songs, touching on both the death of her mother and a blossoming new love in her life.

"I guess you could write a good song if your heart hadn't been broken, but I don't know of anyone whose heart hasn't been broken."

—Lucinda Williams

GREATEST HITS

YEAR	SONG
1982	"Sweet Old World"
1988	"Change the Locks"
1998	"Right in Time"
	"Car Wheels on a Gravel Road"
	"Joy"
	"Can't Let Go"
2001	"Get Right with God"
	"Essence"
2003	"Righteously"
2007	"Are You Alright?"
	"Mama You Sweet"

Picky, Picky!

Williams is known for her exacting standards when recording. Her reputation precedes her into the studio but gets left in the dust when she emerges with the goods. A few Grammy wins, a passel of ecstatic reviews, and pretty soon the labor pains are forgotten. Or should be. Her attention to detail has been called obsessive—like when Williams worked with a succession of great producers to endlessly tweak an album's worth of songs. First Gurf Morlix, then Steve Earle, and finally Roy Bittan all worked over her set of songs, with Lucinda watching their every move. You could call it perfectionism. But when it yields perfection—in this case *Car Wheels on a Gravel Road*—who's to argue?

EMMYLOU HARRIS CALLED WILLIAMS "THE BEST OF WHAT COUNTRY AT LEAST SAYS IT IS." HER *CAR WHEELS ON A GRAVEL ROAD* WON LUCINDA A GRAMMY FOR BEST CONTEMPORARY FOLK ALBUM.

BOB WILLS

March 6, 1905–May 13, 1975

Western swing. It just sounds cool. And it was. A wild stew of musical influences, Western swing combined elements of honky-tonk, blues, and jazz. It was the country version of the big-band sound. And nobody swung like Bob Wills and his Texas Playboys. They were the paragons of Western swing throughout the '40s and into the '50s. Originally in Oklahoma and later in California, Wills stocked his Playboys with excellent musicians, adding members until there were eight male musicians and a pair of female backup singers joining him onstage. He added horns, reeds, drums, and steel guitars to the lineup. Later, after returning from the war, he replaced the horns with electric guitars, becoming one of the first country stars to embrace the new technology that was changing rock and pop so quickly.

Wills had always been a band leader and developed an emcee stage persona that enabled him to showcase others while still being the one with the name on the marquee. His trademark "ah-ha"s could be heard on radio and record, as he bantered with his bandmates and the audience. But above it all, the Playboys could swing. The music was just made for dancing, and hits like "San Antonio Rose" were reworked with the addition of words ("New San Antonio Rose") and became hits all over again.

Wills grew up playing frontier fiddle music with East Texas migrant workers and African-Americans. His Western swing sound was influenced by ragtime, blues, and jazz.

"I think I was singing when I was born."—Bob Wills

By the '50s, as the big-band sound was fading from the pop scene, so, too, did Western swing wane in popularity. Wills' personal problems with alcohol began to affect his professional life, and a series of poor business decisions left him with ever-diminishing options. By the mid '60s Wills was still touring, but the Playboys were no more. Even decades after his death, Bob Wills remains a strong influence and important part of the country music story.

GREATEST HITS

Year	Song
1938	"Ida Red"
	"San Antonio Rose"
1941	"Take Me Back to Tulsa"
	"Cherokee Maiden"
1944	"New San Antonio Rose"
1946	"New Spanish Two Step"
1947	"Thorn in My Heart"
1950	"Ida Red Likes the Boogie"
	"Faded Love"
1954	"Cadillac in Model 'A'"

A Ride with Bob

Ray Benson had been touring with Asleep at the Wheel for more than 30 years, playing Western swing—lots of Bob Wills tunes in particular. In 2005, he had a vision and turned it into *A Ride with Bob*. This theatrical and musical journey involves elaborate sets, 25 actors, and 15 of Wills' best-loved tunes. "San Antonio Rose," "Faded Love," and "Ida Red" play between colorful stories of Will's life. From the 300-seat theater in Austin where it started, *A Ride with Bob* has played in ever-bigger venues. The show was most recently staged for the president and first lady at the Kennedy Center.

LEE ANN WOMACK

AUGUST 19, 1966–

"Take Our Daughters to Work Day" sure worked for Lee Ann Womack. When your dad is a DJ, and you've got the music bug, what could be better? Lee Ann grew up around music, soaking in the classics of country, from Bob Wills to George and Tammy to Dolly Parton. By the time she got to college, majoring in country and bluegrass (you can do that?!), she was honing her gorgeous soprano voice with her college band, Country Caravan.

It had to happen: This girl was Nashville bound. She arrived there in 1990, as a student at Belmont University. Seven years later, after marriage and one child, Lee Ann had paid her dues at local showcases and attracted Music Row attention. Her platinum-selling first album—on the legendary Decca label—was like a blast from the past, with its traditional country sound and Lee Ann's powerful, lilting vocals. Plus, it didn't hurt that she was a knockout. Lee Ann seemed to be channeling the best of the past; she has carved out a place in contemporary country that embraces her heritage while hewing to a straightforward, honest sound—a lot like her friend and booster, George Strait.

Since her first album, Lee Ann has had a wary relationship with pop. Turns out that it's not her best friend. When she treads too close to the mainstream, such as on her 2002 album, *Something Worth Leaving Behind*, her fans don't follow her there. Her new album, due out in 2007, promises to reprise the formula that gave Lee Ann her biggest hit to date, "I Hope You Dance." On that tune, she laid it all out on the table: moving lyrics, great arrangements, and her beautiful voice in perfect control. Go, girl!

GREATEST HITS

Year	Song
1997	"Never Again, Again"
	"The Fool"
	"You've Got to Talk to Me"
1998	"A Little Past Little Rock"
	"(Now You See Me) Now You Don't"
	"I'll Think of a Reason Later"
2000	"I Hope You Dance"
	"Why They Call It Falling"
	"Does My Ring Burn Your Finger"
2002	"Something Worth Leaving Behind"
	"Mendocino County Line" (with Willie Nelson)
2005	"I May Hate Myself in the Morning"
	"Good News, Bad News" (with George Strait)

"Some people take voice lessons to learn how to sing," says Womack, "but I just sat and listened to country records, like George Jones, Dolly Parton and stuff like that."

"It's hard for me to pass up any song that has a lot of ache in it."—Lee Ann Womack

Dance

Lee Ann Womack has described herself as an "old soul." Her wise and lovely greatest hit, "I Hope You Dance," makes it pretty clear that's true. Part mother's prayer, part words of wisdom, the song is dedicated to her two daughters, Aubrie and Anna Lise, who are featured in the video. The song has such universal appeal that it brought Lee Ann huge crossover success. It doesn't sound exactly country, but it has those elements of faith and fortitude that ring true. Her advice to her girls (and fans): "When you have a chance to sit it out or dance, I hope you dance."

TAMMY WYNETTE

May 5, 1942–April 6, 1998

For somebody who became known as the First Lady of Country, Tammy Wynette sure lived a complicated personal life. She could be a simultaneously compelling, exasperating, complicated, and quixotic figure.

Right from her first hit single, "Your Good Girl's Gonna Go Bad," Tammy showed a distinctly different take on the subject of domestic affairs. The narrator claims to be a virtuous woman whose man is out carousing. Instead of berating him, she threatens (or offers?) to decorate up their home like a bar and "be the swingin'-est swinger you've ever had." This was a novel perspective for a country song to project, to say the least.

Next up was "D-I-V-O-R-C-E," perhaps the greatest marriage song ever. Tammy's voice is absolutely in top form. The pathos of trying to keep a domestic upheaval from the kids, and the catch in Wynette's voice vaulted the song to the pinnacle of tragic country relationship songs and cemented Wynette's stature as the reigning domestic arbiter of country music. And yet, all this was but a prelude.

The year 1968 was a turbulent time in gender relations. Women were burning their bras, men were going off to war, and the hippies were inventing "free love" in San Francisco. "Stand by Your Man" hit the country music world like a bomb. Tammy Wynette acquired a signature song, and the country world received a reactionary manifesto. Talk about a feminist's worst nightmare! "And if you love him, oh be proud of him, 'cause after all he's just a man." The song was a huge hit and instantly achieved classic status. For all her other spectacular vocal work, Tammy would be forever tarred as the woman who put those feminists in their place and staunchly defended her right to be subservient.

NUGGET: During the 1992 presidential campaign, Hillary Clinton was interviewed about her marriage on *60 Minutes*. "I'm not some little woman, standing by my man like Tammy Wynette," said the future first lady. A tempest in a teapot ensued. Wynette demanded, and received, an apology from Ms. Clinton.

"I spent 15 minutes writing 'Stand by Your Man' and a lifetime defending it."—Tammy Wynette

The next year Wynette wed George Jones and they began an artistic collaboration that would outlast the marriage. On those duets and her solo work Wynette continued to mine the same familiar yet complicated territory of domestic relations.

NUGGET: In 2003 "Stand by Your Man" was voted the #1 country song of all time by a group of writers, producers, and musicians. When Country Music Television did a special on the list, Martina McBride was given the honor of singing Tammy's signature number.

At Wembley Stadium during the Country Music Festival in 1976. Wynette had twenty #1 hits by the end of the '80s and had sold more than 30 million records.

GREATEST HITS	
YEAR	SONG
1967	"Apartment No. 9"
	"I Don't Wanna Play House"
	"My Elusive Dreams"
1967	"Your Good Girl's Gonna Go Bad"
1968	"D-I-V-O-R-C-E"
	"Stand by Your Man"
1969	"The Ways to Love a Man"
1970	"He Loves Me All the Way"
	"Run Woman Run"
1971	"Good Lovin' (Makes It Right)"
1972	"Bedtime Story"
	"My Man"
	"'Til I Get It Right"
1973	"We're Gonna Hold On" (with George Jones)
1974	"We're Not the Jet Set" (with George Jones)
	"Another Lonely Song"
1976	"'Til I Can Make It on My Own"
	"Golden Ring" (with George Jones)
	"You and Me"
1980	"Two Story House" (with George Jones)

She had Top 10 country hits regularly throughout the '70s. Health problems and declining record sales forced Wynette into retirement during the '80s.

Tammy had one of the greatest voices and most beguiling personalities ever to hit the country scene. "Sometimes it's hard to be a woman," indeed. Tammy showed us all that no matter how hard it was, if you loved hard enough and held your head up high enough, you'd not just be a woman, you'd be a lady—the First Lady of Country.

"STAND BY YOUR MAN" DESCRIBES AN UNDERSTANDING WIFE, BUT WYNETTE WAS KNOWN TO BE PROFESSIONAL AND TOUGH, A "STEEL MAGNOLIA" IN THE COUNTRY MUSIC BUSINESS.

Mrs. Jones

When two country stars collided, especially two known for living the hard lives they chronicled in song, sparks were bound to fly. And fly they did, from the beginning to the end. George Jones had already gotten close to Tammy Wynette; then he happened to be present during a vociferous argument between Tammy and the second Mr. Wynette. At Jones' urging, Wynette and her daughters climbed into his Cadillac, never to return. George and Tammy were married in 1969. Their voices combined as well as their personalities, and they would go on to produce some of the greatest duets in the history of country music.

Take two volatile country stars, a dollop of righteously aggrieved womanhood, and a couple teaspoons of macho boundary issues. Gently stir in the pressures of performing together, add a dash of alcohol—no, make that two dashes; heck, pour in the whole bottle. Shake vigorously, and you have a cocktail unlike any seen in country music before or since.

Jones and Wynette recorded a whole slew of songs together, many of which were about their own supposed domestic bliss. They even released "The Ceremony," which included a "minister" conducting a marriage ceremony, where the principals repeat their vows in song. Then there was "Golden Ring" where the two righteously declare, "only love can make a golden wedding ring." Meanwhile, country's "First Couple" were having offstage domestic problems mostly caused by Jones' prodigious alcohol abuse. They were divorced in 1975.

Years later, in 1980, Wynette and Jones reunited for "Two Story House." The story is of a young couple just starting out at life yearning for a two-story house. In perfect country irony, after years of marriage, the couple indeed gets their two-story house, but "she's got her story, and I've got mine."

TRISHA YEARWOOD

September 19, 1964–

Yearwood came to Nashville to study at Belmont University. She paid her dues as a backup artist and by performing on demos for songwriters.

In an industry littered with yodelers, squeakers, crooners, belters, and passing familiarity with key, Tricia Yearwood has The Voice. It's not just that she can hit a note with bull's-eye accuracy or have that muscular control all through her astonishing range. No, no, it's the emotional control and humanity that make Yearwood's voice unique. She can sell a character like nobody else, her rich, yearning voice dragging listeners into the world of the song. Trisha's voice has an ineffable quality first recognized by Nashville insiders, then the public at large. They say if you can fake sincerity you've got it made, but Trisha exudes realism—she doesn't have to fake it because she's so believable nobody every questions it in the first place.

"What's meant to be will always find a way."—Tricia Yearwood

Yearwood first found success as a backup singer for such country greats as Garth Brooks, Emmylou Harris, Reba McEntire, and Vince Gill, but it was clear from the beginning that she was destined for greater things. Even on her eponymous debut album, people sat up and noticed The Voice. "She's In Love with the Boy" burst onto the Nashville scene in 1991 and quickly jumped to #1. An unbroken string of #1 singles followed as the general public caught on to what Nashville insiders had known for years.

"Thinking about You," "The Woman before Me," and "XXX's and OOO's" continued Trisha's penchant for singing upbeat, emotionally evocative songs that would be huge hits. Between her solo recording, touring, collaborations, and film soundtracks Trisha's voice would form a large portion of the sound of country in the '90s. Expanding the reach and breadth of country music, Trisha even sang with opera star Luciano Pavarotti at the War Children of Liberia benefit.

NUGGET: Tricia recently acted in a recurring role on the television show *JAG*. She played attorney Teresa Coulter, a Navy forensic coroner who assists the title character in defending the innocent and prosecuting the guilty.

Through it all her exquisite technical chops have allowed her to take on an astounding variety of vocal roles, while her musicality and emotion have made her voice such an integral part of modern country music.

Garth + Tricia

Garth Brooks and Tricia Yearwood admired each other as professional colleagues for years, touring together, singing duets, and being married to other people. By 2005 that admiration had turned into something more romantic and less professional. In front of 7,000 fans in Bakersfield one electric night, Garth Brooks asked Tricia Yearwood to marry him. Of course she said "Yes," and the two were wed several months later in a private ceremony at their home in Owasso, Oklahoma. The title of their most recent collaboration, "Love Will Always Win," says it all.

GREATEST HITS

Year	Song
1991	"She's In Love with the Boy"
	"The Woman before Me"
1993	"Walk Away Joe" (with Don Henley)
1994	"XXX's and OOO's (An American Girl)"
1995	"Thinkin' about You"
1996	"Believe Me Baby (I Lied)"
1998	"Perfect Love"
	"There Goes My Baby"
2001	"I Would Have Loved You Anyway"
2002	"Squeeze Me In" (with Garth Brooks)
2005	"Georgia Rain"

FARON YOUNG

FEBRUARY 25, 1932–DECEMBER 10, 1996

You have to start somewhere. Picasso started off by imitating Cézanne, and Faron Young started off by imitating Hank Williams. At least both artists had the good sense to model themselves after the best of their day. Springing up to fill Hank's honky-tonk shoes after his death, Faron soon emerged as a top-notch stylist in his own right. He had good looks, a sweet baritone, and buckets of charm, earning him the nickname "The Hillbilly Heartthrob." Not technically a hillbilly—he was born in Shreveport, Louisiana—Faron appealed to a wide audience, who heard him on *Louisiana Hayride* and The Grand Ole Opry. Throughout the '50s and '60s, Young delivered hit after hit during his years with first Capitol and then Mercury Records.

As a youngster, Faron was drawn more to pop than to country, but after Webb Pierce discovered him singing at a local Optimist Club, he changed his tune. Faron joined the cast of *Louisiana Hayride* in 1951. His fame was just taking off when he was drafted into the army. He served in Korea but continued to record during furloughs. The year 1954 was Young's big breakthrough, with his biggest hit, "If You Ain't Lovin'".

Part of Young's heartthrob status came from his secondary career in acting. Appearing in nearly a dozen movies, beginning with *Hidden Guns* in 1955, Faron soon earned another nickname, the Singing Sheriff. Numerous television appearances followed his films. In 1965, after more than a decade of membership, Young left the Grand Ole Opry to strike out on his own. His success continued for several decades, and Young branched out into real estate and publishing, founding the influential country music magazine *Music City News*. In the '80s Young's popularity had nearly evaporated, and he slipped into despondency; he took his own life in 1996. Faron Young will be remembered as an exuberant, vital part of country music's history.

"LIVE FAST, LOVE HARD, DIE YOUNG" DEFINED THE HONKY-TONK STYLE OF THE DASHING AND FLAMBOYANT FARON YOUNG THROUGHOUT THE '50S THROUGH THE '70S.

A Songwriter's Best Friend

Faron Young had an ear for a great tune and launched careers of many songwriters by recording their songs. Young was among the first to record a Willie Nelson song. His version of "Hello Walls" went to #1 in 1961, and put Willie on the map. And Don Gibson's "Sweet Dreams," later recorded by Patsy Cline, was done first by Young. "Keeping up with the Joneses" was penned by Justin Tubb (Ernest's eldest son), and "Your Time's Comin'" was the work of Kris Kristofferson and Shel Silverstein. Mel Tillis, already an established songwriter, was tapped for Faron's 1967 "Unmitigated Gall."

GREATEST HITS

YEAR	SONG
1952	"Goin' Steady"
1954	"If You Ain't Lovin' (You Ain't Livin')"
1955	"Live Fast, Love Hard, Die Young"
	"All Right"
	"Forgive Me Dear"
1956	"Sweet Dreams"
	"I've Got Five Dollars and It's Saturday Night"
	"You're Still Mine"
1958	"Alone with You"
1961	"Hello Walls"
1965	"You'll Drive Me Back (into Her Arms Again)"
1966	"Keeping up with the Joneses" (with Margie Singleton)
1969	"Wine Me Up"
1971	"It's Four in the Morning"
1972	"This Little Girl of Mine"

Select Discography

Roy Acuff

1951 Old Time Barn Music
1955 Songs of the Smokey Mountains
1961 Once More It's Roy Acuff
1963 Hand-Clapping Gospel Songs
Roy Acuff Sings American Folk Songs
1965 The Voice of Country Music
Roy Acuff Sings Hank Williams
Great Train Songs
1970 I Saw the Light
Roy Acuff Time
1995 So Many Times

Alabama

1980 Alabama
My Home's in Alabama
1981 Feels So Right
1982 Mountain Music
1983 The Closer You Get...
1985 40 Hour Week
Alabama Christmas
1989 Southern Star
1990 Pass it on Down
1992 American Pride
1993 Cheap Seats
1995 In Pictures
1997 Dancin' on the Boulevard
1999 Twentieth Century
2001 When it All Goes South
2006 Songs of Inspiration
2007 Songs of Inspiration, Vol. 2

Eddy Arnold

1955 Anytime
The Chapel on the Hill
Wanderin'
1956 A Little on the Lonely Side
1957 When They Were Young
1959 Thereby Hangs a Tale
1960 More Eddy Arnold
1961 One More Time
1963 Cattle Call
1964 Folk Song Book
1965 My World
The Easy Way
1966 I Want to Go with You
1967 Lonely Again
Turn the World Around
1970 Standing Alone
1971 Welcome to My World
1972 Eddy Arnold Sings for Housewives and Other Lovers
1985 Many Tears Ago

Chet Atkins

1954 A Session with Chet Atkins
1955 Chet Atkins in Three Dimension
1956 Stringin' Along with Chet Atkins
Finger Style Guitar
1959 Chet Atkins in Hollywood
Mister Guitar
1961 Chet Atkins' Workshop
1963 Our Man in Nashville
1964 Guitar Country
1965 More of that Guitar Country
1968 Solo Flights
1969 Chet Picks on the Pops
1970 Me & Jerry
Yestergroovin'
1975 The Night Atlanta Burned
1977 Chester & Lester
Me and My Guitar
1985 Stay Tuned
1990 Neck and Neck

Gene Autry

1955 Champion Western Adventures
Gene Autry Sings Peter Cottontail
Little Johnny Pilgrim
Rusty, the Rocking Horse
1957 Rudolph the Red-Nosed Reindeer
1958 Gene Autry at the Rodeo
1965 Melody Ranch
1994 South of the Border

DeFord Bailey

1998 The Legendary DeFord Bailey: Country Music's First Black Star

Clint Black

1989 Killin' Time
1990 Put Yourself in My Shoes
1992 The Hard Way
1993 No Time to Kill
1994 One Emotion
1995 Looking for Christmas
1997 Nothin' But the Taillights
1999 D'Lectrified
2004 Spend My Time
2005 Drinkin' Songs & Other Logic

Garth Brooks

1989 Garth Brooks
1990 No Fences
1991 Ropin' the Wind
1992 Beyond the Season
The Chase
1993 In Pieces
1995 Fresh Horses
1997 Sevens
1999 In the Life of Chris Gaines
2001 Scarecrow

Brooks & Dunn

1991 Brand New Man
1993 Hard Workin' Man
1994 Waitin' On Sundown
1996 Borderline
1998 If You See Her
1999 Tight Rope
2001 Steers and Stripes
2003 Red Dirt Road
2005 Hillbilly Deluxe

Glen Campbell

1962 Big Bluegrass Special
1963 Too Late to Worry, Too Blue to Cry
1967 Burning Bridges
Gentle on My Mind
1968 A New Place in the Sun
By the Time I Get to Phoenix
Hey, Little One
Wichita Lineman
1969 Galveston

1970 The Glen Campbell Goodtime Album
Try a Little Kindness
1971 The Last Time I Saw Her
1973 I Knew Jesus (Before He Was a Star)
1974 Houston (I'm Comin' to See You)
1975 Rhinestone Cowboy
1978 Basic
1991 Show Me Your Way
1993 Somebody Like That

Bill Carlisle

1958 On Stage with the Carlisles
1965 Carlisle Family: Old Time Great Hymns
1983 Jumpin' Bill Carlisle

Carter Family

1954 Pickin' And Singin' Together
1960 All Time Favorites
In Memory of A.P. Carter
1962 Together Again
1963 The Carter Family
1964 Keep on the Sunny Side
1965 More Favorites by the Carter Family
1967 The Country Album
1973 Mother Maybelle Carter
1976 Country's First Family
2000 Family Album
2003 Sunshine in the Shadows

Johnny Cash

1957 Johnny Cash
1958 The Fabulous Johnny Cash with His Hot and Blue Guitar
1960 Now, There Was a Song!
Ride This Train
1962 All Aboard the Blue Train
I Walk the Line
1965 Sings the Ballads of the True West
1968 At Folsom Prison
1969 At San Quentin
Hello, I'm Johnny Cash
1971 A Man in Black
1974 John R. Cash
1983 Johnny 99
1987 Johnny Cash Is Coming to Town
1989 Boom Chicka Boom
1994 American Recordings
1996 Unchained
2004 My Mother's Hymn Book
2006 American V: A Hundred Highways

Ray Charles

1957 Ray Charles
1958 Soul Brothers
1959 The Genius of Ray Charles
1960 Ray Charles in Person
Genius + Soul = Jazz
1961 The Genius Sings the Blues
The Genius After Hours
1962 Modern Sounds in Country and Western Music
Modern Sounds in Country and Western Music, Vol. 2
1963 Ingredients in a Recipe for Soul
1966 Crying Time
Ray's Moods
1969 Doing His Thing
1970 My Kind of Jazz
1972 Through the Eyes of Love
1973 My Kind of Jazz, Number 2
1985 The Spirit of Christmas
1994 Genius Loves Company

Guy Clark

1975 Old No. 1
1976 Texas Cookin'
1978 Guy Clark
1981 The South Coast of Texas
1983 Better Days
1989 Old Friends
1992 Boats to Build
1995 Dublin Blues
1999 Cold Dog Soup
2002 The Dark
2006 Workbench Songs

Roy Clark

1963 The Lightning Fingers of Roy Clark
The Tip of My Fingers
1965 Roy Clark Guitar Spectacular
1966 Roy Clark
1969 Yesterday, When I Was Young
1970 I Never Picked Cotton
1973 Superpicker
Come Live with Me
1974 Roy Clark/The Entertainer
1978 Banjo Bandits
1979 Makin' Music
1995 Roy Clark & Joe Pass Play Hank Williams

Patsy Cline

1957 Patsy Cline
1961 Patsy Cline Showcase
1962 Sentimentally Yours
1964 That's How a Heartache Begins
Today, Tomorrow & Forever
1965 I Can't Forget You
1966 Stop the World and Let Me Off
1967 Miss Country Music
1985 Heartaches

Floyd Cramer

1957 That Honky-Tonk Piano
1960 Hello Blues
1961 Last Date
On the Rebound
1962 Floyd Cramer Gets Organ-Ized
I Remember Hank Williams
1963 Comin' On
1964 Country Piano/City Strings
1964 Floyd Cramer Goes Honky-Tonkin'
1968 Looking for Mr. Goodbar
Our Class Reunion
1969 With the Music City Pops
1970 Class of '70
1973 Sounds of Sunday
1977 The Floyd Cramer & The Keyboard Kick Band
1980 Dallas
1989 We Wish You a Merry Christmas

1991 The Magic Touch of Floyd Cramer
1997 Blue Skies

Vernon Dalhart
1978 Vernon Dalhart (First Recorded Railroad Songs)
Vernon Dalhart (The First Singing Cowboy on Records)
1980 Ballads & Railroad Songs
1985 Wreck of the Old 97
1999 Inducted into the Hall of Fame, 1981
2005 Lindberg the Eagle of the USA

Charlie Daniels Band
1970 Charlie Daniels
1972 John, Grease & Wolfman
1973 Honey in the Rock
1975 Fire on the Mountain
Nightrider
1976 Saddle Tramp
1977 Midnight Wind
1979 Million Mile Reflections
1980 Full Moon
1982 Windows
1985 Me and the Boys
1987 Powderkeg
1988 Homesick Heroes
1989 Simple Man
1993 America, I Believe in You
1994 The Door
1995 Same Ol' Me
1996 Steel Witness
2001 How Sweet the Sound: 25 Favorite Hymns and Gospel Greats
2002 Redneck Fiddlin' Man

Jimmie Davis
1947 Louisiana
1953 Jimmie Davis
1955 Near the Cross
1957 Hymn Time
1958 Hail Him with a Song
The Door Is Always Open
1959 You Are My Sunshine
1960 Suppertime
1984 Rock 'n' Roll Blues
1985 Sounds Like Jimmie Rodgers
1988 Barnyard Stomp

The Delmore Brothers
1957 Sacred Songs
1964 In Memory
In Memory, Vol. 2
1966 Wonderful Sacred Songs
1970 The Best of the Delmore Brothers
1971 Brown's Ferry Blues
1993 Freight Train Boogie
2002 Inducted Into the Country Music Hall of Fame, 2001
2005 Blues Stay Away from Me 1931–1951
Fifty Miles to Travel
2007 Delmore Brothers, Vol. 2: Later Years 1933–1952

Little Jimmie Dickens
1954 Old Country Church
1957 Raisin' the Dickens
1960 Big Country Songs by Little Jimmy Dickens
1962 Out behind the Barn
1965 Alone with God
Handle with Care
May the Bird of Paradise Fly up Your Nose
1967 Ain't It Fun
1968 Jimmy Dickens Sings
The Big Man in Country Music
1969 Jimmy Dickens Comes Callin'
1994 Straight . . . From the Heart

Dixie Chicks
1990 Thank Heavens for Dale Evans
1992 Little Ol' Cowgirl
1993 Shouldn't a Told You That
1998 Wide Open Spaces
1999 Fly
2002 Home
2006 Taking the Long Way

Steve Earle
1986 Guitar Town
1987 Exit 0
1988 Copperhead Road
1990 The Hard Way
1995 Train a Comin'
1996 I Feel Alright
1997 El Corazón
1999 The Mountain
2000 Transcendental Blues
2002 Jerusalem
2004 The Revolution Starts . . . Now

The Everly Brothers
1958 The Everly Brothers
The Real Everly Brothers
Songs Our Daddy Taught Us
1960 It's Everly Time
The Fabulous Style of the Everly Brothers
1961 A Date with the Everly Brothers
Both Sides of an Evening
1962 Folk Songs of the Everly Brothers
Instant Party!
1963 Sing Great Country Hits
1965 Rock 'n' Soul
Beat & Soul
1966 In Our Image
Two Yanks in England
1967 The Everly Brothers Sing
The Hit Sound of the Everly Brothers
1968 Roots
1972 Stories We Could Tell
1973 Pass the Chicken and Listen
1977 The New Album: Previously Unreleased Songs from the Early Sixties

Freddy Fender
1974 Before the Next Teardrop Falls
1975 Are You Ready for Freddy?
Since I Met You Baby
1976 If You're Ever in Texas
Rock 'n' Country
1977 If You Don't Love Me

1978 Swamp Gold
1991 Christmas Time in the Valley
2002 La Musica de Baldemar Huerta

Flatt & Scruggs

1957 Foggy Mountain Jamboree
1960 Flatt & Scruggs with the Foggy Mountain Boys
1961 Foggy Mountain Banjo
Songs of the Famous Carter Family
1962 Folk Songs of Our Land
1963 Hard Travelin' Featuring the Ballad of Jed Clampett
1964 The Fabulous Sound of Flatt and Scruggs
1965 The Versatile Flatt & Scruggs
Town and Country
1966 When the Saints Go Marching In
1967 Changin' Times Featuring Foggy Mountain Breakdown
Hear the Whistles Blow
Strictly Instrumental
1968 Nashville Airplane
Original Theme from Bonnie and Clyde
The Original Foggy Mountain Breakdown
1970 Final Fling
Breaking Out

Red Foley

1951 Lift Up Your Voice
1954 Red and Ernie
1958 Beyond the Sunset
He Walks with Thee
My Keepsake Album
Souvenir Album
1959 Let's All Sing to Him
Let's All Sing with Red Foley
1961 Company's Comin'
Songs of Devotion
1962 Dear Hearts and Gentle People
1963 The Red Foley Show
1965 I'm Bound for the Kingdom
Songs Everybody Knows
1966 Red Foley
1967 Songs for the Soul
1969 The Old Master

Tennessee Ernie Ford

1948 Keep Lookin' Up
1955 This Lusty Land!
1959 Gather 'Round
1960 Come to the Fair
Sixteen Tons
1961 Civil War Songs of the North
Hymns at Home
1962 Book of Favorite Hymns
Here Comes the Mississippi Showboat
1963 Long, Long Ago
1966 My Favorite Things
1967 Civil War Songs of the South
1970 America the Beautiful
1975 Ernie Sings & Glen Picks
1976 For the 83rd Time

Lefty Frizzell

1952 Songs of Jimmie Rodgers
1953 Listen to Lefty
1959 The One and Only Lefty Frizzell
1964 Saginaw, Michigan
1965 The Sad Side of Love
1966 Great Sound
Lefty Frizzell's Country Favorites
1967 Lefty Frizzell Puttin' On
Mom and Dad's Waltz
1968 Signed Sealed and Delivered

Don Gibson

1958 Oh Lonesome Me
Songs by Don Gibson
1959 No One Stands Alone
That Gibson Boy
1960 Look Who's Blue
Sweet Dreams
1961 Girls, Guitars and Gibson
1962 Some Favorites of Mine
1963 I Wrote a Song
1964 God Walks These Hills with Me
1965 A Blue Million Tears
Too Much Hurt
1966 Great Country Songs
1967 All My Love
1968 I Love You So Much It Hurts
1969 Dottie and Don (with Dottie West)
1970 Lovin' Lies
1971 I Walk Alone
1973 Just Call Me Lonesome
1974 Just One Time

Vince Gill

1983 Turn Me Loose
1984 The Things That Matter
1987 The Way Back Home
1989 When I Call Your Name
1990 I Never Knew Lonely
1991 Pocket Full of Gold
1992 I Still Believe in You
1993 Let There Be Peace on Earth
1994 When Love Finds You
1996 High Lonesome Sound
1998 The Key
2000 Let's Make Sure We Kiss Goodbye
2003 Next Big Thing
2006 These Days

Jimmy Dale Gilmore

1988 Fair and Square
1989 Jimmy Dale Gilmore
1991 After Awhile
1993 Spinning Around the Sun
1996 Braver Newer World
2000 One Endless Night
2005 Come on Back

Merle Haggard

1965 Strangers
1967 Branded Man
I'm a Lonesome Fugitive
1968 Legend of Bonnie & Clyde
Mama Tried
Sing me Back Home
1969 A Portrait of Merle Haggard
Pride in What I Am
Same Train, Different Time
1970 A Tribute to the Best Damn Fiddle Player in the World (Or My Salute to Bob Wills)

1971 Hag
Honky-Tonkin'
Someday We'll Look Back
1971 The Land of Many Churches
1972 Let Me Tell You About a Song
1974 If We Make it Through December
1976 My Love Affair with Trains
1977 A Working Man Can't Get Nowhere Today
1980 Back to the Barrooms
1981 Big City
1982 Going Where the Lonely Go

Emmylou Harris

1975 Elite Hotel
Pieces of the Sky
1977 Luxury Liner
1978 Quarter Moon in a Ten Cent Town
1979 Light of the Stable
Blue Kentucky Girl
1980 Roses in the Snow
1981 Cimarron
Evangeline
1983 White Shoes
1985 The Ballad of Sally Rose
1987 Angel Band
1989 Bluebird
1990 Brand New Dance
1993 Cowgirl's Prayer
1995 Wrecking Ball
1998 Spyboy
2000 Red Dirt Girl
2003 Stumble into Grace

Faith Hill

1994 Take Me as I Am
1995 It Matters to Me
1998 Faith
1999 Love Will Always Win
Breathe
2002 Cry
2005 Fireflies

Sonny James

1957 The Southern Gentleman
1958 Honey
1962 Young Love
1964 The Minute You're Gone
1965 Behind the Tear
I'll Keep Holding On
You're the Only World I Know
1968 Heaven Says Hello
Need You
1969 The Astrodome Presents in Person Sonny James
1970 It's Just a Matter of Time
My Love/Don't Keep Me Hangin' On
1971 Empty Arms
Here Comes Honey Again
1972 When the Snow is on the Roses
1973 If She Just Helps Me Get Over You
Love Letters in the Sand
1975 The Guitars of Sonny James
1989 American Originals
1995 Sunny Side Up

Waylon Jennings

1964 Waylon at JD's
1966 Folk-Country
Leavin' Town
1967 Sings Ol' Harlan
Love of the Common People
1968 Hangin' On
Just to Satisfy You
1969 Waylon Jennings
1970 Waylon
1972 Good Hearted Woman
1973 Honky Tonk Heroes
1974 This Time
The Ramblin' Man
1976 Wanted! The Outlaws
Waylon Live
1977 Ol' Waylon
1978 Waylon and Willie
I've Always Been Crazy
1992 Too Dumb for New York City, Too Ugly for L.A.
1998 Closing in on the Fire

George Jones

1957 The Grand Ole Opry's New Star
1958 Hillbilly Hit Parade
Long Live King George
1959 White Lightning and Other Favorites
1960 George Jones Salutes Hank Williams
1962 George Jones Sings Bob Wills
The Fabulous Country Music Sound of George Jones
1964 George Jones Sings Like the Dickens!
1965 Heartaches and Tears
Mr. Country and Western
I Get Lonely in a Hurry
Trouble in Mind
1966 Love Bug
1967 Walk Through This World with Me
1968 If My Heart Had Windows
1971 George Jones with Love
1972 A Picture of Me (Without You)
1974 The Grand Tour
1976 Golden Ring
1980 I Am What I Am

The Judds

1983 Wynonna and Naomi
1984 Why Not Me
1985 Rockin' with the Rhythym
1987 Heartland
1989 River of Time
1990 Love Can Build a Bridge
2000 The Judds Reunion Live

Pee Wee King

1956 Swing West
1964 Back Again
1965 Country Barn Dance
1975 Golden Olde Tyme Dances
1990 Hog Wild Too!

Alison Krauss

1985 Different Strokes
1987 Too Late to Cry
1989 Two Highways

1990 I've Got That Old Feeling
1992 Every Time You Say Goodbye
1994 I Know Who Holds Tomorrow
1997 So Long So Wrong
1999 Forget about It
2001 New Favorite
2002 Live
2004 Lonely Runs Both Ways

Kris Kristofferson

1970 Kristofferson
1971 Me and Bobby McGee
The Silver Tongued Devil and I
1972 Border Lord
Jesus Was a Capricorn
1973 Full Moon
1974 Breakaway
1975 Who's to Bless and Who's to Blame
1976 Surreal Thing
1978 Easter Island
1979 Natural Act
Shake Hands with the Devil
1981 To the Bone
1986 Repossessed
1990 Third World Warrior
1992 Live at the Philharmonic
1995 A Moment of Forever
1999 Austin Sessions
2003 Broken Freedom Song
2006 This Old Road

Brenda Lee

1959 Grandma, What Great Songs You Sang!
1960 Brenda Lee
This Is . . . Brenda
1961 All the Way
Emotions
Miss Dynamite
1962 Brenda, That's All
Sincerely, Brenda Lee
1963 All Alone Am I
Love You
1964 By Request
Let Me Sing
Songs Everybody Knows
1965 Too Many Rivers
1966 Ten Golden Years
1968 For the First Time
1969 Johnny One Time
1976 Little Miss Dynamite
1997 Live Dynamite
2005 Greatest Gospel Songs

Patty Loveless

1987 Patty Loveless
1988 Honky Tonk Angel
If My Heart Had Windows
1990 On Down the Line
1991 Up Against My Heart
1993 Only What I Feel
1994 When Fallen Angels Fly
1996 Trouble with the Truth
1997 Long Stretch of Lonesome
2000 Strong Heart
2001 Mountain Soul
2002 Bluegrass and Snow: A Mountain Christmas
2005 Dreamin' My Dreams

Lyle Lovett

1986 Lyle Lovett
1987 Pontiac
1989 Lyle Lovett and His Large Band
1992 Joshua Judges Ruth
1994 I Love Everybody
1996 The Road to Ensenada
1998 Step Inside This House
1999 Live in Texas
2000 Dr. T and the Women
2003 My Baby Don't Tolerate

Loretta Lynn

1963 Loretta Lynn Sings
1964 Before I'm Over You
1965 Blue Kentucky Girl
Ernest Tubb and Loretta Lynn
Songs from My Heart
1966 I Like 'Em Country
1967 Don't Come Home a Drinkin' (With Lovin' on Your Mind)
Ernest Tubb and Loretta Lynn
Singin' Again
Singin' with Feelin'
1968 Fist City
Here's Loretta Lynn
Who Says God Is Dead!
1969 Your Squaw Is on the Warpath
1971 Coal Miner's Daughter
One's on the Way
You're Lookin' at Country
1972 Alone with You
God Bless America Again
1973 Louisiana Woman Mississippi Man
2004 Van Lear Rose

Barbara Mandrell

1971 Treat Him Right
1973 Midnight Oil
1974 The Time I Almost Made It
1976 This Is . . .
1977 Lovers, Friends and Strangers
Midnight Angel
Love's Ups and Downs
1978 Moods
1979 Just for the Record
1980 Love Is Fair
1981 Barbara Mandrell Live
1982 He Set My Life to Music
In Black and White
1984 Meant for Each Other
1985 Get to the Heart
1986 Moments
1988 I'll Be Your Jukebox Tonight
1991 Key's in the Mailbox
1995 Fooled by a Feeling
1997 It Works for Me

Kathy Mattea

1984 Kathy Mattea
1985 From My Heart
1986 Walk the Way the Wind Blows
1987 Untasted Honey
1989 Willow in the Wind
1991 Time Passes By
1992 Lonesome Standard Time
1993 Walking Away a Winner
Good News
1994 Good News Radio Special
1995 Ready for the Storm

1997 Love Travels
2000 The Innocent Years
2002 Roses
2005 Right out of Nowhere

Martina McBride
1992 The Time Has Come
1993 The Way That I Am
1995 Wild Angels
1997 Evolution
1999 Emotion
White Christmas
2003 Martina
2005 Timeless
2007 Waking Up Laughing

Reba McEntire
1977 Reba McEntire
1979 Out of a Dream
1980 Feel the Fire
1981 Heart to Heart
1982 Unlimited
1984 My Kind of Country
1985 Have I Got a Deal for You
1986 Reba Nell McEntire
What Am I Gonna Do about You
Whoever's in New England
1987 The Last One to Know
1988 Reba
1989 Reba Live
1990 Rumor Has It
1991 For My Broken Heart
1994 Read My Mind
1996 What If It's You
1998 If You See Him
1999 So Good Together
2003 Room to Breathe

Tim McGraw
1993 Tim McGraw
1994 Not a Moment Too Soon
1995 All I Want
1997 Everywhere
1999 Place in the Sun
2001 Set This Circus Down
2002 Tim McGraw and the Dancehall Doctors
2004 Live Like You Were Dying
2007 Let It Go

Roger Miller
1964 Roger and Out
Dang Me!
1965 The Return of Roger Miller
The Third Time Around
1966 Words and Music
1967 Walkin' in the Sunshine
1968 A Tender Look at Love
1969 Roger Miller
1970 A Trip in the Country
1973 Dear Folks, Sorry I Haven't Written Lately
1976 Celebration
1977 Painted Poetry
1978 Off the Wall
Waterhole #3
1979 Making a Name for Myself
1982 Old Friends
1986 The Country Side of Roger Miller
1994 Green Green Grass of Home
1997 Roger Miller Live!
2000 Live

Ronnie Milsap
1971 Ronnie Milsap
1974 Pure Love
Where My Heart Is
1975 A Legend in My Time
A Rose By Any Other Name
Night Things
1976 20/20 Vision
1977 It Was Almost Like a Song
1980 There's No Gettin' Over Me
1982 Inside
1983 Keyed Up
1985 Lost in the Fifties Tonight
1987 Heart and Soul
1989 Stranger Things Have Happened
1991 Back to the Grindstone
1993 True Believer
2000 Wish You Were Here
2002 Live
2004 Just for a Thrill
2006 My Life

Bill Monroe
1958 Knee Deep in Bluegrass
1959 I Saw the Light
1960 Mr. Bluegrass
1962 Bluegrass Ramble
Bluegrass Special
1964 I'll Meet You in Church Sunday Morning
1965 Bluegrass Instrumentals
1966 The High Lonesome Sound of Bill Monroe
1967 Bluegrass Time
1969 Voice from on High
1973 Bean Blossom
1984 Bill Monroe and Friends
1987 Bluegrass '87
1988 Southern Flavor
1989 Live at the Opry: Celebrating 50 Years on the Grand Ole Opry
1991 Cryin' Holy unto the Lord
1999 Silver Eagle Cross Country Presents Live Bill Monroe
Live from Mountain Stage
2001 Live, Vol. 1
2004 Live at Mechanics Hall

Patsy Montana
1964 The New Sound of Patsy Montana
1977 Precious Memories
1983 The Yodeling Cowgirl

Willie Nelson
1962 And Then I Wrote
1965 Country Willie: His Own Songs
1966 Country Favorites: Willie Nelson Style
1971 Yesterday's Wine
1973 Shotgun Willie
1974 Phases and Stages
1975 Red Headed Stranger
1976 The Troublemaker
1977 To Lefty from Willie
1978 Stardust
1980 Honeysuckle Rose

1985 Funny How Time Slips Away
Me and Paul
1989 A Horse Called Music
1992 The IRS Tapes: Who'll Buy My Memories?
1993 Across the Borderline
1995 Six Hours at Pedernales
1998 Teatro
2003 Run That By Me One More Time
2007 Last of the Breed

Roy Orbison

1960 Sings Lonely and Blue
1961 At the Rock House
1962 Crying
1963 In Dreams
1964 Exciting Sounds
Oh Pretty Woman
1965 There Is Only One
1966 Orbisongs
1967 Cry Softly, Little One
1968 The Fastest Guitar Alive
1969 Roy Orbison's Many Moods
1970 The Big O
1971 Hank Williams in the Roy Orbison Way
1972 Roy Orbison Sings
1973 Memphis
1974 Milestones
1976 Focus on Roy Orbison
1983 Big O Country
1989 A Black and White Night Live
Mystery Girl

Buck Owens

1961 Buck Owens
Buck Owens Sings Harlan Howard
1962 You're for Me
1963 Buck Owens Sings Tommy Collins
1964 Together Again
1965 I've Got a Tiger by the Tail
1966 The Carnegie Hall Concert
1967 Buck Owens and His Buckaroos in Japan!
1968 I've Got you on My Mind Again
1969 Buck Owens in London
Tall Dark Stranger
1970 The Great White Horse
Big in Vegas
Boot Hill
Rompin' and Stompin'
1971 Bridge over Troubled Water
Ruby and Other Bluegrass Specials
1973 Ain't It Amazing Gracie
Arms Full of Empty
1989 Live at Carnegie Hall

Brad Paisley

1999 Who Needs Pictures
2001 Part II
2003 Mud on the Tires
2005 Time Well Wasted
2007 5th Gear

Dolly Parton

1967 Hello, I'm Dolly
1968 Just Because I'm a Woman
Dolly Parton and George Jones
1969 In the Good Old Days (When Times Were Bad)
1970 A Real Live Dolly
1971 Two of a Kind
Coat of Many Colors
1972 The Right Combination
My Favorite Songwriter, Porter Wagoner
1973 We Found It
1974 Jolene
1975 Bargain Store
1976 All I Can Do
1977 Here You Come Again
1978 Heartbreaker
1980 9 to 5
1989 White Limozeen
1998 Hungry Again
1999 The Grass Is Blue
2001 Little Sparrow

Webb Pierce

1955 Webb Pierce
1956 That Wondering Boy
1958 Sing for You
1959 Bound for the Kingdom
1960 Walking the Streets
Webb With a Beat!
1961 Fallen Angel
1962 Cross Country
Hideaway Heart
1963 Bow Thy Head
I've Got a New Heartache
1965 Memory No. 1
1966 Sweet Memories
1967 Where'd Ya Stay Last Night?
1968 Fool Fool Fool
1969 Webb Pierce Sings This Thing
1970 Love Ain't Never Gonna Be No Better
1973 I'm Gonna Be a Swinger
1982 In the Jailhouse Now
2003 Honky Tonk Hero

Elvis Presley

1956 Elvis Presley
Elvis
1957 Loving You
Christmas Album
1958 King Creole
1959 A Date with Elvis
1960 Elvis Is Back
G.I. Blues
His Hand in Mine
1961 Something for Everybody
Blue Hawaii
1962 Pot Luck with Elvis
1963 Girls! Girls! Girls!
1964 Kissing Cousins
Roustabout
1965 Girl Happy
Elvis for Everyone
1967 How Great Thou Art
1969 From Elvis in Memphis
1970 Back in Memphis

Ray Price

1957 Ray Price Sings Heart Songs
1958 Talk to Your Heart
1962 San Antonio Rose
1964 Burning Memories

1965 The Other Woman
1966 Touch My Heart
1968 She Wears My Ring
1969 Sweetheart of the Year
1970 For the Good Times
1971 I Won't Mention It Again
1972 The Lonesomest Lonesome
1973 She's Got to Be a Saint
1976 Hank 'n' Me
1981 Tribute to Willie and Kris
1987 Heart of Country Music
1988 Just Enough Love
1989 American Originals
1991 Sometimes a Rose
1995 Release Me
2000 Prisoner of Love

Charley Pride

1966 Country Charley Pride
1967 The Country Way
The Pride of Country Music
1968 Make Mine Country
1969 In Person
The Sensational Charley Pride
1970 Charley Pride's Tenth Album
Just Plain Charley
1971 Charley Pride Sings Heart Songs
From Me to You
I'm Just Me
1973 Amazing Love
1974 Country Feelin'
1977 She's Just An Old Love Turned Memory
1982 Charley Sings Everybody's Choices
1987 After All This Time
1988 I'm Gonna Love Her on The Radio
1994 My 6 Latest and 6 Greatest
1996 Classics with Pride
2001 A Tribute to Jim Reeves

John Prine

1971 John Prine
1972 Diamonds in the Rough
1973 Sweet Revenge
1975 Common Sense
1976 We're Children of Coincidence
1978 Bruised Orange
1979 Pink Cadillac
1980 Storm Windows
1984 Aimless Love
1986 German Afternoons
1988 Live
1991 The Missing Years
1994 John Prine Christmas
1995 Lost Dogs and Mixed Blessings
1999 In Spite of Ourselves
2000 Souvenirs
2005 Fair and Square
2007 Standard Songs for Average People

Rascal Flatts

2000 Rascal Flatts
2002 Melt
2004 Feels Like Today
2006 Me and My Gang

Jim Reeves

1956 Jim Reeves Sings
Singing Down the Lane
1957 Bimbo
Jim Reeves
1958 Girls I Have Known
God Be with You
1959 Songs to Warm Your Heart
1960 Intimate Jim Reeves
1961 Talkin' to Your Heart
1962 A Touch of Velvet
The Country Side of Jim Reeves
1963 Gentleman Jim
Good 'n' Country
The International Jim Reeves
1964 Kimberly Jim
1966 Distant Drums
Yours Sincerely, Jim Reeves
1967 The Blue Side of Lonesome
1968 A Touch of Sadness

Charlie Rich

1960 Lonely Weekends
1964 Charlie Rich
1965 The Many Sides of Charlie Rich
1966 Many New Sides
1967 Charlie Rich Sings Country and Western
1968 Set Me Free
1969 The Fabulous Charlie Rich
1970 Boss Man
1972 Time for Tears
1973 Behind Closed Doors
1974 The Silver Fox
1975 Every Time You Touch Me (I Get High)
She Called Me Baby
Too Many Teardrops
1976 Original Charlie Rich
Silver Linings
1977 Rollin' with the Flow
1978 The Most Beautiful Girl
1980 Once a Drifter
1992 Pictures and Paintings

LeAnn Rimes

1996 Blue
1997 You Light Up My Life: Inspirational Songs
1998 Sittin' on Top of the World
1999 LeAnn Rimes
2001 I Need You
God Bless America
2002 Twisted Angel
2004 What a Wonderful World
2005 This Woman
2006 Whatever We Wanna

Tex Ritter

1958 Psalms
Songs from the Western Screen
1961 Hillbilly Heaven
The Lincoln Hymns
1962 Stan Kenton and Tex Ritter
1963 Border Affair
1964 The Friendly Voice of Tex Ritter
1966 Sweet Land of Liberty
1967 Just beyond the Moon
Sings His Hits
1968 Bump Tiddle Dee Bum Bum!
Ted Ritter's Wild West
Tennessee Blues
1969 Chuck Wagon Days

Love you Big as Texas
1970 Green Green Valley
1975 Fall Away
1978 Cowboy Favorites
1985 What Am I Bid?
1995 Arizona Days
God Bless America

Marty Robbins
1956 Rock'n Roll'n Robbins
1957 Song of the Islands
The Song of Robbins
1959 Gunfighter Ballads and Trail Songs
1960 More Gunfighter Ballads and Trail Songs
1961 Alamo
Just a Little Sentimental
1962 Devil Woman
1963 Return of the Gunfighter
1965 What God Has Done
1966 The Drifter
1967 Tonight Carmen
1968 I Walk Alone
1969 It's a Sin
Singing the Blues
1970 El Paso
1971 Today
1976 El Paso City
1979 All Around Cowboy
1980 Marty Robbins Today

Jimmie Rodgers
1933 Country Legacy
1957 Train Whistle Blues
1962 Country Music Hall of Fame
1989 My Old Pal
1991 First Sessions
Vol. 5, America's Blue Yodeler
Last Sessions, 1933
1992 The Singing Brakeman
1994 Train Whistle Blues
1996 American Legends #16: Jimmie Rodgers
The Blues
1997 Memorial Album
The Essential Jimmie Rodgers
Father of Country Music
1999 Ultimate Collection
2002 RCA Country Legends
Standing on the Corner
Ultimate Legends
Classic Sides, 1927–1933
2006 The Singing Brakeman

Kenny Rogers
1967 The First Edition
1969 Ruby Don't Take Your Love to Town
1971 Tell It All Brother
1972 Planet Texas
1976 Love Lifted Me
1977 Daytime Friends
1978 The Gambler
1979 Kenny
1981 Share Your Love
1982 Love Will Turn You Around
1983 We've Got Tonight
1984 What about Me?
1985 Heart of the Matter
1986 They Don't Make Them Like They Used To
1987 I Prefer the Moonlight
1989 Something Inside So Strong
1992 Lucille
2000 There You Go Again
2006 American Classic Songbook

Ricky Skaggs
1979 Sweet Temptation
1980 Skaggs and Rice
1981 Waitin' for the Sun to Shine
1982 Highways and Heartaches
Family and Friends
1983 Don't Cheat in Our Hometown
1984 Country Boy
1986 Love's Gonna Get Ya!
1988 Comin' Home to Stay
1989 Kentucky Thunder
1991 My Father's Son
1995 Country Pride
1997 Life Is a Journey
That's It
1999 Ancient Tones
2000 Big Mon: the songs of Bill Monroe
2001 History of the Future
2002 Uncle Pen
2004 Brand New Strings
2006 Instrumentals

Carl Smith
1956 Carl Smith
Softly and Tenderly
1957 Sentimental Songs
Sunday Down South
1958 Lets Live a Little
1960 The Carl Smith Touch
1962 Easy to Please
1963 Tall Tall Gentleman
1964 There Stands the Glass
1965 I Want to Live and Love
1966 Man with a Plan
1967 The country Gentleman Sings His Favorites
1968 Country on My Mind
Deep Water
1969 Carl Smith Sings a Tribute to Roy Acuff
Faded Love and Winter Roses
Take It Like a Man
1970 I Love You Because
1972 If This Is Goodbye
1988 Old Lonesome Times

Hank Snow
1952 Hank Snow Sings
1953 Hank Snow Salutes Jimmie Rodgers
1955 Just Keep A-Movin'
1957 Country and Western Jamboree
1958 Guitar
1960 Hank Snow Sings Jimmie Rodgers Songs
1961 The Southern Cannonball
1962 The One and Only Hank Snow
1963 I've Been Everywhere
1964 More Souvenirs
Songs of Tragedy
1966 Travellin' Blues
1967 Christmas with Hank Snow

1969 Hits Covered by Snow
1970 Cure for the Blues
Hank Snow Sings in Memory of Jimmie Rodgers
1971 Tracks and Trains
1972 The Jimmie Rodgers Story
1975 All about Trains
1980 Lovingly Yours

Sons of the Pioneers
1952 Cowboy Hymns and Spirituals
1953 Western Classics
1955 25 Favorite Cowboy Songs
1957 How Great Thou Art
One Man's Songs
1959 Cool Water
1960 Room Full of Roses
1961 Lore of the West
Westward, Ho!
1962 Tumbleweed Trails
1963 Hymns of the Cowboy
Our Men out West
Trail Dust
1964 Country Fare
1965 Legends of the West
1966 The Songs of Bob Nolan
1967 Campfire Favorites
1968 South of the Border
1973 Riders in the Sky
1990 Empty Saddles

Statler Brothers
1966 Flowers on the Wall
1969 Oh Happy Day
1971 Bed of Roses
1972 Country Music Then and Now
The Statler Brother Sing Country Symphonies in E Major
1973 Do You Love Me Tonight
1974 Carry Me Back
Thank You World
1975 Sons of the Motherland
1976 Harld, Lew, Phil, and Don
1977 Short Stories
1978 Christmas Card
1979 The Originals
1981 Years Ago
1983 Today
1985 Pardners in Rhyme
1987 Maple Street Memories
1990 Music, Memories and You
1993 Home
2001 Showtime

George Strait
1981 Strait Country
1982 Strait from the Heart
1983 Right or Wrong
1984 Does Fort Worth Ever Cross Your Mind
1985 Something Special
1986 #7
1987 Ocean Front Property
1988 If You Ain't Lovin' (You Ain't Livin')
1989 Beyond the Blue Neon
1990 Livin' It Up
1991 Chill of an Early Fall
1992 Holding My Own
1993 Easy Come, Easy Go
1994 Lead On
1996 Blue Clear Sky
1997 Carrying Your Love with Me
1998 One Step at a Time
1999 Always Never the Same
2000 George Strait
2005 Somewhere down in Texas

Hank Thompson
1956 North of the Rio Grande
Songs of the Brazos Valley
1957 Hank!
1958 Dance Ranch
1959 Songs for Rounders
1960 Most of All
this Broken Heart of Mine
1961 An Old Love Affair
At the Golden Nugget
1962 Cheyenne Frontier Days
1963 Live at the State Fair of Texas
1966 A Six Pack to Go
1967 Just an Old Flame
The Countrypolitan sound of Hank's Brazos Boys
1968 On Tap, in the Can or in the Bottle
1969 Smoky the Bar
1971 Next Time I Fall in Love, I Won't
1978 Brand New Hank
1986 Hank Thompson

Floyd Tillman
1962 Let's Make Memories
1967 Floyd Tillman's Country
1968 Dream On
1969 I'll Still Be Loving You
1970 Floyd Tillman and Friends
2004 The Influence

Merle Travis
1956 The Merle Travis Guitar
1957 Back Home
1962 Travis
1963 Songs of the Coal Mines
1964 I'm a Natural Born Gambling Man
Merle Travis and Joe Maphis
1969 Great Songs of the Delmore Brothers
Strictly Guitar
1979 Country Guitar Giants
1980 Light Singin' and Pickin'
1981 Travis Pickin'
1985 Merle and Grandpa's Farm and Home Hour
1986 Rough Rowdy and Blue
2003 Merle Travis in Boston

Randy Travis
1986 Storms of Life
1987 Always and Forever
1988 Old 8 x 10
1989 An Old Time Christmas
No Holdin' Back
1990 Heroes and Friends
1991 High Lonesome
1992 Wind in the Wire
1994 This Is Me
1996 Full Circle
1998 You and You Alone
1999 A Man Ain't Made of Stone
2000 Inspirational Journey

2001 Live: It Was Just a Matter of Time
2002 Rise and Shine
2003 Worship and Faith
2004 Passing Through
2005 Glory Train

Travis Tritt
1990 Country Club
1991 It's All About To Change
1992 A Travis Tritt Christmas: Loving Time of the Year
1994 Ten Feet Tall and Bulletproof
1996 the Restless Kind
1998 No More Looking over My Shoulder
2000 Down the Road I Go
2002 Strong Enough
2004 My Honky Tonk History

Ernest Tubb
1951 Jimmie Rodgers Songs
Old Rugged Cross
1957 The Daddy of 'Em All
1959 The Importance of Being Ernest
1960 Ernest Tubb Record Shop
1961 Midnight Jamboree
1964 Blue Christmas
1965 Country Dance Time
Mr. and Mrs. Used to Be
1966 By Request
1967 Another Story
1968 Country Hit Time
The Terrific Texas Troubadours
1969 Great Country
If We Put Our Heads Together
Let's Turn Back the Years
Saturday Satan, Sunday Saint
1970 Good Year for the Wine
1972 Say Something Nice to Sarah
1992 Walking the Floor Over You

Tanya Tucker
1972 Delta Dawn
1973 What's Your Mama's Name
1974 Would You Lay with Me (In a Field of Stone)
1975 Tanya Tucker
1976 Here's Some Love
Lovin' and Learnin'
1978 T.N.T.
1979 Ridin' Rainbows
1981 Dream Lovers
1982 Live
1983 Changes
1986 Girls Like Me
1987 Love Me Like You Used To
1990 Tennessee Woman
1992 Can't Run from Yourself
1993 Lizzie and the Rain Man
1995 Fire to Fire
1997 Complicated
2002 Tanya
2005 Live at Billy Bob's Texas

Shania Twain
1993 Shania Twain
1995 The Woman in Me
1997 Come on Over
1999 On the Way
2002 Up!

Conway Twitty
1965 Conway Twitty Sings
1966 Look into My Teardrops
1968 Here's Conway Twitty and His Lonely Blue Boys
1968 Next in Line
1969 I Love You More Today
1970 Hello Darlin'
1971 How Much More Can She Stand
1972 Conway Twitty Sings the Blues
Conway Twitty
I Can't See Me without You
1973 Clinging to a Saving Hand
She Needs Someone to Hold Her
1975 Linda on My Mind
1978 Georgia Keeps Pulling on My Ring
1984 Conway Twitty and Loretta Lynn
1987 Borderline
1989 House on Old Lonesome Road
1990 Crazy in Love
1993 Final Touches
1995 Sings Songs of Love

Porter Wagoner
1956 Satisfied Mind
1962 Sings Duets
Slice of Life
1963 The Porter Wagoner Show
Y'All Come
1964 Porter Wagoner in Person
1966 Confessions of a Broken Man
Live on the Road
1967 More Grand Old Gospel
The Cold Hard Facts of Life
1968 Just Between You and Me
The Bottom of the Bottle
1969 Always, Always
The Carroll County Accident
1970 Porter Wagoner and Dolly Parton
1971 Simple as I Am
1972 What Ain't to Be, Just Might Happen
1980 Porter and Dolly
1984 Porter Wagoner and the Right Combination
2000 The Best I've Ever Been

Kitty Wells
1956 Country Hit Parade
Winner of Your Heart
1959 After Dark
Dust on the Bible
1960 Kitty's Choice
Seasons of My Heart
1962 Christmas with Kitty Wells
Singing on Sunday
1964 Especially for You
Country Music Time
1965 Burning Memories
Lonely Street
Lonesome, Sad and Blue
1966 Country All the Way
Guilty Street
Kitty Wells
1967 Love Makes the World Go Around
Queen of Honky Tonk Street
Together Again
1969 Country Heart

Hank Williams

1952 Hank Williams Sings
1955 Hank Williams as Luke the Drifter
1976 Live at the Grand Ole Opry

Hank Williams Jr.

1963 Songs of Hank Williams
1964 Sings Great Country Favorites
Your Cheatin' Heart: Hank Williams' Life Story
1965 Ballads of the Hills and Plains
1966 Blue's My Name
1967 In My Own Way
1968 Time to Sing
1969 Songs My Father Left Me
1972 Eleven Roses
1975 Bocephus
1976 Hank Williams Jr. and Friends
1977 One Night Stands
1979 Whiskey Bent and Hell Bound
1981 Rowdy
1982 High Notes
1984 Strong Stuff
1985 Five-O-Five
1987 Born to Boogie
1995 Hog Wild
2003 I'm One of You

Lucinda Williams

1979 Ramblin'
1980 Happy Woman Blues
1988 Lucinda Williams
1992 Sweet Old World
1998 Car Wheels on a Gravel Road
2001 Essence
2003 World without Tears
2005 Live @ the Fillmore
2007 West

Bob Wills

1951 Bob Wills Roundup
1953 Old Time Favorites
1955 Dance-O-Rama #2
1957 Bob Wills and His Texas Playboys
1959 Texas Playboys
1960 Together Again
1961 Mr. Words and Mr. Music
1963 Bob Wills Sings and Plays
1965 San Antonio Rose
1967 From the Heart of Texas
1969 Time Changes Everything
1974 Fathers and Sons
For the Last Time
1976 Bob Wills: In Concert
1978 'Live and Kicking
1979 Original Texas Playboys
1990 Greatest String Band
2005 Live from Panther Hall: 1963

Lee Ann Womack

1997 Lee Ann Womack
1998 Some Things I Know
2000 I Hope You Dance
2002 Something Worth Leaving Behind
The Season for Romance
2005 There's More Where That Came From

Tammy Wynette

1967 Your Good Girl's Gonna Go Bad
1968 D-I-V-O-R-C-E
Stand by Your Man
1969 The Ways to Love a Man
1970 Christmas With Tammy
Tammy's Touch
The First Lady
1971 We Sure Can Love Each Other
1972 Bedtime Story
1973 The First Songs of the First Lady
1974 Another Lonely Song
Woman to Woman
1976 'Til I Make It on My Own
1977 One of a Kind
1978 Womanhood
1979 Just Tammy
1983 Even the Strong Get Lonely
1987 Higher Ground
1989 Next to You
1994 Without Walls

Trisha Yearwood

1991 Trisha Yearwood
1992 Hearts in Armor
1993 The Song Remembers When
1994 The Sweetest Gift
1995 Thinkin' about You
1996 Everybody Knows
1998 Where Your Road Lives
2000 Real Live Woman
2001 Inside Out
2005 Jasper County

Faron Young

1959 This Is Faron Young!
1961 Hello Walls
1963 This Is Faron
1964 Story Songs for Country Folks
Story Songs of Mountains and Valleys
1968 I'll Be Yours
1970 Wine Me Up
1979 Chapter Two

BIBLIOGRAPHY

Books

Bogdanov, Vladimir, Chris Woodstra, and Stephen Thomas Erlewine, eds. *All Music Guide to Country: The Definitive Guide to Country Music*. San Francisco: Backbeat Books, 2003.

Cantwell, David, and Bill Friskics-Warren. *Heartaches by the Number: Country Music's 500 Greatest Singles*. Nashville: Vanderbilt University Press, 2003.

Cash, Johnny. *Cash: The Autobiography*. San Francisco: HarperSanFrancisco, 1997.

Country Music Foundation. *Country: The Music and the Musicians: From the Beginnings to the '90s*. New York: Abbeville Press, 1994.

Escott, Colin. *Lost Highway: The True Story of Country Music*. Washington: The Smithsonian Institution, 2003.

Guralnick, Peter. *Last Train to Memphis: The Rise of Elvis Presley*. Boston: Little, Brown, 1994.

Kingsbury, Paul, ed. *The Encyclopedia of Country Music*. New York: Oxford University Press, 1998.

Malone, Bill C. *Country Music, U.S.A.*, Second Revised Edition. Austin: University of Texas Press, 2002.

———. *Don't Get above Your Raisin': Country Music and the Southern Working Class*. Chicago: University of Illinois Press, 2001.

———. *Singing Cowboys and Musical Mountaineers: Southern Culture and the Roots of Country Music*. Athens: University of Georgia Press, 2003.

Wolfe, Charles K. *Classic Country: Legends of Country Music*. New York: Routledge, 2001.

———. *A Good-Natured Riot: The Birth of the Grand Ole Opry*. Nashville: Vanderbilt University Press/Country Music Foundation Press, 1999.

Films

Coal Miner's Daughter. Universal Pictures, 1980.

Pure Country. Jerry Weintraub, 1992.

Sweet Dreams. HBO, 1985.

Walk the Line. Fox 2000 Pictures, 2005.

Web Sites

All Music Guide
www.allmusic.com

Country Music Hall of Fame
www.countrymusichalloffame.com/site

Country Music Television
www.cmt.com/artists

Songfacts
www.songfacts.com